Forgotten Women of the Wars of the Roses

Forgotten Women of the Wars of the Roses

THE UNTOLD HISTORY BEHIND THE BATTLE FOR THE CROWN

Jo Romero

Pen &
Sword

HISTORY

First published in Great Britain in 2024 by
Pen & Sword History
An imprint of
Pen & Sword Books Ltd
Yorkshire – Philadelphia
Copyright © Jo Romero 2024
ISBN 9781399066167
The right of Jo Romero to be identified as Author of this work has been
asserted by her in accordance with the Copyright, Designs and Patents
Act 1988.
A CIP catalogue record for this book is
available from the British Library.
Set in Aldine 401 13/16.75
Printed in the UK on paper from a sustainable source by CPI Group
(UK) Ltd, Croydon, CR0 4YY

Pen & Sword Books Limited incorporates the imprints of After the
Battle, Archaeology, Atlas, Aviation, Battleground, Discovery, Family
History, History, Maritime, Military, Politics, Select, Transport,
True Crime, Fiction, Frontline Books, Leo Cooper, Praetorian Press,
Seaforth Publishing, Wharncliffe and White Owl.

For a complete list of Pen & Sword titles please contact
PEN & SWORD BOOKS LIMITED
George House, Beevor Street, Off Pontefract Road, Hoyle Mill,
Barnsley, South Yorkshire, England, S71 1HN
E-mail: enquiries@pen-and-sword.co.uk
Website: www.pen-and-sword.co.uk
Or
PEN AND SWORD BOOKS
1950 Lawrence Rd, Havertown, PA 19083, USA
E-mail: Uspen-and-sword@casematepublishers.com
Website: www.penandswordbooks.com

AUTHOR'S NoTE

While writing this book, it was exciting to uncover not only the lives of these individual women, but their collective impact on the events of the Wars of the Roses. It was important for me to portray them, as far as possible, as living, breathing characters rather than simply names and dates on a page. This objective has spilled out of the confines of the book in related projects which aim to further our knowledge and understanding of these women.

The first is a series of portraits I have created, many based on their effigies and contemporary depictions they would have seen during their lifetimes. They include Cecily Neville, Duchess of York; Anne Neville, Queen of England; Alice Chaucer, Duchess of Suffolk; and Margaret de Vere, Countess of Oxford. I have also drawn Joan Canynges, the wife of Bristol merchant William Canynges. While William is depicted in the city's paintings and stained glass, Joan has been largely overlooked; it was a real pleasure to create a life-like image of her based on the features of her effigy in Redcliffe St Mary's. You can see these portraits on my Instagram accounts @sketcherjoey and @lovebritishhistorypics, along with videos of them being drawn. I'll be producing more, so keep a lookout for reveals of other forgotten women's faces.

I also visited a number of locations known to these women; I walked around their churches, visited their places of work, and in some cases their homes. To bring you closer to them as individuals, I have also created a series of *Forgotten Women* YouTube videos to guide you through many of the places they knew in their lifetimes. You can find these on my blog https://www. lovebritishhistory.co.uk or on my YouTube Channel https://www.youtube. com/@lovebritishhistory.

More forgotten women will be discussed on my blog *Love British History* so do check in there for more stories as I uncover them. Thanks for reading, and keep in touch!

Jo Romero

CONTENTS

KEY FIGURES IN THE WARS OF THE ROSES

King Henry VI
Son of Henry V, victor of Agincourt, and his French queen, Catherine of Valois. Born in 1421, he inherited the throne at the age of nine months and suffered during his lifetime with episodes of mental illness. His inability to control ambitious nobles is one of the major causes of the Wars of the Roses. He lost the throne to Edward IV in 1461 and then regained it briefly in 1470–1471, when Edward once again took control and deposed him. Henry married Margaret of Anjou in 1445 and they had one son, named Edward. He died, imprisoned, in the Tower of London in 1471.

Queen Margaret of Anjou
Margaret was Henry VI's queen and took control of the crown during Henry's illness and inability to rule, though she faced fierce opposition. She is a central figure in the Wars of the Roses, working to claw back the crown from the Yorkists for her husband and for her son, Edward. On Edward IV's regaining power in 1471 she was imprisoned and later exiled to France. She died there in 1482.

Prince Edward of Lancaster
Son of Henry VI and Margaret of Anjou, born in 1453. He married Anne Neville, the daughter of Richard Neville, Earl of Warwick shortly before his death as a teenager at the Battle of Tewkesbury in 1471.

Richard Plantagenet, Duke of York
Husband of Cecily Neville and father to Edward Earl of March, Edmund Earl of Rutland, George Duke of Clarence and Richard Duke of Gloucester. He quarrelled with the Duke of Somerset and the crown, launching his own claim to the throne in the late 1450s. He was killed at the Battle of Wakefield in 1460.

King Edward IV

Formerly Edward Earl of March. Continuing his father's fight for the throne after his death, he deposed Henry VI in 1461. Edward fled to Burgundy during Henry's return to power in 1470–1471 but regained the throne and ruled until his death in 1483. He married Elizabeth Woodville, the daughter of an English knight.

Queen Elizabeth Woodville

Married Edward IV in 1464 she was crowned in 1465 and bore ten children, three sons and seven daughters. She fled to sanctuary at Westminster in 1470 when Henry VI regained power and again in 1483 after Richard of Gloucester took the role of Protector on his brother's death. She lived to see her daughter Elizabeth become queen to Henry VII in 1486. She died at Bermondsey Abbey in 1492.

Jacquetta Woodville, Duchess of Bedford

Elizabeth Woodville's mother and wife of Richard Woodville. Jacquetta was previously Duchess of Bedford, having married Henry V's brother John, Duke of Bedford as her first husband. She played a prominent role during the reign of Henry VI, and later when her son-in-law Edward IV reigned. She died in 1472.

King Edward V

Eldest son of Edward IV and Elizabeth Woodville, Edward was raised under the care of his uncle, Anthony Woodville. He was next in line for the throne after his father's death but was never crowned, his uncle, Richard Duke of Gloucester, agreed to take the throne instead after Edward IV's children were declared illegitimate. He is one of the missing Princes of the Tower, and his fate, along with his brother Richard, Duke of York, is unknown today.

Richard Neville, Earl of Warwick

Husband of Anne Beauchamp, Countess of Warwick. He was the

16th earl, holding the title in her right. He became disillusioned with King Edward IV and defected to Lancaster in the late 1460s, making an alliance with Margaret of Anjou in 1470. He died fighting for Henry VI at the Battle of Barnet in 1471. Warwick is often referred to as 'The Kingmaker' because whichever king he supported during the wars ended up taking the crown.

Richard Neville, Earl of Salisbury

Husband of Alice Montacute, he held the earldom of Salisbury in her right. Father of Richard Neville, Earl of Warwick and a loyal supporter of the House of York. He died after fighting at the Battle of Wakefield in 1460. His effigy, although badly worn, can be seen today at St Mary's Church in Burghfield, Berkshire.

George, Duke of Clarence

Brother of Edward IV, he married the Earl of Warwick's daughter Isabel Neville. She died in 1476, probably from a short illness or complications following childbirth. Clarence defected to Warwick's cause and then back to his brother's. He later faced accusations of treason relating to several events and was executed in 1478. He was the father of Edward Plantagenet, Earl of Warwick and Margaret, Countess of Salisbury.

Richard, Duke of Gloucester, later King Richard III

Edward IV's youngest brother, he conducted various military campaigns on behalf of the king. Popular in the north of England, he married Anne Neville, daughter of Richard, Earl of Warwick. In 1483 he challenged the legitimacy of Edward V on his brother's death and became king himself in July 1483. He was killed at the Battle of Bosworth defending his crown against Henry Tudor in August 1485.

Margaret Beaufort, Countess of Richmond and Derby

Mother of Henry Tudor, she played an active role in her son's fight for the English crown. A constant presence at her son's side once he became king, she lived to see her grandson Henry VIII become king in 1509.

Henry Tudor, later King Henry VII

Henry, Earl of Richmond and from August 1485, King of England. He married Elizabeth of York, Edward IV's daughter, and defeated Richard III at Bosworth in 1485. The threat of usurpers continued however, and he put down at least two Yorkist pretenders that claimed his crown. He died in 1509 and was succeeded by his son, Henry VIII.

Elizabeth of York, later Queen of England

She was the eldest child of Edward IV and Elizabeth Woodville and married Henry VII in 1486. Elizabeth was the sister of the Princes in the Tower. She died from complications following childbirth in 1503.

FORGoTTEN WoMEN ∏T ∏ GL∏NCE

This is not an exhaustive list but highlights some of the forgotten women mentioned in this book who played noteworthy roles in, or were influenced by, the Wars of the Roses.

Elizabeth Clerk
Lived in Reading, Berkshire, near the abbey gateway. She was the wife of a draper and was perfectly placed to witness the aftermath of the king's announcement of his marriage to Elizabeth Woodville.

Alice Chaucer
Duchess of Suffolk, Alice lived in Ewelme in Oxfordshire. Switching her allegiance from Lancaster to York, she married her son to the Duke of York's daughter, Elizabeth. Alice and her husband established almshouses in her village that are still lived in today, and contributed to the building of their local church.

Elizabeth Fitzherbert
Wife to Ralph Fitzherbert, a supporter of Richard III, his effigy depicts him wearing the king's boar emblem. Despite anxieties over the national conflict, Elizabeth carried out her household duties, raising children, managing property, and ensuring their continuing education, from their home in Norbury, Derbyshire.

Ankarette Twynhoe
A Somerset widow who served in the household of Isabel Neville, wife of George, Duke of Clarence. She was accused of poisoning her mistress and was hanged. The controversial handling of her case has been linked with the dramatic fate of her accuser.

Alice Montacute, Countess of Salisbury
Mother to Richard Neville, Earl of Warwick and wife of Richard

Neville, Earl of Salisbury. Alice was personally attainted and declared a traitor during the Wars of the Roses, for her active role within the Yorkist party.

Katharine Gordon

Wife of Perkin Warbeck, a pretender to the throne who claimed to be Richard, the younger son of Edward IV, and one of the Princes in the Tower. She was captured after Perkin's arrest and, despite her precarious position, loyally served in Queen Elizabeth's household and was welcomed into the Tudor court. She is not often acknowledged for her own actions following her arrest but demonstrated quick-thinking in dealing with Henry VII.

Elizabeth Stonor

An often-overlooked woman of letters, her correspondence reveals much about women's roles in maintaining businesses during the period, in Elizabeth's case, in the wool trade. She lived near Henley on Thames with her husband William Stonor and was known to popular characters of the wars.

Agnes Overay

Widow and landholder in Southampton. She managed several properties and tenants around the port and contributed towards the maintenance of the town walls, strengthening its security at a period of uncertainty. She had a wider perspective of the disorder and violence of the wars, having lived through earlier unrest and beheadings in Southampton during the reign of Henry V. Agnes also had links to the port's merchant community and local government.

Margaret Neville, Countess of Oxford

Was asked to borrow money, send men, and equip her husband with saddles and horses ahead of the Lancastrian challenge to the crown in 1470. Wife of John de Vere, Earl of Oxford and sister of the Earl of Warwick, concerns were raised for her financial welfare while her husband was away fighting for the Lancastrian cause.

Gonnora Dowtton
Abbess of Delapré Abbey near Northampton from around 1459 to 1481. She was perfectly placed to witness the Battle of Northampton that took place in the grounds close to the abbey in 1460. With reports that some of the war dead were buried there, Gonnora, as a senior member of the community, would have overseen the burials after the battle.

Marjory Cobbe
Elizabeth Woodville's midwife and traditionally attendant to the queen during her time in sanctuary at Westminster Abbey in 1470. Marjory would have delivered Edward in dubious circumstances. He was born a Yorkist prince while a Lancastrian king was on the throne.

Jane Shore
Edward IV's mistress. Sir Thomas More hinted at her wider influence with the king and his court in helping promote and further the causes of others. Publicly humiliated and ordered to do penance by Richard, Duke of Gloucester after Edward's death, she died an elderly woman during the early reign of Henry VIII.

Alice Claver
London silk woman supplying rich fabrics and accessories to Edward IV. Her work and that of the other silk women helped the monarchy present England as a strong state with wealth and resources, despite the political backbiting that was happening within.

Elizabeth Delabere née Mores
Helped the Duchess of Buckingham disguise her eldest son, Edward

Stafford, to evade detection by Richard III's men following the failed Buckingham Rebellion in 1483. He was restored and became Duke of Buckingham but was later executed on charges of treason by Henry VIII.

Joan Conys
Tenant of the Swan Inn, on Church Street in St Albans, along with her husband John and their son William. The inn was just one street away from the clash of troops at the marketplace during the Second Battle of St Albans in 1461.

Joan Canynges
Wife of influential and wealthy mayor of Bristol, William Canynges, who was said to have entertained Edward IV at their home in September 1461. Joan would have played a key part in the preparations, acting as ambassador for Bristol as well as for her own family.

INTRODUCTION

The Wars of the Roses were fought in England over the space of more than thirty years in the fifteenth century. It wasn't a continual conflict, instead it was marked by periods of peace alternating with political tension, battles and skirmishes. Fuelled by Henry VI's lack of strong government, the English throne changed hands no fewer than six times between 1455 and 1487 as the Houses of York and Lancaster fought for control of the kingdom.

Contemporary sources are dominated by the actions of kings, earls and dukes during this period. However, recent research has examined the influence of many royal women during the conflict, highlighting their individual contributions and, in many cases, challenging stereotypes. Margaret of Anjou, Henry VI's queen, fought tirelessly to regain royal control on behalf of her Lancastrian husband. Elizabeth Woodville's shock marriage to Edward IV paved the way for her and her family to hold influence at the Yorkist court. Their daughter, Elizabeth of York, is often considered to have brought an end to the wars with her wedding to Henry VII. Other well-known and powerful royal women of the period include Jacquetta Woodville, Duchess of Bedford and mother to Queen Elizabeth Woodville, and of course Margaret Beaufort, Countess of Richmond and Derby, the mother of Henry VII.

But what about the thousands of women living in their country estates, towns and cities, who experienced the wars' hostilities?

With some digging, their names and identities began to spill from sources and chronicles. These included a London silk woman whose work dazzled ambassadors and foreign visitors, helping the king maintain a strong and capable image; a young mother who waited anxiously for the fate of her husband, held hostage and under threat of execution; and a duchess who dodged accusations of treason to become a royal mother-in-law. Among them, thousands of wives and mothers waited for husbands and sons to return from battle.

Others ran businesses that profited from the wars, or acted as political ambassadors. Women were also traitors and rebels, covert messengers, companions, and peacekeepers.

For some, their stories have only recently been forgotten. Medieval chronicles record some of them, while legal and court documents reveal others. Historians of later generations, from the sixteenth to nineteenth centuries, preserved more of their stories as they researched women discovered in their own local and family archives. We will challenge some of the opinions these historians formed about these women and attempt to re-evaluate them in the wider context of the Wars of the Roses. Contemporary ballads, poems and local legends also give an insight into women's many roles and duties during the period. In many cases, it is only during the twentieth century that their stories have become absent from many of the history books.

As well as countesses, duchesses and queens at the centre of court, we will also explore the supporting roles played by women as midwives, servants and innkeepers. While there were women who played central, decisive roles in the conflict, others simply lived through it and their experiences are valuable too. Their personal lives reveal some surprising links that existed between some of them.

The first official battle of the Wars of the Roses took place at St Albans in 1455, however, tensions and social unrest had been simmering for some time before this. For this reason, this book considers sources from the 1440s to take account of events leading to early military action, including Cade's Rebellion in the summer of 1450. Similarly, the end of the wars is usually marked by the Battle of Stoke in 1487. However, sources are included from later in the Tudor reign, including those relating to Perkin Warbeck's York-influenced challenge to Henry VII's crown in the 1490s.

Women from all walks of life were affected by the Wars of the Roses, their alabaster effigies lie silent in parish churches today. The hope is that these stories will encourage further research as it is time that their stories were told.

PART ONE:
Family Matters

CHAPTER ONE
CONSEQUENCES OF WAR

By the end of the Elizabethan age the clash of swords and blast of guns had left living memory, but audiences would remember tales passed down of the Wars of the Roses, and William Shakespeare knew it. Intentionally focusing on the agony of mothers and wives in his play *Henry VI*, a son drags his dead father across the stage, while another father carries the lifeless son he has just killed in battle.

The father cries, 'How will my wife for slaughter of my son shed seas of tears, and never be satisfied.' While the son wonders, 'How will my mother for a father's death take on with me and never be satisfied.'[1]

The number of soldiers said to have fought during the wars varies considerably depending on the source. These figures may have been exaggerated for propaganda, confusion, or inaccurate counting. In a letter to John Paston in 1461 the Battle of Towton's dead was recorded at 'gentle and commons, to the number of twenty thousand'.[2] Although numbers of battle casualties are often estimated lower by modern historians, it is certain that over the course of more than three decades and ten major battles, human losses were significant. During these wars tens of thousands of women found themselves affected by warfare as every man that fought and died left behind a daughter, niece, wife, lover, friend or mother.

The Wars of the Roses was not a conflict that affected only the nobility; the military aspect of the wars impacted men and women from all levels of society. The author of the *Croyland Chronicle* wrote that 'besides the dukes, earls, barons and distinguished warriors who were cruelly slain, multitudes almost innumerable of the common people died of their wounds'.[3] Edward Hall, the Tudor historian, described a divided realm with 'many thousands slain'.[4] They were not all trained soldiers either. The author of *Gregory's Chronicle* reported that the captain commanding men at Dunstable in 1461 was actually the town butcher. After the battle the butcher hanged himself, either because of the loss of his goods, said Gregory, or over the guilt of losing eight hundred of his men.[5]

As the Duke of York's army took their positions for that first battle at St Albans in 1455, Henry VI promised to 'destroy them, every mother's son'.[6] Just as Shakespeare's image of mourning mothers was designed to unsettle an Elizabethan audience, the reference to their impending grief in Henry's royal proclamation unnerved and intimidated the enemy.

The Brutality of Battle 'nought else is war but fury and madness'

It is not often we stop to think of battle as a very real and terrifying human experience. Brutal, gory and relentless, men were left dead, or severely wounded, on the field or hastily buried in ditches. Sometimes soldiers fought on despite corpses piling up underneath their boots. Abbot Wethamstede, at the Battle of St Albans in 1455 found 'here one lying with his brains dashed out, here another without his arm, some with arrows in their throats, others pierced in their chests'.[7] Axes, swords, arrows, and daggers maimed, killed and brutalized the enemy, while horses' hooves thundered around the field. Guns were fired blindly into the mist and arrows fizzed through the sky. The Tudor historian Polydore Vergil wrote that, at the Battle of Towton, once the arrows had run out 'the matter was dealt with by hand strokes with so great slaughter that the very dead carcasses hindered them that fought'.[8] According to the chronicler

John Stow, men were called up to fight from the age of sixteen to sixty.[9]

Battle depleted the enemy of its supporters and humiliated its survivors. High-ranking soldiers from the losing side were captured and jostled into marketplaces and beheaded to the yells of baying crowds. Far from bringing matters to an end, this spilled blood only served to fuel further battles and rebellions. According to Stow, 'the children of these, when the world turned, revenged themselves', while nineteenth-century historian Agnes Strickland described the younger generation 'panting to avenge their parents' blood'.[10] A self-perpetuating cycle of brutality, humiliation, and revenge, it's no wonder the exasperated and exhausted Henry VI was said to have written after his capture 'nought else is war but fury and madness'.[11]

Most contemporary chronicles and records give little indication of the real emotional loss experienced by men and women as a result of battle during this period. However, some insight can be provided by Medieval songs and ballads. *The Song of Lady Bessy*, written in around 1485, includes the line 'they blew up their bugles of brass, that made many a wife to cry, alas; and many a wife's child fatherless'.[12] Another song, *The Ballad of Chevy Chase*, was written in the sixteenth century and tells of an early fifteenth-century battle. Describing how women 'bewailed' the deaths of their husbands and 'washed their wounds in brinish tears', it continues 'their bodies, bathed in purple gore, they bare with them away; they kissed them dead a thousand times, ere they were clad in clay'.[13]

Cecily Neville, Duchess of York steadied herself as she waited for news following the Battle of Wakefield in Yorkshire on 30 December 1460. Soon afterwards she would learn of the deaths of her brother Richard Neville, Earl of Salisbury, her seventeen-year-old son Edmund, Earl of Rutland and her husband Richard Plantagenet, Duke of York. A special humiliation was reserved for York by the Lancastrian victors, who fixed a paper crown onto the duke's head in mockery of his regal ambitions. Once decapitated, it was raised onto a spike atop York's Mickelgate Bar. Cecily's anxiety and subsequent grief in the aftermath of Wakefield was a sentiment echoed by countless other women and girls who waited at home, nervously, for news.

Joan, Baroness Strange of Knockin 'my lady at home'

On 22 August 1485 Henry Tudor's forces squared up against those of Richard III in a field near Market Bosworth in Leicestershire. Richard was immediately identifiable, wearing a coronet on his helmet, his substantial and well-assembled army glinting in the sun. But despite this outward show of strength the king was anxious. Richard had doubted the loyalty of the Stanley brothers William and Thomas, and had seized Thomas' son George as a hostage. The reason? Thomas was now Henry Tudor's stepfather, having married Margaret Beaufort, Tudor's mother. Could Stanley and his brother be trusted to support the crown in a battle that aimed to extinguish Lancastrian resistance, or would he be tempted to help Tudor, now his stepson, to the throne? Taking possession of Thomas' twenty-five-year-old heir George Stanley, thought Richard, would ensure the former.[14]

The Song of Lady Bessy, a ballad written to celebrate the outcome of the battle, features Tudor's future queen Elizabeth of York along with Margaret Beaufort. But it also mentions other lesser-known women involved in the events of Bosworth, including Joan, Baroness Strange.

While George was being held under Richard's watchful eye, his wife Joan was at their home in Lancashire. The daughter of Jacquetta Woodville (Elizabeth Woodville's sister) and John Le Strange, Lord Strange of Knockin, she was linked to the Yorkist royal family just as the Stanleys had marital ties to the Lancastrians. On her father's death in 1477 and as his only child, Joan had inherited the title Baroness Strange of Knockin. When she married George in around

1482, he held the title in Joan's right. The couple were newlywed and parents. The dating of the birth of their son Thomas around 1485 means that in August of that year Joan may have been either pregnant or caring for a young child.[15]

As she adapted to the absence of her husband, Joan would have endured some stress and uncertainty over his precarious situation. As servants busied themselves at home, Joan waited anxiously for news. The author of *The Song of Lady Bessy* liked to think that she was in George's thoughts, too. The ballad has King Richard telling George he is soon to die for his uncle William Stanley's treachery for backing Tudor.

'If I should die, said the Lord Strange then,
As God forbid it should so be,
Alas! for my lady that is at home,
It should be long [until] she see me.
But we shall meet at Doomsday,
When the great doom shall be.'

The ballad then relates how George slipped a ring from his finger and asked a gentleman to take it to Lancashire, 'to his lady that was at home'.[16]

The ballad is certainly Tudor-sympathetic. However, it also has potential as a valuable source relating to events at the Battle of Bosworth. Conspirators and soldiers are mentioned by name, and the depiction of Richard III's death is remarkably similar to that supported by recent archaeological evidence, following the discovery of his skeleton by a team from the University of Leicester in 2013. The author of the ballad is thought to have been Humphrey Brereton who was known to both the Stanleys and Elizabeth of York. He may have been an eyewitness to events at the battle or gained knowledge from others present.[17]

The author's careful inclusion of Baroness Strange puts wives at the forefront of men's minds as they prepared for battle, suggesting that this was not at all unusual. Other sources support this. In a letter written by William de la Pole, Duke of Suffolk shortly before his murder in 1450 he conveyed the trust he had in his wife Alice. William Herbert, Earl of Pembroke's wife Anne was also remembered in a personal note written to her in his will before he faced execution in 1469.[18] Joan's individual experience as a 'lady at home' was certainly one of hundreds if not thousands played out across the country during the Wars of the Roses. It is not often however that their presence and individual experiences relating to battle are acknowledged in the context of the wars' history.

In the end, taking George Stanley hostage did not guarantee the Stanleys' loyalty. George's uncle William did indeed support Henry during the battle and his intervention greatly contributed to the Tudor victory. However, despite this, George survived. The seventeenth-century chronicler Richard Baker claims he escaped in the confusion created by Henry's rapid advance, as Richard's men urged him to begin preparations for battle.[19] Once reunited, Joan and George continued to live into the reign of the Tudor kings. Peter Stanley, in *The House of Stanley*, finds that they had seven children, with George fighting at the Battle of Stoke in 1487 as well as in other military engagements up until his death in 1503. Joan died in 1513.[20]

Elizabeth Poynings, née Paston 'contrary to right and conscience'

By the end of May 1487, the new Tudor king, Henry VII, had been ruling for almost two years. As rumours of a new Yorkist claim to the throne trickled into England's villages and towns a widow sat comfortably at her home. The security and tranquillity she conveyed in middle age revealed none of the adversities she had endured in her earlier years.

The daughter of William Paston and his wife Agnes, Elizabeth Paston had grown up with her parents and brothers in Norfolk during the early years of the Wars of the Roses. In the beginning of 1461, now married with a young son, she would soon be plunged into a desperate fight for her livelihood.

Elizabeth's husband Robert Poynings left their home shortly before 17 February 1461 to fight at the Second Battle of St Albans. Before departing, he made a will stipulating that if he should die, Elizabeth was to have 'the rule of all his livelihood', be responsible for paying his debts and use their income to provide for her and their baby son, Edward.[21] Tragedy struck and Robert was killed in the battle. However, despite the couple's sensible forward-planning, Elizabeth's security was dashed when Robert Fynes and Edmund Grey, Earl of Kent took Poynings' lands by force.

In a letter that survives in the Paston Letters, Elizabeth asks for help from her nephew Sir John Paston. She explains to him that, after Robert's death, Fynes seized and did 'great hurt' to their Kent manors, while Edmund took others, passing them to Henry Bourchier, Earl of Essex. In need of her revenues and because the actions were 'contrary to right and conscience' she asks John to speak to the king on her behalf so that 'I and mine assigns may peaceably re-enjoy them'.[22]

By instructing John in the specific steps to take, Elizabeth demonstrates a sound knowledge of legal procedure, something she may have learned while observing her father and brother conducting their legal work. She asks that 'honourable letters' are sent to Fynes, discharging him of the revenues of the properties. Then, 'if any person would attempt to do the contrary, that a commandment, if it please the king's highness, by him might be given to my Lord Chancellor to seal writings sufficient with his great seal'. She signs off, promising to repay any expenses Sir John incurs in petitioning her case.[23]

It is unclear from Elizabeth's writing if the sudden infringement on Poynings' lands was triggered solely by Robert's death in battle. The 'great waste and hurt' she describes taking place does imply a sense of intimidation and fear instigated by the perpetrators and she does refer to Robert's departure when describing the origins of the dispute. The dating of the letter also hints that Elizabeth endured a long fight to restore her lands, with John Fenn dating it to at least four years after the Second Battle of St Albans and Robert's death. What is clear however from Elizabeth's letter is her practical and assertive nature. Intelligent, self-assured and well-informed of legal processes, she also had a strong moral need to see justice carried out.

Elizabeth later married courtier Sir George Browne. Once again however, her marital life would be shattered when George was executed in 1483 for his part in the Buckingham Rebellion against Richard III. Elizabeth had now experienced the loss of two husbands as a direct result of battle and political fallout from the wars. She never remarried and seems to have spent her later days in some financial comfort. Helen Castor, in her work on the Paston family, *Blood and Roses*, finds that her will contained a large number of items including silver plate, furniture and textiles.[24] She died in 1488.

Margaret Beaufort, Countess of Stafford

Back in 1455, while Elizabeth Paston was considering potential husbands in Norfolk, two dukes were bristling over influence and power in London. The animosity between Richard Plantagenet, Duke of York and Edmund Beaufort, Duke of Somerset, both ambitious men with royal blood, would soon tip the country from political tension into armed military conflict. York was being increasingly sidelined by Henry VI and his queen Margaret of Anjou, who continued to promote and elevate Somerset. Croyland wrote that those around the king intentionally set about to tarnish York's reputation, whispering accusations about him that it 'made him to stink in the king's nostrils'.[25] Meanwhile, Somerset continued to rise in status and power. He was raised to duke in 1448 and granted a number of titles including Constable of England in 1450 and two years later, Lord of the Isle of Wight. This was all despite Somerset's military failings in France, while York had been an able and popular commander.[26] With those around the king, including Queen Margaret, continuing to support Somerset, Henry finally stationed York in Ireland, something Alison Weir, in *Lancaster and York*, has called a 'virtual exile'.[27]

As armies buckled on armour in the First Battle of St Albans on 22 May 1455, York's intention at that moment was to remove what he considered Somerset's harmful influence over the king. The end of the battle, fought in the streets of the town, would be marked by Somerset's death, as he was hacked down by York's army outside the Castle Inn. York declared the victory, and Edmund's lifeless body was dragged onto a cart and trundled to the nearby abbey for burial.[28]

Somerset's politically driven murder was one in a long line of Beaufort deaths that would bring endless grief and loss to Edmund's family, in particular, to his daughter Margaret.

As she grew up, Margaret would have waved goodbye to her father as he left for royal negotiations and sailed off to war in France. Her family celebrated her father's growing elevation at court, prayed for his safe return from abroad and would have discussed the implications of York's growing bitterness towards him. Somerset's daughter, Margaret, was never far from politics and war. She would not escape it in adulthood either, as the wife of Humphrey Stafford, son of the Duke of Buckingham.

The First Battle of St Albans would be life changing for Margaret. According to Cokayne, her son Henry was born in 1454. If his dating is correct, Margaret would have been caring for an infant son at the time of her father's death.[29] In 1458 she lost her husband, however Susan Higginbotham has stated that this was down to plague rather than battle.[30] More wars-related tragedy was to come, with the deaths of Margaret's father-in-law Buckingham at the Battle of Northampton in 1460, and her brother Henry's execution at Hexham in the spring of 1464. The deaths of two more brothers followed. John and Edmund were killed at the Battle of Tewkesbury in 1471.[31] As the younger Edmund Beaufort lowered his neck onto the block and closed his eyes, the Beaufort line of the Dukes of Somerset came to an abrupt and bloody end.

Margaret had lost a father, father-in-law and three brothers to battle during the Wars of the Roses. Its violence even continued to affect her and Humphrey's heirs long after their deaths, with the execution of her son Henry, Duke of Buckingham in 1483 for rebelling against Richard III. Her grandson, Edward, would be found guilty of treason under Henry VIII and would be executed in 1521.

It is tempting to imagine a Beaufort curse maliciously hanging over the family long after the Wars of the Roses and into the Tudor era. But as a high-profile family with royal connections, their roles in the conflict were always going to be central. Active in battle and with royal blood of their own the Somersets and the Buckinghams paid the price for their status. Margaret's Somerset relatives also faced death for their unswerving Lancastrian loyalty at a time of Yorkist dominance. We can see in their deaths the revenge pointed out by Strickland, the resolve of younger generations to avenge the spilled blood of their elders. For Margaret and her family, the civil wars were brutal. In just over fifteen years she had lost her brothers, husband and father. The death of her mother Eleanor would also come in around 1468.[32] The experiences of women like Margaret at the edges of the conflict are not often examined, but by switching our perspective we can gain an idea of the challenges she faced and the loss she would have felt, giving our understanding of the wars a new layer of compassion.

Elizabeth Scales 'cast wild fire into the city'

Fathers were lost in the heat of the wars, but not only on the battlefield. Elizabeth Scales was the daughter of Thomas Lord Scales and his wife Ismania, sometimes also referred to as Emma. Both parents were in favour with the Lancastrian royal family, Ismania serving as a gentlewoman to Queen Margaret.[33] Thomas served in Henry VI's early wars in France and in 1450 was involved in suppressing Jack Cade's rebellion.[34] It was Scales, wrote Stow, who 'was left to keep the Tower' when the king, queen and lords fled London as Cade's rebels approached.[35] He is also mentioned in Margaret of Anjou's household accounts 'for his diligent daily attendance in our council' and demonstrated a strong loyalty to Lancaster during the Wars of the Roses.[36]

Richard Neville, Earl of Salisbury had been left in London while the main Yorkist army rode to Northampton to challenge the king's forces. Thomas Scales, fearing for his safety as Salisbury's troops approached, locked himself in the Tower of London with other lords, knights and royal servants. Panicked and hemmed in, Scales and Lord Hungerford ordered guns to be fired across London to repel the Yorkist supporters. It was a catastrophic miscalculation. They 'cast wild fire into the city... whereby they burnt and slew men, women and children in the streets', wrote Stow.[37]

Around two weeks later Scales escaped from the Tower, secretly stole away into the night and boarded a small boat on the inky Thames. Stow writes that he was heading for sanctuary, while Hall thinks he was instead fleeing towards Queen Margaret.[38] Wherever he was going, he never made it. Recognized by a woman on the shoreline, he was set upon by men on the river and murdered, his punctured and blood-stained body discarded on the shore. Gregory calls him a 'notable warrior' whose body was left 'despoiled, naked as a worm'.[39]

As his sole heir, Elizabeth became Baroness Scales on her father's death. By around 1462 she had married Anthony Woodville, Elizabeth Woodville's brother. Although no specific date survives for the marriage, Cokayne found that Anthony was summoned to parliament as Lord Scales in December 1462 and so had received the title, via his wife, by this date.[40]

Thomas' unexpected and violent death would have been a tragic loss for Elizabeth as arrangements were made for his body to be removed from the Thames shore and buried. Elizabeth may have looked back on her experiences at this time ruefully when, in 1469, her husband suffered the loss of his own father and brother due to the wars. Richard Woodville, Lord Rivers and his son John were beheaded after the Yorkist loss at the Battle of Edgecote that summer.[41] Elizabeth would not live to see her own husband beheaded on the orders of Richard, Duke of Gloucester in Pontefract, Yorkshire in 1483. She died on 2 September 1473.[42]

Men heading into battle were able, in some way, to prepare for death. They wrote wills, like Robert Poynings, in an effort to ease the legal and economic transition for their wives into widowhood. They were able to say a tentative goodbye to loved ones before leaving or uttering prayers for the salvation of their souls. For those murdered in the regional brutality of the Wars of the Roses however, there was no time to prepare. Elizabeth's father, husband, brother-in-law and father-in-law would all suffer violent and sudden deaths from events directly linked to the political turbulence of the Wars of the Roses. Her story reminds us that violent and vengeful death threatened those away from the battlefield during this period as much as on it.

Lawlessness and Rebellion 'nothing more than her kirtle and her smock'

Towards the end of the fifteenth century, the diplomat Philip de Commines wrote that in England during the wars, 'neither the country, nor the people, nor the houses were wasted, destroyed or demolished; but the calamities and misfortunes of the war fell only upon the soldiers, and especially the nobility'.[43] Other sources suggest otherwise.

Commines was probably writing based on what he had learned from English dignitaries about pitched battle, but legal records, court documents and chronicles show that residents of towns and cities witnessed the conflict too. Uneasy political tensions, a lack of royal control and bitter disappointment within communities provoked violent attacks on homes, cities and their residents.

Thousands marched with the rebel Jack Cade through London in the summer of 1450, many of them residents of Kent and the southeast of England, focusing on anyone they considered responsible for the recent failures in government. Cade's rebels left a path of beheadings and humiliation, eventually fighting on London Bridge where, Gregory noted in horror, 'many a man was cast in the Thames, harness, body and all'.[44]

One woman's ordeal with Cade's rebels is breathlessly related in the Paston Letters. The wife of J. Payn (her first name is not given) was stunned to find they had broken into her Kent home while her husband was away. Threatening to hang her and her five children, the rebels took all the family's possessions. Payn, in a letter to John Paston, writes that eventually, when they abandoned the home, they left her with nothing more than 'her kirtle and her smock'.[45]

Cade's uprising was not an isolated throng of discontented subjects, but initially a fairly well-organised force with political aims. It also had political consequences. His nickname, 'Jack Amend All', signalled a desire to see reform in Henry VI's government, especially the removal of those he considered were exercising harmful or self-serving influence over the king. His intentions were similar to the reasons for York's animosity towards Somerset before the First Battle of St Albans. Eighteenth-century writer John Noorthouck also noted that, once order had been imposed, the people began to 'listen to the Duke of York's pretensions, which now became a general topic of discussion'.[46]

There were others. The Lincolnshire Rebellion of 1470 was rumoured to have been raised secretly by the now-Lancastrian Earl of Warwick and Duke of Clarence to distract Edward IV; its leader, Sir Robert Welles, implicated them in his confession following his capture.[47] The following year Londoners faced a rebellion led by

Thomas Neville, also known as the Bastard of Fauconberg, a cousin of the Earl of Warwick. He had come to release Henry VI from the Tower, unleashing flame and guns into the city. Cora Scofield, in *The Life and Reign of Edward IV*, highlighted the impact this attack had on the Londoners, the assault destroying a number of houses in Aldgate and thirteen tenements on the bridge.[48]

Private family disputes also ran wild in the heavy political climate, which exacerbated ancient feuds. Local skirmishes, battles and attacks on homes, servants and family members could end in arson, capture or murder. Holinshed wrote that in Northumberland, supporters of the Yorkist pretender Perkin Warbeck 'began the war in most cruel manner, with slaughter of men, burning of towns, spoiling of houses, and committing of all other detestable enormities; so that all the country of Northumberland was by them in manner wasted, and destroyed'.[49]

The idea then that only the soldiers and nobility experienced the sharp end of the wars' violence is firmly disputed by contemporary sources. Reports of illegal gatherings are frequently mentioned in the period's administrative documents and wider rebellions such as those under Cade, Welles and Fauconberg were triggered by existing political struggles and tensions, as the reigning king struggled to maintain control. Fires burned and families were threatened or robbed. It's perhaps no wonder that in 1462 Margaret Paston wrote with a heavy sigh and more than a little anxiety that 'men fear sore here of a common rising', and 'I heard never say of so much robbery and manslaughter in this country as is now within a little time'.[50]

Joan Judde 'a large ransom'

The presence of a band of rebels bursting into the home must have been frightening, but not all citizens ran from Cade's rebels. Surviving evidence reveals that some confronted them and negotiated for safety.

A loyal supporter of Henry VI, John Judde was a London merchant who attracted the attention of the rebels. One, named Lawrence Stokwode, charged into his home and threatened him. The entry in the corresponding Chancery Proceedings specifies a 'false arrest, compelling the wife of the said John to pay large ransom to the rebel Cade'.[51] A 1449 entry in the Calendar of Close Rolls indicates that John's wife was called Joan.[52] Rather than feeling intimidated and submitting to Stokwode, Joan calmly stepped forward and began negotiations for her husband's safety.

This unnerving altercation only seemed to breathe new enthusiasm into John's Lancastrian efforts. In December 1456 he was made Master of the King's Ordnance after promising to deliver sixty guns and a quantity of gunpowder at his own expense.[53] Between 1458–1460 we see him gathering bows and arrows as he was ordered to 'seize all the ordnance and habiliments of war late of Richard late Duke of York and Richard, late Earl of Salisbury'.[54] As it turned out, Joan had only managed to extend John's life by ten years. Both *Bale's Chronicle* and the *Short English Chronicle* record that he was violently murdered while carrying weapons for the king just beyond St Albans, on 22 June 1460. Joan was alive in March 1461, when she appears in an entry in the Close Rolls gifting goods to her daughter, Alice.[55]

The chronicler Fabyan gives another example of a wife intervening for her husband's safety. With Cade ordering the capture of the alderman Robert Horne, he writes, 'his wife and friends made to him such instant labour that finally, for five hundred marks, he was set at his liberty'.[56]

Both Joan and the unnamed wife of Robert Horne showed considerable bravery and steadiness in negotiating with rebels for their husbands' safety. It must have been a frightening experience, but they were able to stay calm under intense pressure, well aware of the arrests and beheadings taking place in the city.

There were also many other unidentified women and girls who witnessed Cade's rebellion. Hall tells us that 'fearful women with children in their arms, amazed and appalled, leapt into the river:

others doubting how to save themselves between fire, water and sword, were in their houses suffocated and smouldered'.[57] For these women, violence came not in organized battle with commanders in charge, but when they least expected it, in their homes and in the streets. Joan Judde, Elizabeth Scales and the wife of J. Payn all represent the hundreds of women affected by rebellion linked to the political struggles of the Wars of the Roses.

Margaret Harcourt 'Lady of the Garter'

Margaret Harcourt's experience during the Wars of the Roses is related in *The Harcourt Papers*, a history of the Harcourt family including transcriptions of family documents, compiled in 1880. Margaret lost her husband to violence, but not in a pitched battle or to politically driven rebels. Robert Harcourt was killed in one of the many family feuds that rippled beneath the national unrest of the wars.

Robert Harcourt had enjoyed a stable career in royal service as Sheriff of Leicestershire and Warwickshire under Henry VI. He was also part of the gathering that met Margaret of Anjou at Rouen for her wedding in 1445. After the Yorkist accession he was made a Knight of the Garter, an honour his wife also received.[58] Rarely given, and even rarer for women, this would have been in acknowledgement of Margaret's own dedicated service to the crown.

The later years of the Harcourt-Stafford feud may have been influenced by the wars; however, their dispute had been ongoing for more than twenty years when Robert was killed in the autumn of 1470. His murderer was Humphrey Stafford, the 'Bastard' of Grafton. The author of the *Harcourt Papers*, Edward William Harcourt, identifies him as a loyal Lancastrian.[59]

The differing allegiances between Robert Harcourt and Humphrey Stafford may be significant. Differing political opinions only fuelled existing animosity between families, and Robert's murder coincided with a surge in Lancastrian resistance during late 1470. With the Earl of Warwick, Duke of Clarence and Margaret of Anjou planning a reinstatement of Henry VI to the throne at this time, Robert's murder, just two months after Warwick's landing, seems politically motivated. It is also possible that it was timed to coincide with Henry VI's new, Lancastrian-sympathetic government, which might treat the murder of a prominent Yorkist more leniently.

Whatever the reasons behind the family feud, Margaret pleaded with the Staffords for compensation over Robert's death, which, she said, had involved Humphrey along with 150 other men. A response from Stafford, or any other evidence of Margaret's success, could not be found.[60]

Eleanor, Duchess of Somerset had been granted funds after her husband was killed at the Battle of St Albans in 1455. Stow records that Henry VI presided over a meeting where the Duke of York agreed to pay her and her son Henry the huge sum of five thousand marks on account of Somerset's death.[61] But Eleanor was a prominent duchess, seeking compensation at the beginning of the conflict. By 1470 battles had taken place all over England and compensation was probably, by now, more difficult to secure.

From the moment she married into the Harcourt family, hostility and war would have been part of Margaret's life. Thrust into a private battle between two warring families, her husband was as much the aggressor as the victim. Not only would she have worried about Robert's safety, but also that of her children and herself, should the Staffords plan a well-timed attack on the home while he was away on royal business.

Margaret lies buried beside her husband Robert at Stanton Harcourt church in Oxfordshire. Robert lies fully armoured with a sword at his side, a Yorkist collar of roses and suns placed over his chest. Margaret wears her Garter ribbon, an honour she would have proudly accepted in life, buckled above her elbow. One of the many women who found themselves tussled by local unrest, Margaret lived in the middle of a regional, family-driven war that simmered beneath the national fight for the crown.

The 'Mad Woman' of Hereford

Consequences of battle, we have seen, were felt by men and women all over the country, even if they did not physically fight in an army. They contended with grief and the unsettling loss of husbands, fathers, brothers and sons, as well as the financial, legal and social implications of these deaths. But one anecdote, related in *Gregory's Chronicle,* suggests a psychological effect, too.

Owen Tudor had married Henry V's queen, Catherine de Valois, after the king's death. Catherine died in 1437 and Owen supported the side of Lancaster during the Wars of the Roses; their sons were half-brothers to Henry VI. Having fought at the Battle of Mortimer's Cross in 1461, Owen was captured by Yorkists and led to Hereford's marketplace, where he was beheaded.

Gregory says that after Owen's head was removed from his body, a 'madde woman' came forward, washing and combing his hair and wiping blood from the decapitated head. She then went to work lighting candles, said to be over 100 of them, around Tudor's head which was placed on the highest point of the market cross.[62]

Nothing more is known about this woman, but she is an oft-forgotten witness to the wars' violent and bloody events. Fifteenth-century attitudes dismissed her as 'mad', but it's possible she was instead suffering from shock, having seen Tudor's hasty execution carried out in her town square. She may even have known him in life, or she may have been suffering from a longer-term mental health condition. Candles were often lit around the body at medieval funerals, vast costs often paid for wax; in this context her actions seem more compassionate than odd. Today, shoppers pass over the plaque in Hereford's marketplace that marks the site of Tudor's death, but the woman that stepped forward to show respect for his memory is rarely acknowledged, even in modern history books. She does however deserve to be remembered, not only as an observer of the wars' bloody nature, but also for the sensitivity and concern she showed to Tudor's memory after his execution.

The voices of the women living through these turbulent and traumatic events are rarely recorded. However, it is possible to find their experiences of the wars in legal and court documents, letters and ballads. Margaret Beaufort, Countess Stafford, Elizabeth Paston, Joan Strange, Joan Judde and Hereford's 'Mad Woman' are just a few of these. Hundreds more filed past publicly displayed bodies of dukes, earls and kings or squinted up at the spiked, severed heads set on York's Mickelgate Bar. They watched as heads tumbled from blocks in marketplaces and waited patiently for news of loved ones in battle. The consequences of war were many: physical, financial, social, emotional and, most likely, psychological.

For their daughters and granddaughters, the words of Shakespeare's victorious Henry Tudor echoed around the theatre. At the end of *Richard III*, the new king triumphantly promises to 'unite the white rose and the red', challenging anyone that 'says not Amen,' reflecting the exhaustion of a nation wrought with internal war for three decades.

They would have listened intently, remembering their older relatives, as a sixteenth-century actor bellowed to a packed Elizabethan audience:

'England hath long been mad, and scarred herself;
The brother blindly shed the brother's blood,
The father rashly slaughtered his own son.
The son, compelled, been butcher to the sire.[63]

CHAPTER TWO
BUSINESS AS USUAL

With the sound of battle trumpets far in the distance, women fulfilled another crucial role during the Wars of the Roses. Responsible for maintaining the home, family estates and servants during their husbands' absences, a number of sources shed light on the daily lives of wives and widows. Account books uncover their expenses, revealing the wide range of responsibilities under their control. Inventories and wills list their domestic surroundings in vivid colour, from the embroidered hangings that decorated their beds to their favourite books and jewels. From these, it is sometimes possible to gain at least a little insight into individual women's personalities.

While women were not permitted to hold positions of local government, we do find them supporting their politician or lawyer husbands away from the public eye, assisting with errands or hosting at important events. In support of her husband, one woman of the wars crossed the sea from Flanders to settle in England. John Utynam was commanded by Henry VI to settle in the country with his wife, children and servants to make stained glass windows for the king's colleges of Eton, St Mary and St Nicholas in Cambridge, also teaching Englishmen his craft. Their charter was made on 3 April 1449, just over a year before Cade's Rebellion.[64] As she sailed with her husband, she must have felt excitement, embarking on this new opportunity for the family. Just over a year later, as news of glowing embers falling from the sky and rebels firing from London Bridge reached her, she must have reconsidered their future.

Many of the wars' wives continued the work of the household, paying servants and maintaining property while their husbands were away fighting, on royal business or building naval fleets. Anxiety and uncertainty often loomed, but for thousands of women it was business as usual.

Managing the Household 'Thou shalt not know where is best to begin'

Medieval ladies didn't spend their days reading illuminated books in their chambers and waving away servants. Evidence shows they had a full, hands-on role in managing estates, buying supplies for the household and caring for family members. All this was even more important with husbands and older sons away, potentially imprisoned, exiled or in sanctuary from the wars. For widows, this arrangement was more permanent. Maintaining continuity in the household was an essential contribution to the war effort.

For wealthier women, servants took care of some of the daily activities of the home, but even they needed to be overseen. The instruction manual *The Book of Husbandry*, published in 1534, explains. On waking, the wife was first to make a sign of the cross, blessing herself and God. Then she swept the house, attended to animals and then woke and dressed the children. Breakfast was next, before baking and brewing. Butter and cheese for the household was handmade and eggs needed collecting from ducks and hens. In the spring it was time 'for a wife to make her garden, and to get as many good seeds and herbs as she can'. The author added that sometimes 'thou shalt have so many things to do, that thou shalt not well know where is best to begin'.[65]

Keeping an eye on servants often took effort and valuable time. Jane Stonor in around 1470 complained that 'servants be not so diligent as they were wont to be'.[66] The medieval instruction book *How the Good Wife Taught Her Daughter* urged wives to 'wisely govern thy house, and serving maids and men. Be thou not too bitter or too debonaire with them, but look well what most needs to be done'.[67] A hopeful Sir John Heveningham chased Margaret Paston with a letter to remind her that she had said her 'will was good' about having his cousin Anneys Loveday in her service but he was still waiting for a decision.[68]

There was also a protocol to wives' behaviour when in the company of others. *The Book of the Knight of the Tower* warned against fidgeting, jealousy and distractedness and advised wives to be 'firm in estate' but also courteous and humble.[69] They were also 'to keep measure in spending', as directed by the *Book of Husbandry*.[70] Margaret Paston wrote to her son John on 5 November 1471 to check the price of pepper, cloves, ginger, cinnamon, almonds, and rice, 'of each of these send me the price of a pound', she asks, 'and if it be better cheap at London than it is here, I shall send you money to buy with such as I will have'.[71] But being frugal didn't mean always buying the cheapest item. Thomas Bradbury, a mercer in London, wrote to Elizabeth Stonor in October 1479 justifying the purchase of 'very fine' sarcenet he considered 'most profitable and most worshipful for you, and shall last you your life and your child's after you'. The cheaper fabric, he sniffed, 'would not endure two seasons'.[72]

The Backdrop of a Woman of the Wars of the Roses

If we could meet one of these women of the wars, what would we see? In an effort to create a three-dimensional perspective of them we can look at their possessions and daily surroundings. Wills, inventories, and surviving artefacts reveal their tastes in decor, treasured possessions, jewels and the books they liked to read.

The marital homes of countesses and duchesses ranged from luxurious moated castles to smaller timber-framed and brick manor and town houses. These homes were much more colourful and elaborate than we imagine today, fitted with rich, brightly dyed textiles and elegantly crafted ornaments. Jane Stonor's inventory of her Oxfordshire house and chapel in 1474 recorded fabrics of 'purple velvet losenged with gold', red and green hangings, 'cushions covered with grey skins' and others 'covered with tapestry work'.[73] Elizabeth Fitzherbert, wife to the Yorkist-supporting Ralph Fitzherbert in Derbyshire, bequeathed in her will green and white hangings, various beds, bolsters, cushions and a 'painted chest'. She also mentions 'a nut harnessed with silver and gilt with a cover of silver and gilt' thought to have been a coconut shell.[74] Anne Holland, daughter of John, Duke of Exeter received a 'white bed with popinjays' from her father in 1447, popinjays (parrots or parakeets) being a popular medieval decoration. Cecily Neville, Duchess of York slept in a 'bed of baudekyn', a richly embroidered fabric often threaded with gold, her chamber also decked out in furnishings of blue satin and white sarcenet.[75]

At this time decorations in the home were often religious. Robert, Lord Hungerford, bequeathed to his sister Lady Margaret Rodney in 1459 'an image of Our Lady in silver gilt, with my arms under the foot thereof' while Anne, Duchess of Buckingham, mentions in her will 'a bed of the salutation of our Lady, with the hangings of the chamber of Antelopes'.[76]

Books were clearly prized possessions, passed down for their material and sentimental value as much as what was written inside. These were also very often religious works, some beautifully crafted. Margaret Hungerford received from her father-in-law 'my best legend of the Lives of the Saints in French and covered with red cloth', while Cecily Neville owned a psalter 'with clasps of silver and gilt enamelled covered with green cloth of gold'.[77]

The pale and worn stone effigies and faded brass etchings of these women that we see today are at odds with the rich materials and bright colours they would have worn in life. Lady Elizabeth Andrews bequeathed a blue gown edged with white fur in her will of 1474, while Lady Ann Scrope in 1498 mentioned a russet-coloured gown, also edged with fur.[78] The wearing of certain fabrics was linked directly to status and power. Displaying rich clothing on public occasions was ever more important as families clung to their established social positions during the changing fortunes of the wars.

Margaret Paston was one lady who reflected the need for dressing to impress. Writing to her husband, in the spring of 1452, after meeting Margaret of Anjou in Norfolk she asks, 'I pray you ... that I may have something for my neck. When the Queen was here, I borrowed my cousin Elizabeth Clere's device, for I durst not for shame go with my beads amongst so many fresh gentlewomen as here were at that time'.[79]

Jewels displayed rank and power but could also convey political loyalty. Margaret Gaynesford, gentlewoman to Elizabeth Woodville and Elizabeth of York, is depicted wearing a collar of suns and roses on her brass, which can be seen at All Saints Church in Carshalton. Margaret Howard, wife of John Howard, the future Duke of Norfolk, owned a similar item, 'a collar of gold with thirty-four roses and suns set on a course of black silk with a hanger of gold garnished with a sapphire'.[80] Roses and suns were adopted as the emblem of the House of York by Edward IV and can be seen on the effigies of many of its supporters. The effigy of Richard Neville, Earl of Salisbury survives at St Mary's Church in Burghfield and although badly worn, parts of his collar of suns and roses can still be seen. John Howard would prove staunchly loyal to the family until his death. If Margaret ever wore the collar publicly, it would demonstrate not only their considerable wealth and good standing with the king, but also their political solidarity as a couple.

Outward displays of right, status, and influence in the suspicious political setting of the Wars of the Roses was important, but some restraint was still advised. The French fifteenth-century writer Christine de Pisan wrote *In the Treasure of the City of Ladies* of a slightly comedic scene involving women wearing large, extravagant headdresses bumping into each other and struggling to get to the front of crowds so they could be seen.[81] Anything too elaborate was to be avoided, but a sprinkling of jewels and a small, confident smile could go a long way in conveying a certain amount of wealth and influence when meeting kings, queens, dukes, and lawyers.

Agnes Overay

A prominent Southampton landowner, Agnes Overay lived in the medieval town off the port's clutter of ship's masts and within its imposing defensive walls. The guns of Catchcold Tower steadily aimed out to sea as salty waves lapped against its grey stone exterior.

Now a widow, Agnes managed a large portfolio of properties in the port town, granted to her after the death of her husband, William. She is listed in the *Southampton Terrier*, an inventory of property owners taken in 1454, as owning thirteen buildings including a cottage and tenement in the old High Street. Her other properties were spread around the town, some not far from those owned by the Earl of Warwick.[82] The town attracted merchants trading in supplies such as wine, wool, and cloth. As barrels of wine rolled off ships and into dark cellars, supplies of salt fish and biscuits were rolled on, for the next leg of sailors' journeys.

John Leland, visiting Southampton in the sixteenth century, noted a landscape Agnes would have known well. Heavy stone walls were punctuated with gates opening onto quays where goods were unloaded. He counted five parish churches, the towering castle and 'many very fair merchants' houses', making special note of those belonging to the town's Italian residents. The High Street, running from the Bargate to the sea, he considered 'one of the fairest streets that is in any town of all England, and it is well builded for timber building'. Leland also notes the 'many fair tombs of marble of merchants' he saw in St Mary's church.[83]

Agnes had strong links to Southampton's political community through her husband William, listed as the town's mayor in 1398 and 1406 and burgess in 1425–1426.[84] Gemma Louise Watson, in her thesis *Roger Machado: a Life in Objects*, links her to the wider merchant community through her first husband, Florentine merchant Bartolomeo Marmora, and discusses the discovery of European pottery and glass excavated from her home.[85] The *Terrier* reveals that Agnes' son Laurence, also a merchant, lived in the town in one of his mother's properties in 1454.[86] These connections linked Agnes to life outside the town and to the wider events of the early Wars of the

Roses. She may have heard grumbling in the port as the Lancastrian, James, Earl of Wiltshire, seized five merchant ships at Southampton in 1460. Insisting he was taking them for the king's service against the Earl of Warwick, he instead used them to escape the realm.[87]

Agnes was responsible for overseeing her many properties and managing tenants. She would have negotiated rents and terms, managed disputes and filled vacated homes. As a property owner Agnes also contributed to the physical defence of the port, the *Terrier* marked out the individual section of the port's defensive walls each resident was responsible for maintaining. This was vital to the safety of Southampton's residents as well as its ability to continue to function as a busy port and centre of business. The port's security was made a priority towards the end of the fourteenth and beginning of the fifteenth centuries following a devastating raid in 1338 when many buildings were burned, and residents lost their lives. In the mid-fifteenth century Southampton was still vulnerable, due to its position on the south coast close to France. This was particularly important as hostilities between the nations continued during Henry VI's reign and again under Edward IV, as he contemplated war with France in the 1470s. The section of wall the landowners were allocated to maintain was directly affected by the amount of property they owned; Agnes contributed significantly to the maintenance of the town's defence.

The shriek of gulls and the rumble of barrels would have been the soundtrack of Agnes' life. Living in the town she was also well placed to have witnessed the earlier political turmoil of Henry V's reign. Dishevelled traitors, including the Duke of York's father, the Earl of Cambridge, were led to their executions outside the town's Bargate following the Southampton Plot of 1415. The king left for France a few days later, through the town's fortified Westgate. As murmurings of fresh riots, traitors and beheadings filtered into the port in the 1450s, Agnes must have wondered at history's compulsion to repeat itself.[88]

Agnes was a woman living through the early Wars of the Roses but is rarely mentioned in its context. Her story supports the role of women as property owners who, during the wars, continued their activities despite the looming threat of civil unrest. By the time a town clerk scrawled Agnes' name into the *Southampton Terrier* in 1454, the Wars of the Roses was on the verge of fracture. Cade had already set upon London with his rebels, and tensions continued to smoulder between the dukes of York and Somerset. Her unique viewpoint of the wars came from not only the conspiracies, plots and beheadings of the 1450s, but with hindsight of earlier turmoil too. Continuing to work behind the scenes, she was allocated responsibility towards maintaining the defensive walls of the port, which was vital for its defence. Finally, her close ties with the merchant community gave her a wider understanding of the wars' effect on the seas, as merchants struggled with piracy and the seizure of their ships.

Elizabeth Stonor 'a good woman and well disposed'

The sixteenth-century explorer John Leland paused to look up at Stonor Park's gardens, woods and rabbit warrens. 'The mansion place standeth climbing on a hill', he recorded, 'and hath two courts built with timber, brick and flint.'[89] Around fifty years before Leland's visit, this was the home of Elizabeth and William Stonor.

Just three miles from Henley on Thames, Elizabeth settled into her new marital home at Stonor Park, with its rolling fields, spacious rooms and private chapel. Her husband was the son of Jane Stonor, who was identified by historian Charles Kingsford as the illegitimate daughter of William de la Pole, Duke of Suffolk. The latest in a line of Stonor heirs that dated from the thirteenth century, William married Elizabeth in 1475, the year she is first mentioned in the family's letters.[90]

Like the Pastons in Norfolk, the Stonor correspondence gives valuable detail about fifteenth-century life, as well as revealing something of their individual personalities. Elizabeth seems to have been business-minded, brought up as the daughter of a London mayor. She had been married previously and was now widowed.[91]

The Stonor letters show that William developed an interest in the wool trade soon after his marriage to Elizabeth, something Kingsford claims was driven by his wife. Employing Thomas Betson as their agent in Calais, her influence can be seen as she travelled, dealt with her husband's clients, and passed on recommendations for the sale of wool.[92]

Elizabeth also came into contact with some key characters of the Wars of the Roses. She knew Elizabeth, Duchess of Suffolk, sister of Edward IV and wife of John de la Pole, Duke of Suffolk. She was present at a meeting in October 1476 between the king and his mother, Cecily, Duchess of York, which she described as 'a very good sight'. She also corresponded, on William's behalf, with Sir Francis Lovell, a resolute and loyal Yorkist.[93]

Elizabeth's letters also reveal a softer side to her personality. She wrote to her husband, 'I wist full heartily diverse times that you had been here' and offered to ride from London to Oxfordshire, a forty-mile journey, to see him, if he is unable to make the trip to see her.[94] There are also glints of her boldness. Elizabeth had heard that her brother-in-law was grumbling about her expenditure, and that she had been 'plucking' William's livelihood. She starts her attack artfully. 'I pray you greet well my brother Thomas Stonor from me', before adding 'I marvel greatly what ... moved him to say such language by me as he does'.[95] Considering Elizabeth's visible efforts in the family's wool trading business, her indignant reaction to Thomas' insult is not surprising. Elizabeth died in late 1479, one family member consoling William that she was 'a good woman and well disposed'.[96]

Elizabeth Stonor is less well-known than her contemporary woman of letters Margaret Paston, but her contribution is a valuable perspective of a woman's life during the Wars of the Roses. She fulfilled duties at the centre of court and had contact with some of the wars' major characters. She also supported her husband practically in business, conveying love and loyalty to him when they were away from one another. Trustworthy and dedicated, she was also not afraid to confront her opponents when necessary.

Margaret Howard, Duchess of Norfolk

Over the course of Edward IV's reign John Howard was commissioned to build a number of fleets to resist the king's enemies, in particular, for military campaigns in Scotland. His wife Margaret stayed at the family home while her husband was away, and was the main point of contact for servants, suppliers and tradespeople. The family's surviving household accounts reveal a great deal about the expenses she had responsibility for, as well as how they maintained a smooth transfer of financial control while he was absent.

The expenses Margaret paid for were varied. In a number of entries in the accounting books Margaret buys a bird, travels with a servant to buy oxen and purchases ale. She also makes an offering to the shrine at Walsingham.[97] She pays wages and travelling costs to servants, including one George Daniel for 'all parcels that he laid out at Harwich, boat and all' and a payment for 'men that were with the horses'.[98] She also oversees building work, settling bills with workmen including tilers, carpenters, a brick maker, pond makers and glaziers. She buys a lamb and a pair of pigeons and finds time to give alms.[99]

These entries dispel the myth that wealthy women in the fifteenth century spent their days sewing and left all the business activity to their husbands. During the wars in particular, when husbands were away building fleets, arresting rebels and safeguarding the seas, women's roles in the running of the household had to be full and active for their estates to continue to run smoothly.

The Howard's accounts also reveal a seamless transfer of financial control between the couple. A note is added at the point John leaves home and Margaret's accounts begin with no interruption or pause. Even if a household servant physically noted the sums, Margaret's trace is still visible as she is named as the payee, authorizing the transaction. This wasn't just confined to Margaret and John Howard. Christine de Pisan also promoted the importance of couples discussing finances and making agreements as to expenditure and budgeting.[100]

Howard was a diligent record keeper, recording every dinner taken at an inn, every purchase of horse feed and every penny spent towards the war effort. Margaret would also have recorded each payment she made at home while he was away, declaring all sums and ensuring paperwork was up to date. P. J. P. Goldberg, in *Women in England c1275–1525*, highlighted medieval women's roles 'as household managers, economic partners, and, in their husband's absence, acting heads of household able to answer for their husbands vis-a-vis the wider community'.[101] Margaret perfectly demonstrates this view.

John Howard supported Edward IV and would continue to back Richard III when he came to the throne. Richard made him Duke of Norfolk in 1483, and Margaret became his duchess. Howard would only enjoy his dukedom for two years; he was killed at the Battle of Bosworth in 1485 defending Richard III's throne. Margaret died nine years later, requesting in her will that she be buried in the 'quire of the Church of our Lady in Stoke, before the image on the side of the high altar'.[102]

'Remember and read often my bill of errands'

While messengers rode through towns and cities with letters of insurrection and war, women darted house to house conducting local business. We have seen the examples of Agnes Overay, Margaret

Howard and Elizabeth Stonor, all fulfilling different business-related roles in the undercurrent of the wars.

Some occupations saw workloads increase during the uneasy political climate of the period. Sheriffs were busy arresting rebels and putting down insurrections. Lawyers could spend months working on complex property disputes caused by generations of heirs killed in a single battle. The evidence demonstrates that the wives of these men were expected to assist. They knocked on doors and chased replies or wrote letters to request legal documents. One minute they would be acting as a family diplomat, gaining the support of an influential lord, and the next sending medicine for an aching knee.

We have seen the example of Elizabeth Stonor, who wrote often to her husband during their marriage informing him of the results of their wool trade and her interactions with lords and duchesses. Margaret Paston, the wife of lawyer John Paston in Norfolk wrote to her husband in the same way. Like Elizabeth, her letters convey a sense of duty and practicality. They include updates on legal cases, rents, sales of wool and the care of three horses she bought for him at the fair.[103] Her letters demonstrate knowledge of John's clients and cases as well as the legal process in general. She was often guided by John who wrote to her in 1465 urging her to 'remember and read often my bill of errands ... and send me answer of your good speed'.[104]

News of the wars also trickled into their communications, as wives spread the wider news to their families and local communities. Margaret Paston informed her husband of Margaret of Anjou's visit to Norfolk in April 1452 and in around 1466 wrote of difficulties between the lords and residents of Kent. In 1469 she acted as family diplomat, trying to secure Anthony Woodville, Lord Scales' favour on a trip to Norwich that year.[105]

The unrest and lawlessness associated with the wars could cause complications and slowed down the flow of travel, which was vital for communication and the movement of people and belongings.

Margaret Paston wrote that her aunt refused to send twenty marks in cash by road 'for fear of robbing, for it is said here that there goeth many thieves betwixt this and London'. In around 1458 Agnes Paston expressed fear, after she heard of pirates kidnapping residents, that it was 'a perilous dwelling by the sea-coast'.[106]

Husbands turned to their wives too, for assistance with health. Margery Paston, Margaret's daughter-in-law, was requested by her husband to send an ointment that eased knee pain and asked to include instructions on how to use it.[107] Elizabeth Stonor also seems to have had a keen knowledge of medicine, sending her husband 'powder to drink when you go to bed, for it is wholesome for you'.[108] In another letter she urges him to drink a mixture containing nutmeg. John Gerard's sixteenth century book *The Herball, or General History of Plants* notes that nutmeg was used medicinally for digestive problems or stomachache, possibly one of the symptoms with which William was suffering.[109]

The work carried out by the Paston and Stonor women is preserved in their letters. But there were many other women fulfilling similar roles all over the country whose letters and notes have not survived. Working quietly during the wars while husbands were away working, imprisoned or called on for royal service to support the wars, they maintained households and supported family businesses.

Wives in the Shadows of Royal Service

Isabella More, in her slim-fitting, round-necked gown and veiled butterfly headdress, was married to William More, also known as Gauwain. Their brass inscription at St Michael's Church in Tilehurst, Berkshire tells us that he was one of the marshals of the king's court, a role which saw him responsible for organizing the court and seating visitors and residents according to their rank and status. *The Book of Courtesy* also reveals that marshals were to keep order within the court. 'In absence of steward he shall arrest, whomsoever is rebel in court or feast', the medieval manual states.[110] With such an important and sensitive role, we can but wonder what tales William might have shared with Isabella after a day's work. He may be the William More mentioned in a pardon granted to John Hampton over a 'robbery and the breach of the peace of the late king [Henry VI], with which William More charged him'.[111] Certainly, he would have had inside knowledge of the king's visitors and was responsible for calming any hostility or altercation that took place. The power and authority given to marshals could also make them a target for violence. In 1465 a Marshal of the Hall in Edward IV's court was wounded in an altercation with an Esquire of the Body, Thomas St Leger.[112]

Isabella and William had three sons and two daughters, all shown kneeling underneath their parents on their brass. It's not known whether Isabella also served at court, although if she did it's likely this would also have been recorded on the brass. The couple are otherwise absent from the records, suggesting they lived a peaceful, law-abiding life. They died within a short space of one another in 1469, William on 28 September and Isabella on 2 November. The timing and close proximity of their deaths hint at them being possible victims of a local virus or an outbreak of plague during the period.

There is little evidence of these wives' direct involvement in the events of the wars, despite being married to men with inside knowledge of the court. However, it is worth considering the supporting roles wives like Isabella may have played, or the secret knowledge they may have been aware of. Elizabeth Stonor, Margaret Paston and Margaret Howard all assisted their husbands economically and emotionally. There is no reason to suggest that wives of court officials and royal servants did otherwise. In fact, because of their relative anonymity they may have been more likely to have been trusted with secrets and inside knowledge of court events disclosed by their husbands. Agnes Chesham was the wife of Henry VI's 'writer of the court hand' John. They are mentioned in the Calendar of Patent Rolls shortly after the Battle of St Albans and the death of Edmund Beaufort, Duke of Somerset.[113] During the reign of Richard III Alice Fowler was the wife of Thomas, an Esquire of the Body to the king in 1484.[114] What might she tell us today about rumours surrounding the disappearance of the Princes in the Tower, or Richard's accession to the throne?

One source might reveal tantalizing evidence about a wife's secret knowledge. Thomas Penn, in *The Brothers York*, sees potential significance in an unusual payment made by Richard III to the widow of his servant Miles Forrest in 1484. Miles was later rumoured to have been involved in the disappearance of the princes.[115] It is not unreasonable that wives of powerful and well-connected men may have had second-hand knowledge of confidential or dangerous information relating to events of the wars. Wisely, if they did, it appears they chose to keep it secret.

Political Women of the Wars

In the Medieval ballad *Robyn Hood and the Potter*, the Sheriff of Nottingham's wife features not as a timid, subservient woman with no interest in her husband's business, but as an intelligent administrator and hostess. On finding out her husband has been tricked by the outlaw and has had his horse stolen, she laughs, shrugging off the horse as payment for pots the disguised Robin gave her earlier in the day. In the tale she invites Robin for dinner, knowing all about her husband's plan to find Robin and later consoles the sheriff that they may have lost their horse, but at least they still have his pots.[116]

But are there any traces of women during the wars working in local government and political affairs? Women were not permitted to openly and actively work in politics, but their presence can still be felt alongside that of their husbands. Wives of sheriffs, mayors and men of status appear to have carried out subtle roles to assist them. Others, however, chose to be more vocal.

Catherine Moleyns 'There should go no penny for your life'

While Isabella More was kneeling at prayer in leafy Berkshire, Catherine Moleyns was over a hundred miles away near Colchester overseeing her marital estates. Her husband was John Howard, the man who would later marry Margaret and raise a fleet for Edward IV. Catherine was John's first wife, and the Victorian historian Charles Martin Torlesse found they had five children; a son, Thomas, who would succeed his father, and four daughters: Anne, Isabel, Jane, and Margaret.[117]

The Howards lived in Stoke by Nayland near Colchester; John rapidly gained the recognition of the Yorkist kings. Knighted after the Battle of Towton in 1461 he was made Sheriff of Norfolk and Suffolk, as well as Constable of the Castle of Norwich.[118] Catherine must have celebrated the beginning of her husband's rise, but her pleasure might well have been tarnished by one particular local dispute.

A legal wrangling would bring John and Catherine up against the Paston family. The Pastons were in a dispute with John Howard's cousin, John Mowbray, over the ownership of Caister Castle following the death of its owner, John Falstolf. In August 1461 a letter to John Paston from his son records an altercation between Paston and one of Howard's men. The man lunged at Paston with a dagger and tried to stab him twice, but he was saved by the thick material of his doublet.[119] Edward IV summoned Paston to court, but he resisted. His brother Clement wrote to him, urging him to come to London, warning that Howard was in favour with the king: 'Also if you do well come right strong, for Howard's wife made her boast that, if any of her husband's men might come to you, there should go no penny for your life'.[120]

Catherine was clearly not afraid to voice her frustrations and even issue veiled threats. Her reply shows anger, boldness and a good knowledge of the dispute. Helen Castor in *Blood and Roses* has pointed out that Catherine was indirectly linked, through family, to another Paston quarrel, the Moleyns' claim to Gresham. Catherine's bitter response likely reflected a deeper frustration, as she grew tired of hearing so many complaints about the Pastons.[121]

By September 1465 Catherine was in ill health. The family's household records hint at a lingering illness, with payments for 'reward in looking to my lady', 'medesynes' and sugar candy, along with 'water of honysoclys for my lady'.[122] In John Gerard's *Herball* it is noted that honeysuckle water 'in times past' was used for soothing the throat and mouth, either from general soreness or ulcers. It was also used, he said, to heal blood passed in the urine. Catherine might then have been experiencing these symptoms towards the end of her life.[123]

Catherine lived for a few more weeks and died around 13 November 1465, when her husband paid ten shillings to the friars of Colchester to sing for her soul.[124] At her funeral torches and tapers flickered inside St Mary's Church and sixty-eight children were paid to sing in the choir. Black cloth was also purchased to make gowns for the mourners.[125]

A brass monument of Catherine, in St Mary's Church in Stoke by Nayland in Suffolk, portrayed her with hands in prayer, wearing a high-necked gown and mantle embroidered with her family heraldry. Images on brasses are not normally taken to be likenesses, but there is something in the poise of the figure etched in the metal that conveys something of the strong personality and confidence Catherine would have demonstrated during her lifetime.

Joan Canynges 'The Hostess'

It was against the backdrop of creaking masts and the cry of gulls that Edward IV visited Bristol in September 1461. Wealthy merchants watched for their ships carrying wine, cloth and spices to port, as sacks were slumped lazily along the harbour. Bristol's merchants traded with countries including Wales, Spain and Portugal and foreign coins from the period, excavated from the river Avon, can be seen in Bristol's M-Shed Museum. A cosmopolitan community, the air was filled with different languages as mariners, merchants, and townspeople shared news, conducted business arrangements and unloaded ships.

One man with a keen interest in the commercial activity of Bristol was William Canynges. First a wealthy merchant, he rose to become Bristol's mayor, a post he held five times. An inscription above his tomb in St Mary Redcliffe Church states this fact, calling him 'the richest merchant of the town of Bristol'. As mayor, he carried out local administration and enforced the law under a Lancastrian government, in 1450 fortifying the medieval town with 'certain guns and other stuff necessary for defence'.[126] Now, as William stood at the entrance to the town's gate wearing his official robes, he welcomed the Yorkist king, nineteen-year-old Edward IV.

According to local legend,[127] Canynges hosted Edward at his home in Bristol's Redcliffe Street. The official town records simply state that the king 'was full honourably received, in as worshipful wise as ever he was in any town or city', while Stow says that he was 'most royally received'.[128]

It was not unknown for kings to stay with wealthy citizens. Their opulent homes offered a spontaneous and convenient stop with more security and privacy than a local inn. The stay would have been important for William, to show his loyalty to the recently crowned Yorkist king on behalf of his family as well as his town. With no alternative record of the king's lodgings during his 1461 visit, the legend may well be true.

William lived with his wife Joan in a grand house towering above the huddled buildings backing onto the water. A visitor to the building in the nineteenth century marvelled at the intricately carved wooden ceilings, medieval wall paintings and staircases inside. It had a private chapel, library and a banqueting hall. Traces of gilt that once shone on the Canynges' ceiling could still be seen in 1854.[129]

In the weeks before the visit Joan and her servants would have been busy preparing the house for their royal guest. Responsible for drawing up sleeping arrangements and purchasing food and drink, Joan would also have had the Canynges' best tapestries carefully unfurled over the home's plastered walls. Christine de Pisan encouraged wives to have a hands-on approach when receiving guests, overseeing the serving of food from the kitchen as well as maintaining a respectful, pleasant manner.[130]

Special occasions could be lavishly celebrated, and a host's generosity was praised during the period; the Earl of Warwick was well-known for this. Stow relates that when the earl came to London 'every tavern was full of his meat, for who that had any acquaintance in that house he should have had as much sodden and roast as he might carry upon a long dagger'.[131] Elizabeth Stonor's account book for Christmas 1478 lists a similarly elaborate feast including eighteen geese, a dozen capons, six dozen larks and two dozen chickens.[132] A visit from a new monarch would have demanded lavish hospitality, and Joan would have been busy selecting and purchasing the best meat and drink for the king and his entourage.

A 1918 painting by Ernest Board in the collection of the Bristol Museum and Art Gallery depicts the young king feasting at Canynges' house in Redcliffe Street, intently watching the entertainments. It's not clear whether the artist has depicted Joan among the women in the scene, but she would certainly have been present, signalling discreetly to servants to top up the king's wine or serve the next course.

Joan can be seen today in a lifelike, painted effigy at St Mary Redcliffe Church in Bristol. Her alert eyes are fixed on the inside of a tomb canopy painted with golden stars. Angels prop up her head, which rests on a plump pillow. Joan's face is framed by the folds of a white headdress, and she wears a long red gown, matching that of her husband lying next to her. Gold rings are slipped onto her fingers and a leather girdle with a gold buckle hangs softly around her waist.

William Canynges' illustrious mercantile and political career is well documented in the modern city's history books, stained glass windows and art. He achieved great wealth and conducted business around the world. Any contribution Joan made to William's success, however, has been largely forgotten.

At the least, Joan would have managed their household in Bristol while William was away in London or attending to business. Although the law prevented Joan from entering politics in her own right, it would be unrealistic to suggest that, as a constant presence by his side, she knew nothing of his work. Drawing on the examples of Catherine Moleyns, Margaret Howard, Elizabeth Stonor and Margaret Paston, it's certainly probable that Joan had first-hand knowledge and experience of William's business and political activities. It's plausible then that Joan would have once hurried through Bristol's streets, following up on correspondence and running errands for her husband.

One written source does credit Joan's part in her husband's rise. Written in the nineteenth century, *The Antiquities of Bristol* records one theory that was doing the rounds about Canynges, 'that his wife had unfairly possessed herself of the grand secret of the Elixir of life, and that such was the real source of her husband's wonderful wealth'.[133] While it is encouraging to see at least some acknowledgement of Joan in the historical record, the real contribution she made to William's career was no doubt far more straightforward. She acted as ambassador for the port of Bristol as well as for her family and most likely assisted William to some degree in his business, also providing moral support to him during his troubles. If the Bristol legend is correct, her role extended to welcoming King Edward 'most royally' at her home. William entered a career in the church after Joan's death and died in November 1474. He is buried next to her at St Mary Redcliffe Church.

CHAPTER THREE
THE BUSINESS OF MARRIAGE

Marriages could mark decisive moments in family fortunes. They could also sway the course of wider events during the Wars of the Roses. A marriage to a member of the opposite faction could signal a switch in allegiance or bolster a family's wealth and influence, leading to animosity from others. The marriages of the Woodville family to prestigious and wealthy spouses cemented their rise in status after Elizabeth's introduction to parliament as queen in 1464. It was a marriage, after all, that hoped to unite the Roses and put an end to the wars, when Henry Tudor and Elizabeth of York wed at Westminster Abbey in January 1486.

Women were as involved in prenuptial negotiations as the men of the family. Elizabeth Stonor wrote to her husband William that when questioned about the potential marriage of one of her children, 'I could not answer that matter without you nor nought would do'.[134]

The marriage process involved seeking out potential suitors and gauging their interest, opening negotiations and maintaining good relationships throughout. Payment of any dowry would be discussed, along with timelines for the wedding date. However, the political action of the Wars of the Roses would often make the wedding, and its negotiations, more complicated. Nuptials were contrived for political and economic gain and bloodlines were ridiculed as inferior.

In the summer of 1453, one woman's wedding celebrations descended into violence.

Maud Stanhope, Lady Willoughby 'The covenants of marriage'

The carts and retainers of a wedding party bumbled through the lanes of Heworth just north of York on the warm afternoon of 24 August 1453. They didn't suspect the group of men stooping in the shadows on either side of the track ahead. Armed with swords and daggers, they sprang an ambush as the party drew near, men clashing hand to hand in the Yorkshire countryside. In the history books, if she is mentioned at all, Maud, the unfortunate bride, is pictured as the helpless damsel in distress whose wedding was ruined by fighting.

Maud was the daughter of Sir Richard Stanhope, a knight from Rampton in Nottinghamshire. Following the death of her parents, Maud and her sister Joan were placed under the protection of their uncle, Lord Ralph Cromwell. Cromwell, their maternal uncle, had served Henry VI as Lord High Treasurer and Constable of Nottingham Castle and Warden of Sherwood Forest.[135] Maud had first been married to Robert, Lord Willoughby of Eresby, but on his death Cromwell secured another advantageous marriage for her, connecting her to the wealthy Neville family. Her licence to marry Thomas Neville, son of Richard, Earl of Salisbury was entered into the Patent Rolls on 1 May 1453.[136]

Maud's wedding to Neville didn't just benefit the bride; she stood to inherit a portion of her uncle's vast estate which would descend, through her marriage, to the Nevilles. This angered their enemies, the Percys of Northumberland, as some of these lands had once been possessions of their own family.

The trace of Maud in the records suggests she was practical, determined and resilient. Far from a woman of anonymity, she lived among key characters of the wars. KL Clark, in *The Nevills of Middleham*, finds that she had a 'fiery temper and a quick wit', and was attendant at Queen Margaret's churching ceremony in 1453.[137] She would also have come into contact, at Margaret's court, with women such as Alice Chaucer, Jacquetta Woodville and Cecily Neville, all strong and influential women of the Wars of the Roses. Her mother-in-law was the bold Alice Montacute, Countess of Salisbury. Maud may well have felt inspired by her interactions with these formidable women.

Maud's husband Thomas Neville was killed during the Battle of Wakefield in December 1460, leaving her a widow. She married again, to Sir Gervais Clinton, and found herself entangled in a dispute with Anthony Woodville, Lord Scales.[138]

Far from a tragic bride whose mundane contribution to history was the violent interruption of her wedding, Maud was a strong personality in her own right. Briefly one of the Nevilles of Yorkshire, she would have been privy to conversations during the early years of the wars and its escalation. Her father-in-law Salisbury was one of the leaders of the Yorkist party and his wife Alice was also directly involved.

Maud died in August 1497, and is buried near her uncle, Lord Cromwell, in Tattershall. A brass commemorating her survives, depicting her in widow's clothing and wearing long robes. She was an integral part of the escalation in hostilities between the Percys and Nevilles and one of the rare women to find herself ducking sword blows in the centre of battle, Maud is rarely mentioned at length in relation to the Wars of the Roses. However, she lived an active life among notable characters of the wars at the dawn of the conflict, surviving into the reign of Henry VII.

Anne Boleyn, née Hoo 'as lowly as ye list'

Maud Stanhope's newly married life might not have gone smoothly, but by the summer of 1453 Anne Hoo (great grandmother to Henry VIII's second wife) was already settled down with a man whose wealth and prominence were on the rise. She was the daughter of Thomas Baron Hoo and Hastings and his wife Elizabeth Wichingham. A loyal soldier and advisor, Thomas served Henry VI in the French wars and was appointed Knight of the Garter in 1445. Elizabeth would have taken on extra duties around the home while her husband was away in France. She died before 1446 and he married Eleanor Welles, daughter of Lionel, Lord Welles.[139]

Anne found a husband in Geoffrey Boleyn, an ambitious social climber who would serve as Mayor of London. Well-known and respected, he appears in several chronicles and documents ensuring peace was kept in the city, and in 1457 received a commission to deliver over a thousand archers for Henry VI.[140]

Geoffrey was certainly ambitious and keen to increase his social influence through trade, politics, and wealth. But his marriage to Anne gave him a significant advantage. Elizabeth Norton, in *The Boleyn Women*, points out that Geoffrey was the first Boleyn to be matched to a member of the nobility, although underlines that Anne's father's title was a new one and bestowed after her wedding.[141] Even so, their union must have boosted Geoffrey's influence; he was now married to the daughter of one of Henry VI's prominent advisors.

Anne's efforts in her daughter's marital negotiations, as well as a trace of her forceful personality, can be found in the Paston Letters. The Paston brothers discussed her movements in April 1469, as she rode through the Norfolk countryside with her daughters, paying visits to potential suitors. The event seems to have unnerved the younger John, who was hoping to be considered for her daughter Alice. His elder brother, also named John, advised him on how to speak with her. 'Bear yourself as lowly to the mother as ye list', he wrote, 'but to the maid not too lowly, nor that ye be too glad to speed, nor too sorry to fail'. The suitor had best be calm and measured, not excited for the marriage nor dismissive. The recommendation that Anne in particular needed delicate handling might indicate that he thought her proud in character or easily offended. She was certainly outspoken, adding that 'if he and she can agree I will not [prevent] it, but I will never advise her thereto in no wise'.[142]

Anne's firm and outspoken nature and Geoffrey's ambitious and loyal character seem to have made them a good match. CL Kingsford, in *Prejudice and Promise in Fifteenth Century England* included Geoffrey Boleyn as one of the characters of the wars from whom 'the new nobility was to spring'.[143] Anne deserves this same credit as ancestress of the Boleyns that would rise to power during the Tudor age.

Elizabeth Clerk 'great consultations'

Elizabeth Clerk was the wife of Thomas, a draper of the town of Reading, an area already well-known for its cloth industry. She lived not far from the heavy wooden doors of St Laurence's Church, a short walk from the nearby marketplace. Deeds show that the couple lived at their tenement in New Street (today's Friar Street) from May 1458. Just a short walk from the entrance to Reading Abbey, the couple would have noticed a bustle of well-dressed visitors whenever parliament was held there, usually when escaping the threat of plague in London. Thomas had died by 1476, as in that year Elizabeth signed over their tenement to John and Joan Langeham, recording herself on the deed as Thomas' widow. Elizabeth had then lived on New Street for almost twenty years and was perfectly placed to witness one of the most politically decisive events of the Wars of the Roses.[144]

She may not have known the reason for the groups of agitated noblemen gathering outside the abbey walls, but within Reading Abbey Edward IV had just dropped a bombshell. He had chosen this meeting, on 29 September 1464, to announce his secret marriage to Elizabeth Woodville. Lords diligently bowed in her presence, but they were secretly furious, especially Richard Neville, Earl of Warwick. It was said that Warwick had been eyeing an alliance with a foreign princess for the king in a diplomatically driven match. *The Baker Chronicle* suggests that an alliance with France would have been a sensible option at the time, to ease tensions between the countries as well as eliminate its support for Margaret of Anjou.[145]

'Edward and the Earl of Warwick have come to very great division and war together', wrote the Milanese Ambassador in February 1465. A letter in the Milan Archives dated October 1464 noted the people's disappointment over the marriage, 'and for the sake of finding means to annul it, all the nobles are holding great consultations in the town of Reading, where the king is'.[146] Edward IV's surprise wedding to Elizabeth Woodville has long been considered one of the triggers of

Warwick's defection to the Lancastrian cause during the wars.

Elizabeth's family were quickly and effortlessly promoted to influential positions at court and married into wealthy families. The Woodvilles were on the ascendant. In the few minutes it had taken to utter her wedding vows, Elizabeth had gone from a young widow with two sons to Edward IV's queen. But there were several other women on the fringes of a royal wedding during the wars, too. The marriage of Henry VII and Elizabeth of York was a landmark moment in the conflict; however, evidence suggests their wedding was not always a foregone conclusion.

Henry Tudor: The women who might have been his queen

Maud Herbert, playing in the lush grounds of Raglan Castle, would have been naively unaware of her family's full role beyond its strong, stone walls. Her father, Sir William Herbert, had risen to prominence during the reign of Henry VI, but at the outbreak of civil war, took the side of York. He was made a Knight of the Garter and served as MP of Hereford. In 1468 he captured Harlech Castle in Wales. Maud's mother, Anne Devereux, was the daughter of a Hereford knight, Sir Walter Devereux and his wife Elizabeth.[147]

In February 1462 the five-year old Henry Tudor joined the family at Raglan, an entry in the Patent Rolls confirming that Herbert paid the large sum of £1,000 for his 'custody and marriage'.[148] It later became clear who he intended as Tudor's bride. In Herbert's will, written hastily before his execution in 1469, he revealed that Henry was to marry Herbert's daughter, Maud.[149]

The wedding between Maud and Henry, as we know, would never take place. Following Herbert's execution by Lancastrian forces Henry was taken into exile by his uncle Jasper, returning to England in 1485 to take the throne. With Henry overseas and Herbert dead, the marriage to Maud was shelved.

But what if events had turned out differently? Had Herbert

survived the Battle of Edgecote and retained his wardship, Henry's marriage to Maud would likely have gone ahead, probably within a few years, meaning they may have had a string of heirs by the time Henry took the throne in 1485. As his wife, Maud would have taken her place as Queen of England. Strickland, who took a particular interest in Henry's love life, called Maud 'his former love'; however, the marriage devised by Herbert was likely conceived for reasons other than romance, Henry being just twelve years old on Herbert's death.[150]

By 1483, with Maud now married to Henry Percy, Earl of Northumberland, Strickland claims Henry considered another Herbert sister as a bride, Katherine.[151] While a fondness may have developed between Henry and one (or both) of the Herbert sisters while he lived at Raglan, neither of them were, in the end, destined for a crown.

There were other women hovering around Tudor during the early 1480s. Another woman Strickland identifies that Henry was 'in love' with was Katherine Lee, the daughter of one of his attendants in exile.[152] Bernard André, a chronicler in the English court writing in around 1500 and in a position to have heard the story from Henry himself, wrote about a potential match with Anne, daughter of Francis, Duke of Brittany, although he stated that Henry, diplomatically, refused to agree to the wedding without the assent of his advisors.[153] Depictions of Anne show her with large, round eyes, her dark hair just visible under a French hood. She may have been an attractive woman in adulthood, but Anne was just six years old in 1483 and so Francis' proposal was certainly politically driven. Henry, meanwhile, would have understood the importance of furnishing the royal nursery with legitimate heirs as soon as possible, to ensure a stable transfer of power after the uncertainty caused by the wars. At his accession he was approaching his thirtieth year.

Whatever his feelings for any of these women, the marriage that took place between Henry and Elizabeth of York on that cold January day in London in 1486 was essential for the end of the York-Lancaster conflict. They swore oaths to one another against a backdrop of silks, tapestries and glittering jewels, in a dazzling work of propaganda and political showmanship.

Isabel Mede 'her base blood'

Elizabeth of York's marriage to Henry VII was negotiated around the strength of her bloodline. The same was not true of Isabel Mede.

Daughter of a wealthy merchant Philip Mede and his wife Isabella, Isabel had been raised in Somerset, her father having served as alderman and Mayor of Bristol.[154] Isabel may even have been able to glimpse Edward IV from the crowds on his visit in 1461. Joan Canynges and her husband William were well known in the town and considering the similarity in her father's and William's roles, it's likely that the Medes would have known the couple.

At the altar on her wedding day in 1465, Isabel stood with her husband-to-be, Maurice Berkeley. A brother of the existing Lord Berkeley, Maurice was clear-headed and tenacious. A young widow, Isabel brought lands in Somerset and Gloucestershire to the marriage; the couple lived in Thornbury with their children.[155] The Medes bestowed heirs, land, money and local influence on the Berkeleys. But not everyone was content with the match.

Isabel's story was recorded by seventeenth-century historian John Smyth of Nibley in *Lives of the Berkeleys*. Smyth considered Maurice's older brother William relentlessly ambitious and of a 'high and pompous mind'.[156] He said that William complained openly of Isabel's unworthy background and sniffed at her 'base' family origins. During the reign of Edward IV, William started to sell his estates to the crown to gain further titles and influence, an act Smyth claims was done 'lest any of her [Isabel's] base blood should inherit after him'.[157] The family estates disposed of, Maurice, along with any children of his and Isabel's marriage, were disinherited.

This seems a particularly cruel and bitter action on William's part. The Medes were a relatively new family of wealth, and not an ancient high-born family like the Berkeleys, who had held their title since 1068.[158] But it was not unusual for merchant families to marry men and women considered to be above them in social status. Geoffrey Boleyn's marriage to Anne Hoo is another example. Merchants could become incredibly wealthy and influential, but it seems that there was still a snobbishness towards those considered lower down the social ladder. William de la Pole, Duke of Suffolk was a key advisor and favourite of Henry VI, but still attracted resentment according to Victorian historian Mary Ann Hookham. In *The Life and Times of Margaret of Anjou* she wrote that in de la Pole, the nobility resented 'the preference given to one of inferior birth to themselves, and who was but the descendant of a merchant'.[159]

The political and social upheavals related to the Wars of the Roses didn't help. Titles, lands and wealth that generations worked hard to build up over centuries could be seized by the king in the time it took for a scribe to scratch the order onto parchment. This wealth could then be distributed amongst the king's favourites and servants. The sudden deaths of wealthy young nobles in battle also interrupted the traditional timeline of inheritances, meaning heirs came into their titles earlier than before and as we have seen, legal disputes over property could spill into warfare. The established medieval social hierarchy was the foundation of daily life. What you wore, who you bowed to, as well as what you could realistically hope to achieve was all dictated by social status and bloodline in the fifteenth century.

The wars may have jolted the perceived security of the medieval social system, but by the 1460s Maurice's wedding to Isabel was by no means sensational. William's hostility towards Isabel was far more likely to have been a result of a longer-running hostility between the brothers with Isabel simply a target for William's enmity. John Maclean has pointed out that the brothers were likely estranged by William's death, as Maurice is unusually not mentioned in William's will as an executor or beneficiary.[160]

After William died, Maurice successfully regained many of his lands through the law courts. He died in 1506, buried at the Church of the Augustinian Friars in London, leaving Isabel widowed for a second time. She never remarried. Smyth writes that Isabel was 'a virtuous lady, and evermore content with better or harder fortunes'. She died in Coventry in 1517, at the age of seventy, overseen by her secretary Thomas Try and priests reciting orations.[161]

During the Wars of the Roses marriage could raise a person's status to unimaginable heights. It could also highlight the differences in status, some spending their married lives in the shadows of higher born in-laws. At least one wedding party was disrupted by battle, while another signalled a crucial political switch and a dreaded return to civil war.

CHAPTER FOUR
RAISING THE CHILDREN

Running family estates, businesses and organising marriages were all essential parts of a woman's work, but there was another role they played that linked directly to the events of the Wars of the Roses: motherhood.

Caring for wards, admonishing children, even when they were adults, and overseeing education and etiquette, were just some of the responsibilities of motherhood. During the wars women also soothed family dissension and mediated in relationships where children were pitched on opposite sides of the conflict. They also sheltered children at risk of being pursued by enemies.

Children in Hiding 'ever in feare to be knowne'

When the tide turned and prominent families found themselves on the losing side of battle or fortune, their fears often turned towards their children. This was particularly true for the eldest who would have gone on to inherit the family estates. By hiding them from the glare of their enemies, the child could emerge in different political circumstances to claim their birthright.

There are examples of this in the sources, including Cecily Neville's steps to separate her sons after the siege of Ludlow in 1459. York fled to Ireland with their second son Edmund, Earl of Rutland while the Earl of Salisbury and Warwick escaped to Calais with the eldest, Edward, Earl of March (later Edward IV). Cecily stayed at Ludlow with the two youngest, George and Richard. The following year, after their father's death, she sent her two younger sons to Burgundy.[162] By distributing the York heirs to the four corners the survival and prospects of the family were more assured should one or more of them be captured.

Some were more secretive. Thomas Clifford, son of Lord Clifford was, according to Holinshed, 'brought up with a shepherd in poor habit, ever in fear to be known, till king Henry the Seventh obtained the crown, by whom, he was restored to his name and possessions'.[163] Stow writes that Richard III and his council in 1483 actively feared Elizabeth Woodville would send her younger son, Richard, overseas for his safety. That this was outwardly discussed and dreaded indicates it occurred so often that it was Elizabeth's expected response as the prince's mother.[164]

The story of the Yorkist Pretender Perkin Warbeck also depended on the concealment of a prince. In 1493 he claimed to be Edward IV's son in a letter to Queen Isabella of Spain. A man sent to kill him, he says, instead kept him alive but made him agree to keep his identity secret. In the end Warbeck turned out not to be the prince he claimed. However, the tale of a long-lost child returning from abroad to seize their rightful inheritance was certainly considered plausible in England and at the European royal courts.[165]

Elizabeth Mores 'put him in a maiden's raiment'

Kinnersley Castle in Herefordshire in 1483 was the scene of a dramatic bid to preserve the eldest son of the Duke of Buckingham at the time of the duke's fall. The story is told in a sixteenth-century paper found among the documents at Thornbury Castle in Gloucestershire and was published, along with several other documents relating to the family, in 1869, by Charles Robinson.[166]

As Henry Stafford, Duke of Buckingham realized his rebellion against Richard III had failed, he looked towards the safety of his children, in particular his eldest son, Edward. The Thornbury paper states that the duke brought his wife Catherine and their two sons to Weobley, sending his eldest to live with Sir Richard Delabere at Kinnersley 'for to keep until he sent for him by a token'. A token is often mentioned in Wars of the Roses' correspondence and would have been a ring or other object known to both parties so that they took any communication from messengers to be genuine. This was especially important in this paranoid age of switching allegiances and accusations of treason.

The account states that Richard III offered a reward for the capture of either Buckingham or his son. As searchers flocked into Herefordshire, Elizabeth, Delabere's servant, 'shaved my Lorde Stafford's beard and put upon him a maiden's raiment and so conveyed him out of Kinnersley to Newchurch'. Stafford was a young boy at the time, and so most likely didn't have a beard to shave, so this is either a misunderstanding or an error made when making the Tudor copy or Victorian transcript. In any case, the context is clear. Elizabeth disguised Edward as a young girl to prevent arousing suspicion.

Searchers came twice to Kinnersley. Elizabeth and William ap Symon removed Edward from the castle each time, met the men at the door and claimed 'there was none such Lord there, and that shall ye well know for ye shall see the house searched'. Eventually, Elizabeth took Stafford to a nearby stream and sat with him until the coast was clear. Riding through Hereford, Edward rode behind Elizabeth and ap Symon 'aside on a pillow like a gentlewoman... in gentlewoman's apparel'. They rode on to the house of a trusted widow in the town, a friend of Elizabeth's.

The 1575 account is a copy of an earlier document and reads as an eyewitness account of events. It does mention the involvement of specific people including William ap Symon and Sir William Knyvet as well as the Hereford widow and a Mistress Oliffe who contributed to the young boy's safety. Specific locations are given, demonstrating that the writer had, or was given, a thorough knowledge of Kinnersley Castle and its grounds.

We will never really know if Edward Stafford was hidden exactly as the account describes. However, the concept of concealing high-born children in times of political uncertainty was firmly rooted in medieval consciousness, and women were very much involved. It is Elizabeth in this story who drives the momentum for Stafford's concealment and disguise and takes responsibility for him until the coast is clear. She met suspicious searchers at the castle drawbridge, having Edward whisked away in advance. For her to do this she would need to have had prior knowledge of their approach, perhaps organizing scouts to keep watch.

But what was Elizabeth's motivation in helping the young heir to the Buckingham estates? Sensing a child may have been in danger, she would have felt a moral duty in helping Stafford. But there is also evidence that Elizabeth's actions were provoked by political motives.

The Thornbury account explains that Elizabeth was once a servant in Richard Delabere's household. But there's a plot twist: later in the tale she is described as Dame Elizabeth Delabere.

It is possible that Elizabeth had initially served as a gentlewoman to Delabere's first wife Anne, the daughter of Lord Audley and remembered on the knight's brass in Hereford Cathedral. Their marriage licence reveals that he and Elizabeth were granted permission to marry on 28 July 1483, and were therefore in a relationship, and intending to marry, before the Buckingham Rebellion and the events described in the Thornbury paper.[167] Although Elizabeth was a servant of Delabere's, she was, at the time of these events, also his future wife.

There is also evidence of the Delaberes' alignment to the new Tudor regime. On Henry VII's accession in 1485, Stow records that Elizabeth's husband Richard was made a Knight Banneret.[168] Her father is named on the brass Elizabeth shares with Richard (and his first wife) as Henry VII's Sergeant of the Hall. Could Elizabeth and her family have been rewarded for their loyalty towards the combined causes of Edward Stafford, Henry, Duke of Buckingham and Henry Tudor?

Unfortunately for Edward Stafford, as we know, Elizabeth's actions could not save him from the executioner's block. He was restored his title and inheritance in 1485 but was beheaded on charges of treason by Henry VIII in 1521.[169] Henry VIII's relentless pursuing of noble bloodlines well after the end of the fifteenth century demonstrates the lingering paranoia and threat to his rule that existed into the early sixteenth century.

Elizabeth Delabere is depicted with her husband and his first wife Anne in early sixteenth-century clothing. Laid into the floor of the south transept of Hereford Cathedral, Richard is portrayed on his brass in full armour, his hands joined in prayer and a sword by his side. Elizabeth wears an early-Tudor headdress and long gown. Below are shown twenty-one children. Underneath Anne are the figures of four girls and one boy. Underneath Elizabeth are ten sons and six daughters. That this monument is laid in Hereford Cathedral suggests that Richard Delabere had links there, perhaps as a regular visitor or benefactor. The links Elizabeth had with Hereford women, like Mistress Oliffe and her widow friend, may have extended to others, such as Elizabeth Jones, the wife of Andrew Jones, a cider maker in the town who died in 1497, buried in the cathedral's crypt with her husband.[170]

Today, Elizabeth's etched likeness is unnoticed by many of the thousands of tourists that visit Hereford Cathedral each year. But it stands as a reminder of the woman who, according to a forgotten account in the papers of Thornbury Castle, was reported to have disguised, concealed and protected the young son of a traitor during the unsettled later years of the Wars of the Roses.

Anne Herbert 'her maternal arms'

John Leland took in the imposing towers of Raglan, describing it as a 'fair and pleasant castle', with 'goodly parks', although disappointedly noted the town nearby was 'bare'.[171] Inside its richly decorated chambers a young woman kept a watchful eye over her children. Among them played the Herberts' ward, Henry Tudor, a five-year old boy with watchful blue eyes.

Anne is depicted in a manuscript made in the late 1450s, *The Troy Book and The Siege of Thebes,* now in the collection of the British Museum. Believed to have been made as a gift to Henry VI, it shows Anne and her husband William Herbert kneeling either side of the king. These likenesses might represent how the couple appeared in life, painted in shimmering colour to remind Henry of them and their loyalty whenever he picked up the book. Anne kneels, wearing a grey and red gown, the mantle lined with fur. A large pendant hangs from her neck and on her head rests a gold-coloured butterfly headdress, the thin veil folding out towards the back.

Lavish gifts to Lancastrian kings aside, William, as we have seen, chose during the wars to ally with Edward IV, who rewarded him well in the early years of his rule. With her husband often away on royal business, Anne would have been responsible for the day-to-day care of young Henry. His days at Raglan would have been spent eating with the other children, playing, and receiving an education under Anne's watchful eye. Strickland describes the countess as 'good and merciful', taking Henry in 'her maternal arms', and raising him with her other children.[172]

Henry remembered it differently.

In around 1485 when the adult Henry prepared to sail to England, he told Philip de Commines that he had been imprisoned since he was five years old.[173] Vergil wrote that at Raglan he was a 'prisoner, but honourably brought up with the wife of William Herbert'.[174]

Henry's use of the word 'prisoner' is interesting. It's unlikely he was locked up in the traditional sense, behind bars or separated from the rest of the household. Henry's interpretation more likely comes from an emotional longing, missing his mother, his uncle Jasper and the servants he would have known from his younger years. Despite the use of the word, there is no suggestion that Anne treated him harshly or any differently from her own children. In fact, Vergil's insistence that she had raised Henry 'honourably' suggests that the king later had a good opinion of Anne. As we have seen, Henry may have formed bonds with some of the Herbert children, particularly Maud and Katherine who he would later consider as potential brides.

Towards the end of July 1469 Anne waved William off as he headed for battle, as she had done many times during their marriage. He was travelling to fight for Edward IV against the Earl of Warwick's and Duke of Clarence's forces at the Battle of Edgecote. Before he left, the couple discussed what would happen should he die; Anne had promised she would remain a widow. While this may seem a purely romantic gesture, her motivation was financial. As a widow she retained control of the family estates in her own right, but if she married, it would transfer to her new husband.

Fortune was not on their side. William was captured, along with his brother Richard. Preparing for death, he hastily scribbled a short will. Giving instructions for his burial, he bequeathed funds to religious houses and allocated money for prayers and songs for his soul and 'all the souls slain in the field for two years'. He reminds her twice of her oath, revealing its purpose. 'Wife, that ye remember your promise to me, to take the order of widowhood, as ye may be the better master of your own, to perform my will and to help my children, as I love and trust you'.[175]

Henry VI, temporarily back on the throne in 1470, reinstated Jasper Tudor as Earl of Pembroke. Speedily, he regained custody of his nine-year-old nephew and sailed with him to Brittany. Anne's role in Henry's childhood is not often acknowledged, but she had the responsibility of caring for the young boy who would, although she wouldn't know it, one day be king. Henry may have considered his time at Raglan as some form of imprisonment, but this assessment was undoubtably driven by the separation from his own family and, in hindsight, his position as a political and social pawn.

'Be your own purse bearer'

Family life during the Wars of the Roses was rarely straightforward.

Anne, Duchess of Exeter found herself torn between her father, fighting for the House of York, and her husband, battling for Lancaster. Cecily Neville, Duchess of York, would face turmoil when her son George, Duke of Clarence plotted against his brother Edward IV to reinstate the king they had once deposed, Henry VI.

Parents living through the wars had to do their best to ease political tensions, but there were also other family differences to settle. Surviving sources provide us with a rounded and intimate look at the challenges of parenting during the Wars of the Roses.

Some of the issues they faced are familiar to modern parents. In one of her letters Margaret Paston wrote to her son, Sir John, imploring him to contact his father after a disagreement. 'You should not spare to write to him again as lowly as ye can', she urges, 'beseeching him to be your good father'. She adds a typical telling-off in the next line, wishing that 'ye [guard] of your expenses better [than] ye have been before this time, and be your own purse-bearer.'[176] The Paston letters frequently mention requests from Sir John for money while he is dealing with their property business in London; this may have been the cause of their disagreement.

Parents also kept tabs on the diligence of their children while they were in education. Agnes Paston asked in 1457 'how Clement Paston hath done his endeavour in learning. And if he hath not done well, nor will not amend, pray him that he will truly belash him till he will amend'. In the same letter she urged her daughter Elizabeth, later Elizabeth Poynings and at that time in the de la Pole household, to be told to 'use herself to work readily, as other gentlewomen do, and somewhat to help herself therewith'.[177]

Sir John was the recipient of another telling-off from his mother when Margaret felt he was not doing enough to assist when the family found itself under siege at Caister in 1469. On 12 September, while John was in London trying to secure support, Margaret scribbled a letter giving 'the greatest rebuke to you that ever came to any gentleman, for every man in this country marvelleth greatly that ye suffer them to be so long in so great jeopardy without help or other remedy'.[178]

Elizabeth Fitzherbert 'God's blessing and mine'

Inside the stout stone church of St Mary and St Barlock in Norbury, Derbyshire, lies the alabaster effigy of Elizabeth Fitzherbert. Her fingers are decorated with rings, and she wears an intricate collar worked with tiny roses from which hangs a pendant showing the image of the Virgin with Child. The folds of a long, fitted gown fall from her frame.[179] Beside her is her husband Ralph, in his armour, complete with a Yorkist collar of suns and roses. The boar badge, an indication of his loyalty to Richard III, is pinned to his chest.

We only know a few key facts about Elizabeth's life. Her monument states that she was the daughter of John Marshall of Upton in Leicestershire, and this is probably where she spent most of her childhood. A lost inscription recorded as once being at Upton church gives John's date of death as September 1432, so Elizabeth may have lost her father while still young.[180]

Elizabeth's father-in-law, Nicholas Fitzherbert, was a Derbyshire constable, responsible for keeping peace in the county and enforcing order. Nicholas was one of those ordered to arrest the men raising rebellions in Derbyshire in 1462.[181] In 1472 he is named in a commission of array (an order to muster troops) along with George, Duke of Clarence, Richard, Duke of Gloucester and William Hastings.[182] Ralph was also summoned, in 1473 and 1483, to chase up sums owed to the king in Derbyshire, and in 1484 he appears in a commission to raise troops for Richard III.[183]

While Ralph was busy on the king's business, Elizabeth was at home in Norbury taking care of the household and overseeing the children. They lived at Norbury Hall, a two-storey manor house built by Ralph's ancestor Henry Fitzherbert in the early-fourteenth century.[184] The grounds would have been scented with flowers and herbs, a thick wooden door leading to an oak staircase and onto the upper floors within. The couple had seven sons and eight daughters. One of her sons, Sir Anthony Fitzherbert, has been suggested as the Tudor author of the *Book of Husbandry*. If so, his advice for housewives might reveal a little of what he learned from his mother. He writes that wives 'should be idle at no time', 'keep measure in spending' and should get up early.[185] Elizabeth may have had servants to carry out these tasks for her, no doubt watched by the young Anthony.

Elizabeth, the owner of the silver-harnessed coconut we saw earlier, was clearly a fashionable lady. She particularly liked the colour violet, with three gowns of the colour mentioned in her will, one of them 'furred with grey'.[186] Her effigy at Norbury church was once vividly painted. A nineteenth-century visitor commented that traces of green could be seen on her gown, red on her mantle and gilt on her headdress.[187] Ralph died in March 1484, having written his will the previous December; after his death Elizabeth continued living at Norbury as a widow. Towards the end of her life, in October 1490, she made provision for her children.

In her will, Elizabeth makes arrangements for the marriage of her daughters, divides the family lands and expresses concern that some of her sons have not yet received the inheritance from Ralph's will. She also asks her eldest son John to ensure his younger brother Anthony has enough funds to continue his education. As a result of this clause Anthony would complete his legal training and become a successful Tudor lawyer. Anticipating arguments between the brothers, she names them her executors and asks that they be 'content according to this my will without making further strife, suit or debate … as they will have God's blessing and mine'.

Warning them lovingly, from beyond the grave, to get along, Elizabeth clearly had a good relationship with her adult children as well as their husbands and wives, who she also mentions in the will. It was common to include a statement of good mind and healthy body in wills, but Elizabeth only mentions she is 'steadfast of mind and of good remembrance'. Perhaps at the time of writing she had suffered a long illness and expected death to come soon. She died the following year.[188]

While much of what we know of Elizabeth comes from one document, glimmers of her personality still trickle through. There is a sense of organization in the bequeathing of every household item right down to the last cooking pot. She may also have inspired the writing of a household manual. She had a love of fine fabrics and bright colours and would have marvelled at her silver harnessed coconut shipped from a distant land. The tone of the writing of her will is controlled and assertive and in it, she displays intuition by pre-empting a potential dispute between her children.

Elizabeth's married life with Ralph must have had its anxieties and upheavals because of the uncertainty of the wars. By the time Ralph wrote his will in the chilly December of 1483, the young Edward V had been deposed by his uncle who was now ruling as Richard III. Ralph bequeathed his suit of armour to his eldest son and heir, perhaps out of thrift or nostalgia but more likely because in the continuing and changeable political climate, he sensed he would come to need it.[189]

The Lady Gwladys Gam 'The Star of Abergavenny'

There are some well-known, spirited mothers of the Wars of the Roses. Jacquetta, Duchess of Bedford, the mother of Elizabeth Woodville, is thought by many to have been instrumental to her family's rise and success under Edward IV. Margaret of Anjou was present at battles, negotiated with allies and affirmed her son's right to rule, despite repeated military efforts against her. Cecily Neville, Margaret Beaufort and Elizabeth Woodville were also courageous, bold mothers of soldiers, statesmen and royalty. But what about Gwladys Gam?

Gwladys was born towards the end of the fourteenth century, the daughter of famous Welsh soldier David Gam. She was married twice, first to Sir Roger Vaughan of Tretower, who lost his life along with her father at the Battle of Agincourt in 1415. She then married Sir William ap Thomas of Raglan Castle, who died in 1446.[190] The nineteenth-century historian TJ Llewellyn Prichard found Gwladys had thirteen children between both marriages.[191] One of these would achieve notable success under the wars' Yorkist government: William Herbert.

The husband of Anne, who we have already seen raising the five-year-old Henry Tudor at Raglan, was an ambitious and bold military commander. His story evokes tenacity, resilience and courage. But is it possible to see Gwladys' influence in William's later success? A poem written by the Welsh poet Lewis Glyn Cothi shortly after her death calls Gwladys 'the Star of Abergavenny', referencing her piety and describing the elaborate tomb erected in the Priory Church of Abergavenny where she was buried with her second husband. Cothi describes it carved with sculptures of Christ, the Apostles and angels. Torches flickered and wisps of incense curled as 3,000 people, he says, came to pay their respects at her funeral. Cothi praised Gwladys as a communicator, able to speak both Welsh and English and refers to her as 'an arm [a support] to Gwent and the land of Brychan'. Celebrated as a patron of poetry, special note is given to her ancestry as well as her status as the ancestor of 'the race of kings and golden earls of Gwent'.[192]

Gwladys demonstrated resilience, coping with the loss of her father and first husband to war. She developed skills in language and had a love of literature, particularly Welsh works. Widowed twice, she oversaw a growing brood of children, among them not only William but other notable warriors of the wars such as Richard Herbert and Thomas Vaughan, who both lost their lives to its bloodshed.

We can see some similarities in William's life. He also lost his father in early adulthood, established his own family at Raglan and remained faithful to the Yorkist cause despite military setbacks.

We have seen his particular concern for the care of his children in the note to his wife Anne that he added to his will. His library at Raglan was said to contain books in both Welsh and English, with one ninth-century work by the Welsh writer Geraint Bardd Glas y Cadair recorded there in the mid-seventeenth century.[193] Tenacious and adaptable with notable similarities in their actions and values, it's just possible to see Gwladys' early guiding hand and influence in her son's later successes. However, she would not live to see the pinnacle of his rise. She died in 1454 and was buried with her second husband.

As the mother of soldiers, one of them a significant military statesman of the wars, Gwladys should be remembered in the historical context of the Wars of the Roses. Living through the early fifteenth century, she would have seen the first tensions between York and Lancaster take root, and the emergence of the early rebellions against Henry VI's rule. Gwladys left more than a trace of her bold, resilient nature in the personalities and characters of her children, including the future Earl of Pembroke, Sir William Herbert.

CHAPTER FIVE
WoMEN OF THE WARS IN WoRK

We have seen events of the wars spilling into women's homes as they encountered rebels or witnessed executions and the murmurings of angry courtiers in their marketplaces. But contemporary sources show that its drama overflowed into women's workplaces too.

One woman worked for decades at the centre of local justice, carrying out the king's orders and taking battle captives into confinement. Others found the wars provided difficulties and dangers to their trade, while some directly profited from the movements of armies and retainers across the kingdom. A small number saw for themselves decisive events play out as they witnessed subtle seizures of power, fled from rebellion and mopped spilled blood from their courtyards.

Elizabeth Venour 'fair mistress of the Fleet'

By the 1460s, the Fleet Prison was already ancient. Dating to the end of the twelfth century, it was the reluctant home of those who accumulated debt, damaged property or breached contracts. Wat Tyler's rebels had set fire to the building during the Peasant's Revolt in 1381, but by the 1460s it stood firmly once again in London's skyline as an essential, but widely dreaded, part of the medieval city's legal system.

Within these imposing walls the Warden of the Fleet, Elizabeth Venour, attended to the prison's daily business. The position of warden had descended to her via her father Roger Saperton. Elizabeth acted as warden with her husband William, taking an active role in the upkeep, administration, and duties within the prison.[194] When Bishop Hooper complained in 1553 that 'while I came down thus to dinner and supper, the warden and his wife picked quarrels with me', he recorded to history the clear visibility of the Fleet's wives, as well as their husbands.[195]

Standing alongside the Fleet River, the prison was known for its squalid living conditions. In 1355 Edward III wrote to the Mayor of London concerning the prison ditch being 'obstructed and choked up by filth from latrines built thereon ... and the abominable stench which there prevails, many of those there imprisoned are often affected with various diseases and grievous maladies, not without serious peril unto themselves'.[196] Nothing had changed by the 1540s when Henry Howard, Earl of Surrey, wrote to the Privy Council complaining it was a 'noisome prison whose pestilent airs are not unlike to bring some alteration of health'.[197]

The role of warden had social influence, status and was also lucrative. Prisoners paid for their food and lodging costs, handing over extra cash for services, including the attendance of servants. However, the position also came with high levels of responsibility. Wardens personally oversaw prisoners and were accountable for their debts, Elizabeth herself attending court in 1467 over allegations she had allowed a debtor to leave the prison without satisfying his debt.[198]

A grant gives the Venours' wardenship of the Fleet in July 1434 and Elizabeth left the position in around 1468.[199] In that time, she would have admitted debtors, thieves and fraudsters through the Fleet's heavy doors. Some of these characters were directly linked to the Wars of the Roses. When Cade's rebels demanded the release of William Cromer, Sheriff of Kent, on 3 July 1450, Elizabeth would have been there to assist. Stow states that Cromer had been admitted to the Fleet for 'certain extortions' he had committed while in office. Cade's rebels however had a different version of justice in mind. After leaving the Fleet, Cromer was led to Mile End where he was beheaded, his head spiked on a pole on London Bridge.[200]

Henry Percy, son of the Earl of Northumberland, was also one of Elizabeth's prisoners. She would have led him through the musty corridors, keys jangling from the leather belt on her waist. Percy's father, also named Henry, had lost his life at the Battle of Towton in 1461 fighting for the Lancastrians. The uneasy atmosphere of the dark, stuffy rooms must have been disconcerting for the young boy who had been brought up in comfort. He was allowed some luxury, albeit at a cost. The Issues of the Exchequer show that Edward IV paid £1 6s 8d each week (the equivalent of £857 today) 'to provide for his table and four persons to attend upon him in the king's prison of the Flete during two months and four days'. Edward also rewarded three of the men serving the young Percy with sixpence per day.[201] As for Elizabeth, her name appears in a pardon in December 1467 over the escape of four inmates, but soon after, she disappears entirely.[202]

Elizabeth, in her work as Warden of the Fleet Prison, played a crucial part in the Wars of the Roses, but is rarely acknowledged. She helped administer justice, leading prisoners to their lodgings and appearing in court with them when required. She crossed paths with some key characters of the wars, such as Margaret and John Paston and was known to their son, Sir John. She would have known and worked with John Prysot, Justice of the Peace, who is often referred to in Patent Rolls concerning the movements of inmates at the prison. Elizabeth may even have ordered the release of William Cromer to Cade's rebels and oversaw the keeping of Henry Percy, the Lancastrian heir to the Northumberland estates. We can only imagine at Elizabeth's many other interactions with characters of the wars that went unrecorded.

Sir John Paston referred to Elizabeth in a letter as his 'fair mistress of the Fleet'.[203] Because evidence of Elizabeth's own words is scarce, it is difficult to speculate on her personality. However, it is likely she had a bold, no-nonsense approach, commanding the confidence needed to run a notorious medieval prison and its inmates for three decades. But there is a hint in one source of Elizabeth's softer and more trusting side. Over the thirty years she worked at the Fleet, she would have admitted prisoners in varying states of emotional distress. Some were cast into prison for the first time, all helpless and distraught, many knowing they could not pay their debts. A letter written in around 1453, and preserved in the Paston Letters, gives us a glimpse into Elizabeth's more empathetic nature. Writing to John Paston, a man (who is not named) relates how his wife was committed to the Fleet, and after her arrest prematurely delivered the baby she was carrying. Writing that he and his wife both feared for her life, he reveals that 'afterward my wife was some deal eased by the labour of the warden of the Fleet'. Although both Elizabeth and her husband William were managing the prison at this time, it is more likely it was Elizabeth's efforts that are referred to in this letter. Soothing and calming the distressed woman, childbirth was very much a woman's responsibility in medieval England.[204]

Merchants of the Wars

With their prominence in society and potential for raising large amounts of cash, it is not surprising that merchants often became entangled, both willingly and unwillingly, in the events of the Wars of the Roses.

Fleeing the realm after the Lancastrian recovery of power in 1470, Edward IV enlisted the help of merchants who provided him with a safe passage to exile. Commines wrote that he sailed to his brother-in-law in Burgundy in ships with two merchants and around 800 followers.[205]

Merchants were present at more tranquil royal events too. In November 1480 Richard Cely, the West Country wool merchant, saw Edward IV's baby, princess Bridget, at Eltham and wrote with news of Margaret of Burgundy's visit to England in the same year. The merchant class, with their connections overseas were also a channel of news during the wars. Cely also shares with his brother George the king's preparations at the Tower of London to 'see his ordnance and to admit gunners and see that all things be made ready'.[206]

With their connections and wealth, some merchants made the

move to local government and wielded political influence, as we have seen. Philip Mede, William Canynges and Geoffrey Boleyn were all merchants who were later elected mayors of their towns and cities. In 1470, says Commines, London merchants even managed to convince the Earl of Warwick against war with Burgundy as it would interfere with the prosperity of their trading centre at Calais.[207]

Not all merchants' involvements in the Wars of the Roses went smoothly. Some were caught out funding the 'wrong side'. Vergil explains that Edward IV did 'vehemently rebuke with many words diverse others, whether they were citizens or merchant strangers, whom he knew to have given money to King Henry for levying of an army and greatly complained of their offences'.[208] Other merchants found their ships seized by pirates or faced other dangers on the seas. A ship owned by William Neville, Lord Fauconberg, appears in a complaint of piracy against merchants in the Patent Rolls of 1458. In the same year mariners on board a vessel owned by Sir Thomas de Ros were also accused, as was one belonging to Sir Hugh Courtenay in 1461.[209]

They could also be manipulated politically. As Edward IV considered war with France, the French king, Louis XI, issued a sharp warning against it, pointing out the commercial consequences. 'Which war, if it continue,' he said, 'shall neither be profitable to you, nor to your nobility ... and especially to merchant men shall bring both misery, poverty and calamity'.[210] Later, in response to Margaret of Burgundy's support of the Yorkist pretender Perkin Warbeck, merchants found their work disrupted as Henry VII angrily banished trade with Burgundy.[211]

Along with England's civil wars, merchants also had to navigate tensions with old foreign enemies, sometimes fuelled by past wrongs or foreign policy. Stow tells how, in 1457, the French, 'in revenge of old injurie' sent two fleets to rob Sandwich in Kent, murdered the mayor and 'robbed and spoiled two great galleys or ships laden with merchandise coming to London'.[212] This also posed a threat during the relatively peaceful years of the wars. Bohemian visitors to England in 1465 were shot at by mariners suspecting they were French, while in 1480 William Cely wrote of two Frenchman chasing an English ship off the coast of Calais.[213]

Merchants continued to work despite the risks of piracy, political sanctions, and general uncertainty on the seas. But their duties were not confined to waving off ships and counting coins. The letters of the Cely family reveal that they packed, transported, shipped and handled their goods, overseeing not only the ship it was loaded onto but recording its exact location onboard. They spent days chasing debts and settling bills along with dealing with unexpected setbacks. One of these occurred on a cold January morning in 1482 when the Celys found a disgruntled harbour resident had thrown horse dung through the window of their wool house at Calais, spoiling their goods.[214]

All this was certainly challenging for the merchants running a business during the Wars of the Roses. It was no less challenging for the women who also made a living from the sea.

Alice Chestre 'at all times be ready to do us service'

Timber-framed houses and inns huddled tightly along Bristol's winding streets as the towers of medieval church spires pierced the skyline. The billowing sails of merchant ships limp into view, heavy with stocks of fish, textiles and wine. Among the merchants overseeing their business, discussing news and crossing off inventories is Alice Chestre.

Alice's husband, the merchant Henry Chestre, died in March 1471. He requested his burial to take place near his seat at the medieval All Hallow's Church in Bristol, near its high cross. Alice, his sole executor, was responsible for settling her husband's debts and making religious donations on his behalf.[215] As mourners filed out of the church, Alice decided she would continue her husband's livelihood, and trade in her own right.

There were other female merchants operating during the wars, including Margaret Croke, who shipped goods from Calais in the summer of 1478.[216] In York, several women were members of the Mistery of Merchants, with Mariona Kent appearing on its committee in 1472.[217]

Bristol was not immune to the challenges faced by other merchants in England. Fabyan tells how in 1458 a Bristol merchant named Sturmyn had his ship, laden with green pepper and other spices, captured and 'spoiled' on its way back to England.[218] Bristol merchants William Whityngton, John Poke and Thomas Sexten also found their ships hijacked by Cornish pirates in 1472.[219] According to Howell Thomas Evans, in *Wales in the Wars of the Roses*, the threat came from geographical as well as social factors. He observes that during the time of the wars, 'merchants who plied their trade in the west were the prey of a godless nobility and a brutalized peasantry... the estuary of the Severn swarmed with pirates, every creek giving shelter to its seadogs who had their accomplices in the towns'.[220]

Bristol merchants could be called on to assist in the king's business too. Scofield stated that in 1474, Edward IV offered them goods 'laden in and out custom free and pass free for the first voyage' if they built ships which would 'at all times be ready to do us service'.[221]

Alice certainly found success working as a merchant and her decision to continue her husband's business after his death surely demonstrates that she had been actively assisting in it during their marriage. The wealth she amassed, and the comfort in which she lived, is revealed in the expensive gifts she bequeathed to Bristol's churches in her will, including various items of silver, gilt and a number of torches. She also owned a robe trimmed with fur and three girdles decorated with silver and gilt: one red, one violet and one black.[222]

On 17 November 1472, shortly after her husband's death she drew up a contract with local carpenter Stephen Morgan. He was commissioned to build her a new home on Bristol's High Street with a shop, hall and two further chambers. In the document, which can be seen at Bristol's M-Shed Museum, she specifies the addition of oriel windows and agrees Stephen can take away and keep any timber salvaged from the old house.[223] It's possible Alice would have known William Canynges' wife Joan during the 1450s and 1460s. Alice's husband Henry witnessed a grant for the endowment of a chantry in November 1450, with William Canynges adding his signature to the document.[224] The families certainly had much in common, lived near to one another and were part of the same commercial community.

She didn't just sit in her new house quietly enjoying her wealth, however. Alice took steps to improve Bristol's local merchant community by paying £41 for a crane to be built, easing the job of loading and unloading goods. It also generated income for the town in rents.[225] Alice therefore left a legacy for future merchants and innovated medieval Bristol, bringing in new and much needed fifteenth-century technology.

Like the Celys, Alice and the other women merchants working through the Wars of the Roses would have taken responsibility for the packing, transport, and shipping of their goods, adding a few devout prayers for their safe arrival overseas. She would have worked within rules on taxation, customs, and administration and been affected by trade restrictions caused by military or political events. Alice would have worked despite the risks, adversities and restrictions imposed as a result of the wars, continuing to trade as a member of a bustling community, seeing five successive monarchs proclaimed between 1470 and her own death in 1486. She was buried with her husband at All Hallows in Bristol.[226]

Prostitutes of the Wars 'available day and night'

There is very limited evidence of prostitutes and brothels in the recorded history during this tumultuous period, but that doesn't mean they should not be considered. Prostitutes were an ever-present part of medieval life and would have encountered many individuals we know from the wars' history books.

John Howard's accounts record a payment of twenty shillings lent to 'my said lord of Norfolk when he lay at the stewe' in May 1465.[227] Stews were bathhouses where prostitutes were often known to ply their trade; they were also simply places where travellers could take a bath, so the interpretation here is vague. Another source however is anything but ambiguous.

MW Greenslade, in *A History of the County of Stafford* tells of one Lichfield prostitute who claimed to have profited greatly from the movement of men around the country. She stated that she earned £3 (the equivalent of £1,923 today) by being available to the men of the Duke of Clarence's household while they lodged in the town in 1466.[228] Courtiers and gentlemen from high-status households such as Clarence's – George, Duke of Clarence was Edward IV's brother – would have been active during the wars and therefore travelling frequently on royal business.

Both PJP Goldberg and Lynda Telford have alluded to one 'Cherrylips', otherwise known as Margery Gray, a prostitute banished from the city of York in 1483. Lynda Telford has argued that this expulsion was no coincidence and was ordered to avoid embarrassment or offence during Richard III's planned visit.[229] Fabyan supports this timeline of events, stating that Richard did indeed head north after his coronation at Westminster to invest his son Edward as Prince of Wales.[230] Expulsion was certainly not a punishment particular to York. Ruth Mazo Karras stated in *Common Women: Prostitution and Sexuality in Medieval England*, that the banishment of prostitutes had also been carried out in Sandwich in Kent.[231]

While brothels and prostitution certainly existed during the fifteenth century, the lack of written evidence connecting it with the Wars of the Roses is not proof that they were not part of it. The period saw a considerable movement of armies, messengers, mariners and households around the country, and it is naive to think that prostitutes were not called on for their services as the populations passing through towns, cities and ports grew. The lack of written evidence for this aspect of women's work is not surprising, especially considering the verbal nature of their transactions. The tantalizing glimpses of the woman from Lichfield and York's Margery Gray are two examples. It's certain there were many more.

The White Hart, Southwark 'The wife of the house'

Medieval innkeeping was not exclusively a man's trade. Many women were registered as owners or tenants of inns, where travellers refreshed themselves before a long journey or lodged while away from home. Their establishments provided a base for communication as well as a place to rest. For some, decisive events of the wars would play out in their dining halls and courtyards.

In the summer of 1450, the rebel Jack Cade rode into the courtyard of The White Hart in Southwark and demanded a room from the wife of the house. Cade's presence here is well documented in sources including in a letter by J. Payn to John Paston. Payn confirms the inn as the place where Cade and his men robbed him, later forcing him to fight on London Bridge with the rebels.[232]

Southwark was famous for its inns and taverns and would have attracted travellers of all kinds. Bale records that Cade and his rebels frequented a London tavern too, called The Crown.[233]

The White Hart in Southwark no longer stands. A ground plan of the old inn drawn in the nineteenth century and based on its older foundations, reveals a large premises with a network of lodgings, stables, stores and yards. An entrance gate opens out to the first courtyard from the High Street, the gate Cade would have galloped through in the summer of 1450. It was estimated, at the time of drawing the plan, that due to its size, the inn could lodge up to two hundred guests.[234]

As we have seen, Cade and his rebels arrested and executed officials they considered either corrupt or an otherwise negative influence on government. According to Stow, after James Fiennes, Lord Say was beheaded, his headless body 'drawn naked at a horse tail upon the pavement from Cheap into Southwark to the said Captain's inn', which, according to Gregory, as we will see, was the White Hart.[235] *The Chronicle of the Greyfriars* also states that 'at the White Hart, in Southwark, one Hawaydyne of Saint Martin's was beheaded'.[236] Cade's connection to the White Hart was still on the lips of Londoners during the Elizabethan period, with Shakespeare placing the rebel here in his play, *Henry VI Part Two*.[237] Later, when Cade went on the run, the wife of the inn mopped Fiennes' and Hawaydyne's dried blood from her courtyard. But her role in the rebellion wasn't over yet.

Cade was eventually apprehended and killed in the struggle ensuing from his arrest. According to Gregory, Cade's body was brought naked in a cart 'and at the Hart in Southwark the cart was made to stand still, the wife of the house might see him if it were the same man or no that was named the Captain of Kent, for he was lodged in her house in his previous time of his misrule and rising'.[238] That the wife of the inn was chosen to identify Cade shows she had dealt closely with him during the rebellion and his stay there. Her positive identification of the punctured, lifeless body at her door led to Cade's ritual beheading and quartering as a traitor.

Sadly, the name of this woman wasn't recorded. However, the names of other female innkeepers during the period can be found. Joan Walter jointly owned The Belle in Lombard Street, London with her husband in 1450 and Alice Hayward owned The Swan on the Hope in Bishopsgate Street 'with a great gate, shops and solars' in 1452.[239]

Among their responsibilities were keeping order, maintaining the building and safeguarding guests' property as much as was possible. Not only providing a bowl of food and a cup of ale, they gave guests a warm welcome too, as Schaseck, a Bohemian visitor to London in

1465 found. He wrote that, on arrival at an inn, 'the hostess comes out with her whole family to receive them', although this enthusiasm may have been out of curiosity for their foreign guests.[240]

In the treacherous political climate, lodging or drinking at a tavern or inn had its dangers. *The Ballad of Lady Bessy* warns: 'sit not too long drinking the wine, lest in heart thou be too merry, such words thou may cast out'. It also places conspirators at an inn, 'changing his inn in every town, and let his back be from the bench lest any man should him know'.[241]

While building a military fleet for Edward IV, John Howard paid visits to several inns, as his household accounts show. In 1463 he paid three shillings and four pence 'to the wife of the Cardinal's Hat for my master's boots'.[242] Among payments for procuring gunpowder and men on horseback to 'make scout watch' he pays for dinner at The Mermaid in Fleet Street.[243]

With no modern postal system in medieval England, news travelled as fast as a messenger could ride. Inns provided a secure location where these letters could be sent and received. Hall wrote that at this time of uncertainty 'letters never ceased, their messengers never slept'.[244] Innkeepers were trusted to keep sensitive correspondence for their patrons as changing allegiances, plots, battle outcomes, movements of armies and changes in government were communicated. Sir John Paston wrote on 28 September 1471 'I pray you send me word hereof by the next messenger, and if it come to Mrs Elizabeth Higgens at the Black Swan, she shall convey it to me'.[245] Jane Stonor also directed a letter sent 'in haste, at the Sword in Fleet Street'.[246]

Joan Conys 'The Swan'

Joan Conys was the proprietor of The Swan Inn on Church Street in St Albans, having agreed to the lease in 1459. She leased the inn jointly with her husband John and their son William. The document confirms their neighbours, John Newbury, who ran an establishment called The Peacock on the same street and John Vessey, landlord of The George, on the opposite side.[247]

As Joan cleared bowls from wooden candlelit tables in the days before 17 February 1461, she would have noticed an increased military presence in the town, perhaps even glad of the extra custom. However, she would soon find her familiar duties interrupted by war as a rain of arrows shuddered into the sky. The Earl of Warwick's Yorkist forces engaged against the royal Lancastrian army, The Swan Inn close to the action. The commotion spilled into St Peter's Street, the town full of the thud of battle, the crying of the injured and the chaotic shouts of commanders. Stow gave an account of arrows falling in the town 'as thick as hail' and the 'sharp encounter' between the Lancastrian and Yorkist armies.[248]

A letter from a Milanese ambassador reported that the fighting started at around midday and continued until six o'clock in the afternoon.[249] Did Joan slam shut the windows and barricade her wooden doors at the sound of battle outside? She may have hidden inside with her family or run out onto the street in panic to get away from the battle. As the town fell silent in the early evening, Joan and her neighbours would cautiously have emerged to survey the damage and the bodies of the dead.

The contribution of innkeepers to the Wars of the Roses was rarely political. Instead, they worked behind the scenes as hosts, receivers of sensitive correspondence, and provided a place for meetings and lodging. Their establishments were scenes of rebellion and war, one wife condemning a traitor's soul and another at the centre of battle. At their inns, women welcomed guests whose heads rested for the night on straw-filled pillows, only to tumble the following morning from a makeshift executioner's block.

'A Bloody Rain'

We have seen how women supported husbands in work and set up their own trades during the conflict, providing services and goods. But others, absent-mindedly going about their daily business, inadvertently slipped into the wars' timeline too.

The *Davies Chronicle* relates how, in around 1459, a woman in a town in Bedfordshire, taking in her sheets after hanging them out to dry found them covered in a 'bloody rain'.[250] We see this in modern times, as dust particles fall with drops of rain, giving the appearance of rusty-coloured marks on clothes and buildings. To the medieval superstitious and religious mind, these 'red drops' proved to be an eerie prophecy and evidence of God's displeasure at England's civil war. She wouldn't know it, but bringing in her washing, she secured a place in the history books.

Another tale in the *Croyland Chronicle* tells of a heavily pregnant woman in Huntingdon, whose unborn baby could be heard 'weeping as it were and uttering a kind of sobbing noise' in reaction to the country's turbulent events. Although not likely to be the desperate wails of an unborn child, rather the gurgling of a cramped digestive system, it was of course committed to history as one of what he calls the 'wondrous signs' as 'even the children unborn deplored our impending calamities'.[251]

One unnamed Lancashire woman going about her business in the countryside stumbled upon a lost John Howard and his men, making war preparations. She stopped and gave them directions. The only evidence of her existence is a scrawl in Howard's accounts book in 1463 as having 'taught the way over Tyddysbery forthe' (Didsbury). She was rewarded with a penny.[252]

Joan Conys wasn't the only woman to find herself accidentally in the throng of battle. While John Leland was travelling through Yorkshire, locals told him of a woman who had become involved in the Battle of Wakefield in 1460. With his father, the Duke of York, killed, the teenager Edmund, Earl of Rutland, frantically searched for a place of safety. 'The common saying is there', writes Leland, 'that the earl would have taken there a poor woman's house for succour, and she for fear shut the door and straight the earl was killed'.[253]

This woman of Wakefield must have been terrified at the armoured man hammering, panic-stricken, on her wooden door as the shouts from his pursuers drifted closer. Despite Leland not naming her, her role was decisive and may have changed the course of history. With the earl saved, the York brothers might have been a more stable force after Edward's accession. George and Richard would have been further down the line of succession and with an older brother living, Richard might never have been king. It is difficult to imagine the closing years of the Wars of the Roses without King Richard III's valiant fight at Bosworth, or the disappearance of the princes in the Tower, but this is the impact this one forgotten woman might have had on history. Instead, on 30 December 1460, she sealed his fate. With nowhere to run, he was cut down by Lancastrian soldiers and killed. Leland noted on his visit that a cross had been set up in remembrance of the earl.

There is one more mysterious tale involving an unsuspecting woman of the wars. Holinshed relates the account of the Duke of Buckingham's capture in 1483. He had taken refuge in Humphrey Bannister's house, who, hoping for a reward, gave him up to Richard III. According to the Tudor historian, Bannister's children suffered for their father's greed. His daughter was 'of excellent beauty', but 'was suddenly stricken with a foul leprosy'. Her brothers also suffered, one of them having 'waxed mad and so died in a bores sty'.[254]

As mysterious as the story is, Holinshed would have found a popular angle here for his readers, with Bannister showing loyalty to Henry VII's enemy, Richard III. For his 'treachery', he implies, Bannister and his family suffered God's divine disapproval. It should be remembered that we are seeing Holinshed's interpretation of the event through Tudor-influenced eyes. Connecting Bannister's tragedies to divine wrath, he is reinforcing Henry VII's God-given right to rule, as the rightful conqueror of Bosworth.

CHAPTER SIX
THE WHEEL OF FORTUNE

One of the common illustrations found in medieval England was the Wheel of Fortune. It was usually depicted as a wooden cartwheel, sometimes held by a woman, with people clambering up one side, and falling down the other. Hall described Fortune as a woman 'which turneth the wheel at her will and pleasure'.[255] Anywhere the wheel was seen, whether in manuscripts, books, or paintings, it served as a bleak warning. Your fortunes could rise but could also suddenly fall.

Families certainly experienced dramatic shifts in status and prosperity during the Wars of the Roses. As well as the military cost, where entire generations of a family could perish in battle, there were material and financial sacrifices too. Lands could be seized; titles could be stripped, and widows might find themselves under scrutiny, singled out for their wealth. For at least one woman, her tumble would come decades after the wars were supposed to have ended. It was a time of uncertain alliances, power struggles and falls from favour, and it could depend on something as simple as the presence of royal blood in your veins. Shakespeare summed it up best in *Henry VI*, 'Ah, gracious lord, these days are dangerous; virtue is choked with foul ambition'.[256]

Catherine Woodville Duchess of Buckingham

Catherine Woodville is often overlooked when discussing the Wars of the Roses. But not only was she close to the royal court and politics of the period, she also saw her fortunes dramatically rise and fall as a result of them.

The daughter of Richard and Jacquetta Woodville, Catherine was the younger sister of Elizabeth Woodville, Edward IV's queen. A large family, the Woodvilles had settled in Northamptonshire in the village of Grafton, both her parents were in the service of Henry VI's Lancastrian government. Her father was knighted by the king in 1426 and served as Governor of the Tower of London.[257] Catherine's mother Jacquetta was Duchess of Bedford, once sister-in-law to Henry V and present in the household of Margaret of Anjou. Catherine would see her fortunes rise however under a new Yorkist regime, at the head of which was her sister.

With Elizabeth established at Edward's court towards the end of 1464, Catherine's earliest memories would have been of ceremonies, celebrations, and royal palaces. It was appropriate then that she would secure a marriage that promised both social and financial security, as well as one of the grandest titles of the realm. In around 1465 a marriage was arranged for her to Henry Stafford, Duke of Buckingham. Henry was the son of Margaret Beaufort, Countess of Stafford.

How happy the couple was has been debated by historians. The Italian visitor, Dominic Mancini, holds the traditional opinion on the state of their marriage. He noted in the 1480s that Buckingham's resentment towards the Woodvilles was fuelled by his marriage to Catherine, which had been arranged when they were young.[258] However, there are inconsistencies with this assessment. The couple went on to have four children over an almost twenty-year marriage and in an account we have already discussed, Catherine is placed at her husband's side during a time of intense danger. Sarah Gristwood, in *Blood Sisters,* has pointed out that Mancini may have been influenced in his writing while in England by anti-Woodville sentiments existing at court.[259]

As a member of a prominent family during the Wars of the Roses, it was inevitable that tragedy would strike. In the summer of 1469 Catherine's father, Richard, and brother, John, were executed after Warwick's victory at the Battle of Edgecote. She would later grieve for the loss of her mother Jacquetta in 1472. The death of Edward IV brought another political blow in 1483 when Richard, Duke of

Gloucester, took the young king into custody for his coronation, only to have himself crowned ruler in his place. Elizabeth was in sanctuary with her younger son and daughters, and Catherine's brother, Anthony Woodville, had been executed. Accusations of illegitimacy and unchaste living were levelled against other members of the family. As Mancini saw it, Richard systematically removed 'those who had been the closest friends of his brother and were expected to be loyal to his brother's offspring'.[260] The Woodvilles, with their family bonds and positions of influence in the princes' households, were surely at the top of that list.

Events would take another dramatic turn in the autumn of that year when Catherine found herself at the centre of the fallout over the Buckingham Rebellion, which aimed to remove Richard from power. The plot, involving her husband, failed, and Buckingham ran. The Delabere account of events at Kinnersley recorded that Catherine was by his side with their sons before they separated to make their escape. Eventually he was captured and beheaded at Salisbury on 2 November 1483, his property and title taken into Richard's hands.[261] Catherine, on her return to London, would have learned of the news of her husband's death and realized she was now the widow of a traitor. With the Buckingham lands and livelihood in the hands of the crown, Catherine must have been anxious over her position, although the Patent Rolls of 1484 record that Richard did grant her an annuity of 200 marks.[262]

Catherine soon found some stability, however. She married the king's uncle, Jasper Tudor, in a match swiftly arranged by Henry VII on his accession. Henry reversed Buckingham's attainder, restoring Catherine to her lands, and created Jasper Duke of Bedford. Interestingly, the Bedford title had now returned, full circle, to the Woodvilles. Catherine now held the title her mother held as a teenager when she married Henry V's brother John, Duke of Bedford, in 1433. Catherine's marriage to Jasper wasn't a long one. He died in December 1485, leaving Catherine a widow for the second time. She remarried, to Richard Wingfield.[263]

It is not often we stop to consider Catherine's story and how she was affected by the political turmoil of the Wars of the Roses. Rising at a young age from relative obscurity in the Northamptonshire countryside, she quickly became a duchess of the realm, profiting financially and socially from her sister's marriage to the king. Escaping major consequences following the accession of Richard III and then her husband's failed rebellion, she was restored to status, albeit under close Tudor watch. Catherine suffered with the deaths of family members from battle and execution, as well as the heartbreaking disappearance of her nephews, the princes. There is little evidence that Catherine played a politically active role during the wars and while it is tempting to speculate on her thoughts or actions during Buckingham's Rebellion, there is no further evidence, other than the Thornbury account that places her by Buckingham's side.

Chroniclers and history books focus on the Duke of Buckingham's contribution to the wars, as well as his involvement in the early reign of Richard III. But Catherine's experiences also shed light on the changes in wealth, status and security that could be faced by a woman close to the royal court. When things went wrong for Catherine, there was nowhere to hide. As a Woodville, a prominent Yorkist, and wife to two leading dukes of the Yorkist and Tudor realms, her life was always going to be tussled by the events of the Wars of the Roses.

Alison Fitzgerald, Countess of Kildare 'The Great Earl'

On 24 May 1487, in the late spring sun, a boy was crowned King of England inside Dublin Cathedral. As the crown was lowered upon his head, his eyes flicked over the dignitaries present. Powerful men in jewelled collars and expensive, colourful robes nodded their approval. They crowned him Edward Plantagenet, son of George, Duke of Clarence, nephew of Edward IV. In their eyes, he was the rightful heir to the throne of England.

As cheers for the new king rang out in Ireland, the real Edward Plantagenet lay behind lock and key in the Tower of London. Henry VII, receiving word of the coronation, steadied himself for the defence of his realm. At the head of those supporting the imposter, Lambert Simnel, was Gerald Fitzgerald, eighth Earl of Kildare.

Fitzgerald had been loyal to the House of York since the reign of Edward IV. His father Thomas was the Duke of York's deputy from 1454 to 1460, also serving as Lord Justice and Chancellor of Ireland. Gerald succeeded his father in 1477, serving all Yorkist kings as either Lord Deputy or Lord Justice.[264] Outwardly cooperative to the new Tudor king, Gerald clearly still harboured Yorkist sympathies. When Lambert Simnel arrived in fine robes claiming to be of Yorkist descent, the earl rallied to his cause, not only to remove Henry VII from the throne, but also perhaps motivated by wider-reaching political implications. Carmel McCaffrey, in *In Search of Ireland's Heroes*, sees Irish support for Simnel as a strong statement to Henry that Ireland could make its own political decisions, separate from the English crown.[265] For all his popularity and charm however, FitzGerald must have known that he was treading a dangerous path.

Likely to have been with Gerald among the cheering crowds at Dublin Cathedral was his wife, Alison. Her father Roland FitzEustace had served as Lord Treasurer of Ireland and was created Baron of Portlester by Edward IV in 1462. Ten years later the king elected him a Knight of St George.[266] Alison would therefore have grown up with an idea of what a life in public service involved as her husband and father served loyally under the House of York. After her marriage to FitzGerald, she would have settled into the earl's home, likely at his main seat at Maynooth Castle, in County Kildare.

Alison's life in the imposing thirteenth-century residence would have been luxurious, as expected for the wife of a wealthy and prominent Irish earl. It was also well-defended, the walls up to nine-feet thick in some places. Looking out of the windows, her eyes would have rested on the estate's parks, outbuildings and the fields beyond. She held daily worship in the private chapel and took her dinners in the candlelit hall.[267]

Her husband Gerald was a smooth-talking statesman, witty and able to discuss his way out of potentially serious situations. On one occasion Henry VII asked Gerald why he had tried to burn down a religious house run by one of his enemies. 'By my troth', he is said to have answered, 'I wouldn't have done it, but I thought the bishop was in it'. During her husband's dealings with Simnel, Alison would also have been caring for their two-year-old heir, Gerald, who was born in 1485, although the specific date of his birth is not known.[268]

With her husband away fighting or summoned to London, Alison, like other women of the wars, would have been the household's main point of contact. But she also had strong family connections to Irish politics of her own, through her father. Could she have played a decisive role in the Wars of the Roses?

The fifteenth century chronicle *The Annals of Ulster* hints at Alison's individual part in the Simnel affair. It describes the 'great fleet of Saxons' descending on Ireland to meet Simnel, 'who was exiled at that time [and living] with the Earl of Kildare, namely, Gerald, son of Earl Thomas'.[269] If FitzGerald was indeed hosting Simnel at their home in 1487 then Alison would certainly have known about it and likely took an active role in ensuring he had everything he needed. She would also have known at least a few facts about his campaign to seize the Tudor throne. With her father and husband carrying out loyal service during the reign of the Yorkist kings, Alison may have shared this political leaning and been more inclined to support her husband's activities relating to the pretender.

In the end, their support of Simnel would turn out to be a catastrophic miscalculation. Henry defeated him and his army at the Battle of Stoke on 16 June 1487. Lambert Simnel was a boy of around ten years of age, and it was clear he had been used as a figurehead for a wider Yorkist challenge to Henry's rule. On realizing that the boy himself posed no threat to him, Henry famously had the pretender set to work in the royal kitchens. The Simnel threat now over, Henry remained understandably suspicious of Gerald. Rumours began to reach the king that the earl was now involved with another Yorkist pretender, Perkin Warbeck. Henry's patience had worn out. Because of this and rumours that he was involved in other conspiracies and charges, Gerald was imprisoned in the Tower of London for two years, on 5 March 1495.[270]

Alison's anxiety must have been immense. She may have feared attacks or reprisals, not only from Tudor, but from local enemies taking advantage of her husband's absence. *The Annals of Ulster* record a number of battles, skirmishes and attacks on properties at this time, and Alison was a potential wealthy target. Cokayne places the date of her death as 22 November 1495, just eight months after Gerald's imprisonment. He and other historians have maintained that she died of grief, but with her husband held under guard 400 miles away and amid fears of local unrest, a stress-related condition could equally have been responsible. She was buried at the abbey of Kilcullen.[271]

In 1475, Alison had wealth, power and security as well as the ear and protection of the 'great earl'. At this time she was arguably one of the most influential women in Ireland. But by 1495, suspicions over Yorkist loyalties and the backing of usurpers hung in the air. Separated from her usually politically agile husband, Alison died at a deeply troubling time for the family. Her story demonstrates that falls from status and power could be both heavy and sudden during the wars, and that its turbulence was felt not only in England but further afield, too.

Elizabeth de Vere, Countess of Oxford 'put in fear of her life'

Presiding over his first parliament, Henry VII reversed attainders imposed by the previous Yorkist government against Lancastrian supporters. John de Vere, Earl of Oxford, a committed soldier and commander, was once again restored to his forfeited estates. But there was a problem. The lands he now owned did not include those of his mother, Elizabeth de Vere.

Elizabeth was the wife of John de Vere, Earl of Oxford. John had been knighted by the four-year old Henry VI at Leicester in 1426 and was on the young king's Privy Council. John and Elizabeth had married by 1429, when she was around nineteen years of age. A keen Lancastrian, John was executed on the orders of Edward IV in 1462 with his eldest son and was buried in the Austin Friars in London.[272]

The earl's surviving son, John de Vere, shared not only his father's name, but also his passion for the Lancastrian cause and fought tirelessly for its reinstatement. He invaded St Michael's Mount in Cornwall, was imprisoned in Calais by Edward IV and, after Henry VI's death, switched loyalty to Henry's next heir, Henry Tudor. But when John returned from fighting, he discovered that Elizabeth had signed his inheritance over to Richard, Duke of Gloucester.

John petitioned Henry VII in parliament in November 1485, stating that Elizabeth, who had since died, had given her lands to Richard unwillingly after being 'put in fear of her life and imprisoned' by the duke. John argued that this transfer should be made void and given permission to enter once again into his mother's lands. He insisted that because she had signed her lands over to Gloucester unwillingly, he had lost a large part of the inheritance due to him. Henry considered the circumstances and ruled in de Vere's favour.[273]

However, there is a line in the Parliament Roll for that year that gives the suggestion Elizabeth herself was an active and loyal supporter of Lancaster. John's petition states that Gloucester's motive for targeting Elizabeth was 'for the true and faithful allegiance and service which she, as well as the same John de Vere, owed and did the aforesaid most blessed prince King Henry.[274]

Elizabeth's son may well have believed that Gloucester was punishing Elizabeth for her Lancastrian loyalties, but it was also a convenient angle to now present to Henry. It demonstrated that

John, Elizabeth and Henry had all been on the same side, likely hoping that Henry would indeed reward the Oxfords' loyalty and steadfastness by ruling in his favour. But we can also see Gloucester's point of view. Seizing Elizabeth's significant estates in a hurried deal prevented her from financially supporting any further Oxford-led campaigns against his brother's Yorkist crown. As Elizabeth's estates would eventually pass to John, Richard's actions at the time were also an indirect attack against Oxford, removing him from his inheritance.

John de Vere was successful in securing his mother's estates, but Elizabeth died with the knowledge that her son's inheritance was in Richard's hands. Whether Richard's motive was to secure her wealth, punish her and her son's loyalties, or diminish her influence, Elizabeth de Vere gives us a greater understanding of the risks posed to older widows, particularly those opposed to the king, during the Wars of the Roses.

Margaret Pole, Countess of Salisbury 'very strange, not knowing her crime'

In 1536 another elderly widow must have looked back on the events of the Wars of the Roses as if they were old news. Margaret Plantagenet had been a young child during the later bloodshed. Born in 1472, she was just four years old when her mother died and only five when her father, George, Duke of Clarence, was executed on the orders of her uncle, Edward IV. Her portrait on the Rous Roll, sketched around 1483, shows her as a young girl, eyes cast down softly, wavy hair tumbling around her shoulders. She would have been around her eleventh year. Drawn at the beginning of the reign of her uncle Richard III, the lines convey a sense of the girl who had already experienced so much personal devastation from conflict.

However, by 1536 Margaret had been married, widowed, and had children of her own. Her husband Richard Pole died in 1504. She had even been a member of the flourishing court of Henry VIII, serving in the household of the princess Mary.[275] The fear and bloody violence of the Wars of the Roses, Margaret must have thought, was long gone.

It would have been a surprise to her then, when in 1539 she was arrested. She had inadvertently become associated with the activities of her son Reginald Pole who had strongly criticized the king, particularly over his divorce from Catherine of Aragon and subsequent marriage to Anne Boleyn. Evidence was presented that convinced Henry of Margaret's guilt, and her complicity in the views and actions of her outspoken and rebellious son. But perhaps the Poles' other problem was that they were of Yorkist blood. Margaret's grandfather was the Duke of York who, a century before, had been granted the right to rule after Henry VI's death. York supporters could make a York-inspired bid for the crown through Margaret and her sons' descent. Henry VII had ordered her brother Edward executed in 1499 for his involvement in the Perkin Warbeck plot. Perhaps the royal blood of the Poles kept his son awake at night, too.

Half a century had passed since Henry Tudor had won at Bosworth. And yet Margaret stood implicated in what Henry regarded as charges of treason. But was Margaret even that much of a danger to Henry? Any risk Margaret herself posed to the crown was negligible. She had lived within the Tudor court for decades and had been granted her ancestral title in 1513. The Salisbury title that she now used conjured up hazy memories of the fiercely Yorkist Richard Neville and his countess, Alice. Even then, up until 1539 neither monarch, not even the wily and suspicious Henry Tudor fresh on his throne, considered Margaret, the Duke of York's granddaughter, a threat.

Sentenced to death, Margaret was led to the wooden block on 27 May 1541. The ambassador Chapuys noted that she 'found it very strange, not knowing her crime' and guessed she was around ninety years old. Margaret was in fact just sixty-seven but may have looked older and more tired due to the stress and anxiety endured during her capture, interrogation and imprisonment. The sight of the fragile woman struggling to comprehend events as she was directed to the block must have been a heartbreaking sight for the 150 or so spectators that Chapuys said attended. She laid down her head and an inexperienced, masked executioner ended her life with the blade of an axe. According to Chapuys, the beheading was especially bloody and frantic as the executioner missed her neck and took hacks at her shoulders and head instead.[276]

Margaret Pole was a member of the Yorkist royal family, her uncles and cousins destined to be kings. As a child she lived through the later wars and escaped its violence, eventually building a new life and was welcomed into the Tudor regime. But although Henry insisted she was being executed for treason, her bloodline seems to have been a factor he took into his calculations. The lingering doubts and hostilities that had initially grown during the Wars of the Roses turned her royal blood into a traitor's, and it is possible that as far into his reign as 1539, Henry saw the shadow of Yorkist challengers falling threateningly over his realm.

PART TWO:
Political and Social Survivors

CHAPTER SEVEN
OVERLOOKED ROYAL WOMEN

Royal women were at the very heart of the Wars of the Roses. But what about other royal women that are often overlooked? Anne Neville, the queen consort of Richard III, is often passed over in discussions on the wars, with chroniclers more concerned with the adventures of her husband and her father, the Earl of Warwick. There are foreign royal women too, some with surprising links to the wars' politics. Queens like Isabella of Castile and Mary of Guelders, who skilfully managed relationships with English rulers on both sides of the conflict during unexpected and dramatic events. We will also discuss one of the wars' 'lost' princesses and the secluded life she spent well away from the royal palaces.

These women have been discussed far more widely by historians than for example the wars' innkeepers or housewives. Agnes Strickland, in particular, referred to many of them in her *Lives of the Queens of England* series, published in 1854. We will look at the attitudes of Strickland and other historians and evaluate whether their assessments of these royal women are still relevant today. Stateswomen, peacekeepers and women of power, these fascinating characters widen our perspective and understanding of the Wars of the Roses.

Isabella of Castile 'turned in her heart'

Isabella of Castile is most widely remembered as the mother of

Catherine of Aragon, Henry VIII's first wife. She formed a potent force with her husband Ferdinand in bringing stability to Spain and famously funded Christopher Columbus' voyage to the Americas.

As it turns out, Isabella was being considered as a possible wife to Edward IV in the early 1460s. Only recently on his throne, Richard III received a visit from her ambassador Granfidius de Sasiola on 8 August 1483. Conveying a statement from Isabella, he told Richard how she had 'turned in her heart from England in time past, for the unkindness the [sic] which she took against the King last deceased [Edward IV], whom God pardon, for his refusing of her, and taking to his wife a widow of England'.

Because of this rejection, she says, she allied away from Edward and towards the French Louis XI. Louis assisted the Lancastrian cause in the 1460s, being Margaret of Anjou's cousin and also wary of Edward IV's loyalty to his enemy, Burgundy. Isabella points out, although it was hardly necessary, that the Woodville marriage also caused 'mortal war between him and the Earl of Warwick, the [sic] which took ever her part to the time of his death'. Isabella hoped for a new partnership with England, 'now the king is dead that showed her this unkindness', adding soothingly that it was always her nature to 'love and favour England'.[277]

Born in 1451 Isabella would have been just thirteen years old when she heard, apparently highly insulted, about Edward's marriage to his subject Elizabeth Woodville in 1464. However, by 1483 she was on the prowl for beneficial political connections and had a brood of daughters that she was looking to marry. She may have sent Sasiola to gauge Richard's interest in a marriage between one of her daughters and his young son, Edward of Middleham.

As for her political switching, it is highly unlikely that Edward's refusal to marry Isabella was the reason for her allying with Lancaster. It is probable that Sasiola had been sent because Edward had now died. Alliances and treaties made between nations usually involved complicated and lengthy negotiations pinned on far more than a teenager's revenge over a broken heart. The 'displeasure' she felt when Louis broke the terms of their agreement, added as a short side, probably had far more to do with her move in 1483 towards the Yorkist court. However, as she conveniently shifted the blame onto the now silent Edward IV, a new friendship between Spain and England could be formed without Richard raising awkward questions over her past.

Contemporary depictions of Isabella portray her with her hair often loose, a long nose and heavily lidded eyes. She died in 1504. Isabella would, in the end, achieve a partnership with England, through her daughter's marriage to the Prince of Wales, but it would not be Edward of Middleham. Catherine of Aragon would build the foundations of Henry VII's Tudor dynasty by marrying his eldest son Arthur in 1501 and later, his brother Henry VIII, in 1509.

Cecily Neville 'The right excellent princess'

Cecily Neville experienced the full force of the wars. As Duchess of York, she witnessed its triumphs as well as its bloody aftermath, grieved the violent deaths of loved ones and looked on helplessly as her family fractured over rivalry and ambition. Two of her sons would become king, but as far as anyone knew in the autumn of 1460, it was Cecily who was next in line to wear a crown.

The wife of Richard Plantagenet, Duke of York, Cecily has often been labelled pompous and arrogant. Strickland wrote that she welcomed guests seated on a throne as if she was a queen. Her Household Ordinances give her the title 'right excellent princess', with a surviving letter addressing her in the similar 'most gracious and excellent princess'.[278] But evidence shows that Cecily's character was far more rounded than the one-sided caricature of the 'Proud Cis' her Fotheringhay locals were said to have called her.

Cecily was born in 1415, the daughter of Ralph Neville, Earl of Westmoreland, and Lady Joan Beaufort. She had royal blood, descended from John of Gaunt, son of Edward III. Her husband, who was of course to actively promote his claim to the throne during the Wars of the Roses, was also related to Edward III, through the king's granddaughter Philippa, daughter of Lionel, Duke of Clarence.[279] We do see Cecily referred to as a princess after her son Edward IV's accession to the throne, which was to be expected as the king's mother. As Mary Anne Everett Wood pointed out, Margaret Beaufort similarly signed her letters 'Margaret R' following the accession of her son, Henry VII.[280]

Cecily was present for the very first crackles of civil war. She married the duke in around 1424, remaining loyal to him up to his death in 1460.[281] After that, she would remain steadfast to York's cause through their children and grandchildren. When he processed to London to lay his claim to the throne, he sent for Cecily. Gregory wrote that she travelled in a blue velvet chair as trumpeters announced their progress through the country.[282] Amy Licence, in *Cecily Neville Mother of Kings*, states that evidence shows she travelled a great deal with her husband within England as well as overseas. A relic mentioned in her will as 'a pix of the flesh of St Christopher' may have been carried, then, for protection on these journeys with St Christopher the patron saint of travellers.[283] In October 1460, parliament agreed that Henry VI should retain the throne only up until his death. After that, Richard Duke of York would become king, and Cecily his queen.

As well as successes, Cecily also suffered the wars' adversity. Fabyan placed her at Ludlow during the Lancastrian attack on the town and castle in 1459 with her two young sons.[284] She saw the wars' bloodshed in the executions, deaths in battle and humiliation of loved ones but Cecily remained ruthlessly loyal to her family and its cause.

The traces Cecily left behind in documents show that she was a confident and resilient woman. She and her husband raised similarly ambitious and capable daughters including Margaret of York (who would later become Duchess of Burgundy), Anne Duchess of Exeter and Elizabeth Duchess of Suffolk. William Wolflete was another who could attest to Cecily's determination. She wrote to him on 19 August 1495 with the ominous warning 'that you fail not hereof as you will avoid the awful peril that may ensue with our great displeasure and heavy ladyship'.[285]

Cecily certainly wasn't a lady to be messed with. But she also had a softer side. Her will included thoughtful gifts to her children and grandchildren, along with payments to servants.[286] She bequeathed *The Revelations of Saint Bridget* to the Prioress of Syon and three more religious texts to her granddaughter Bridget, who entered Dartford Priory. A special gift was reserved for Arthur, the grandchild next in line to the throne. She bequeathed him a bed depicting the Wheel of Fortune, perhaps a reminder of the twists and turns she had seen in her own sons' lives.[287]

Cecily's Household Ordinances record that towards the end of her life she woke around seven, spent time in prayer, met guests and enjoyed conversation with her ladies, retiring to bed by eight.[288] It was an appropriate schedule for a woman who had endured decades of the wars' wild and turbulent events. She died, eighty years old in 1495, and in her will asked to be buried with her 'most entirely best beloved lord and husband' at Fotheringhay in Northamptonshire.[289]

Anne of York, Duchess of Exeter 'an atrocious character'

Cecily's daughter, Anne, didn't catch the eye of many nineteenth-century historians, but Agnes Strickland certainly had something to say about her. In a footnote to her *Lives of the Queens of England*, she dismissed her as 'rapacious' and an 'atrocious character' who 'divorced and despoiled her first husband, and caused the death of her second'.[290] But how far does Anne of York really deserve this assessment?

Anne was born at Fotheringhay Castle on 10 August 1439 and

married Henry Holland, Duke of Exeter by 1447.[291] The arranged marriage had taken place while Anne was still a child, and before the start of the Wars of the Roses. The couple had one daughter also named Anne. As political tensions grew and the Duke of York began to fight resolutely for power, Holland chose to reject his father-in-law's ambitions, and remained firmly aligned to Lancaster and the promotion of Henry VI's cause.

Anne's husband's support of Henry VI might have been an annoyance and embarrassment to the Yorks, but from Edward IV's accession it was treason. Edward wasted no time in transferring Exeter's lands to Anne and her heirs.[292] Anne, who seems to have been close to her younger brother, wasn't shy in using her influence with him, several cases recorded in the Patent Rolls brought 'on supplication of the king's sister'. She was also the driving force behind her divorce from Exeter in 1471, Stow writing that it was carried out on 12 November that year 'by means of her own suit'.[293] Holland quickly fled into exile and spent the next few years plotting and campaigning for Lancastrian support.

Following her divorce, Anne married the Yorkist courtier Thomas St Leger. Holland turned up dead soon after, Fabyan recording his death with appropriate suspicion. 'In this year was the Duke of Exeter found dead in the sea between Dover and Calais, but how he was drowned in certainty is not known'.[294] It is often speculated that Holland, ever a thorn in the side of his royal brother-in-law, may have been thrown overboard and drowned, but there is no evidence for this.

St Leger would eventually share Holland's bad luck. After Anne's death in 1476 he remained loyal to Edward, joining the ill-fated Buckingham Rebellion after his death when he was captured and executed.

But what about Strickland's evaluation of the duchess?

Certainly, Anne divorced Holland and played a role in 'despoiling' him, swiftly taking control of his estates as he continued to fight against the crown for Lancaster. As for the assertion that she caused the death of her second husband, this is more difficult to establish. He died in 1483, seven years after his wife, having taken part in a rebellion that she could never have known would happen. Of course, had St Leger never married into the royal family he would have been further away from the heart of the wars and perhaps less politically active, which might have saved his life. It is fair to say however, that it was St Leger's own actions that led to his death, and certainly not his late wife's.

Anne was the loyal sister of Edward IV and a prominent figure at court during the wars. She was also one of those Croyland saw as important for reuniting her brother Clarence with the king after his defection.[295] Her choice too, of a second husband already allied to the family's cause, could indicate a conscious smoothing out of her political and personal lives.

A drawing of Anne on her monumental brass shows her kneeling, wearing a mantle lined with ermine, a crucifix around her neck and a long gable hood with coronet. She has a slim, long face and alert eyes. The traces of her short life in the sources suggest she was persuasive, ambitious and loyal to her family. Her brass stated that she died in 1476, in her mid-thirties. Anne was buried in St George's Chapel in Windsor Castle.

Margaret of York, Duchess of Burgundy

Another of Edward's sisters would become particularly zealous in her promotion of the House of York during the closing years of the wars. Margaret of York had married Charles, Duke of Burgundy in 1468. A letter from John Paston to his mother describes the pageants, processions and jousts that welcomed the young bride on her arrival.[296] Their union secured an English-Burgundian alliance which would prove crucial to Edward's success, although he would never have known it at the time. Just two years later, his brother-in-law would aid in his reclaiming of the throne after Henry VI's brief retaking of power in 1470-1471.

Like her mother and sister, Margaret was a loyal Yorkist as well as a shrewd and calculating stateswoman. With Anne she acted as peacemaker between their brothers in 1471. Commines also wrote of her exerting power in Burgundy during her marriage and also as Dowager Duchess, overseeing the reign of her stepdaughter Mary.[297]

In contemporary portraits Margaret wears a tall, conical headdress with a veil, fine gowns with lacing at the bodice and colourful jewels. She often appears with a white rose, a symbol of her York roots. But Margaret's boldest political acts during the Wars of the Roses would come after the end of the York dynasty, and during the reign of Henry VII.

Richard Baker called Margaret 'the common and sure refuge for all rebels against King Henry VII' while Bernard André in his *Life of Henry VII*, compared her to the mythical figure of Juno, stopping at nothing to champion the Yorkist cause.[298] To them, the duchess seemed willing to lend her support to anyone intent on overthrowing the Tudor government to restore the House of York, however tenuous their claim.

Margaret was implicated in the attempts of both major pretenders to the Tudor throne. In 1487 she assisted Lambert Simnel, who we have seen crowned in Dublin Cathedral. He claimed that he was her nephew, Edward, Earl of Warwick, and Margaret equipped him with a force, said Hall, of 2,000 soldiers.[299] She also backed the later attempted invasion of Perkin Warbeck, who claimed to be one of the 'lost' princes in the Tower, the younger Richard. Hall pins Margaret as the driving force behind the deception, instructing him on 'the secrets and common affairs of the realm of England' and decking him out in the York livery of murrey and blue.[300] Warbeck however failed to generate support in England and was captured by Henry VII. Hall touches on the pretender's arrival in a country weary of generations of war. He describes men deciding not to follow the imposter, 'remembering what evil chances their forefathers had, and how small a profit such as have rebelled have gained'.[301]

It is not known if Margaret truly believed the claimed identities of the two pretenders or had any real faith in their chances of success in England. Despite now living overseas, she remained fiercely loyal to the Yorkist cause, believing only perhaps that she was doing the right thing for her family's legacy by fighting for it. There is also the possibility that Margaret simply wished to be a nuisance to Henry, the man who killed her youngest brother and took his throne. Margaret died in 1503, and is buried in Mechelen, Belgium.

Mary of Guelders 'fugitives and suppliants'

In the summer of 1460, Margaret of Anjou and her son Edward glanced up at the tall towers and stone arches of the Collegiate College of Lincluden, north of the town of Dumfries. They had escaped to Scotland via Wales, following the Battle of Northampton on 10 July that year, her Lancastrian army suffering a disastrous defeat. With Henry VI now captured and under the control of Yorkists, Margaret was scouting out for possible allies.

On her way to meet the royal exiles was Scottish Queen Mary of Guelders with her son, King James. Mary was in mourning for her husband who had recently been killed in a cannon accident at the Siege of Roxburgh Castle. Now regent, Mary was overseeing the reign of her young son, James III. Travelling through the bumpy, rural tracks to Lincluden, she would have carefully considered Margaret's situation. Henry VI was a captive and battles and riots were springing up all over England in an attempt to wrestle power from the crown. The blood of the king's subjects had been spilled and the queen and prince were in hiding. The House of Lancaster had completely lost its grip on government. Strickland writes that Margaret and Edward came to Scotland as 'fugitives and suppliants'.[302] Mary would have sensed, weighing up Margaret's predicament, that there was a deal to be made. Within Lincluden's red sandstone walls the two queens hashed out their terms.

Mary agreed to back Lancaster, furnishing Margaret and Henry with an army. In return she requested a royal marriage between Prince Edward and Mary's daughter as well as the long-contested town of Berwick in the north of England. Mary's men would have been among the 18,000 soldiers Stow reported were with the Lancastrian army at the Battle of Wakefield. The battle would prove an outstanding victory for Margaret. The duke was outnumbered (Stow says he had less than 5,000 men) and was killed, along with his son.[303] Mary's support to Margaret then, was a decisive moment in Lancastrian fortunes.

However, it also unnerved the Yorkist party and sent shockwaves across Europe. On 1 June 1461 Papal Legate Francesco Coppino wrote to inform the Pope of events in England, in a letter that survives today in the Calendar of State Papers. Specifying the agreement made between Mary and Margaret at Lincluden, he wrote about rumours of a Scottish-Lancastrian invasion of England with support from the French. He also reveals that the Duke of Burgundy had written to Mary, his niece, to try to control the developing political heat.[304]

As it turned out, Berwick was eventually recaptured by the English and the marriage between the Scottish princess and Prince Edward never happened.[305] However, Mary's contribution to the Wars of the Roses was still significant. She led negotiations with Margaret of Anjou and provided military assistance to the Lancastrian cause, changing the course of the entire conflict at Wakefield. She also turned the distress of two royal exiles on her doorstep into a chance for political and financial gain. She died in 1463.

Anne Neville 'The unhappy Duchess of Gloucester'

We all know about Anne Neville, the daughter of the Earl of Warwick and wife of Richard III, but she is not often discussed in detail. There

117

is a real lack of evidence about her as an individual, with chronicles instead focusing on the adventures and exploits of the men in her life. When she is remembered, Anne is often portrayed as a sad, subservient pawn who offered no contribution to history except as Richard III's depressed and tragic queen.

Tudor chroniclers pitied Anne, the wife of the man they considered a tyrant. Thomas More, in his *History of King Richard The Third*, conjured an image of her with 'weeping tears' on hearing malicious, but clearly untrue rumours of her death.[306] After her death, Hall considered it 'most likely' that Richard had poisoned her, while Vergil said it might have been 'sorrowfulness'.[307] To Strickland, she was 'the unhappy Duchess of Gloucester'.[308] Perhaps it's time to reconsider Anne.

Anne Neville was born in June 1456 at Warwick Castle, the daughter of Richard, Earl of Warwick, and Anne Beauchamp.[309] Both parents had strong personalities and backgrounds. Her father was charismatic and generous, a brave soldier and calculating statesman, her mother diplomatic, intelligent and resilient. The women in Anne's extended family were also bold and assertive. Her grandmother was Alice Montacute and among her aunts were Margaret Talbot, Countess of Shrewsbury, and Margaret Neville, Countess of Oxford. From a young age Anne and her sister Isabel would have seen these women asserting their rights and assisting in their husbands' war efforts. With these role models close to her in childhood, perhaps Anne wasn't the meek and submissive woman of the chronicles.

Anne's main entry into the history books comes in 1470, when she married Edward, Prince of Wales, son of Henry VI and Margaret of Anjou. The marriage was intended to demonstrate Warwick's new Lancastrian loyalty to a suspicious Margaret. It provoked some alarm, in particular with Philip de Commines, who called it 'an unaccountable match ... to dethrone and imprison the father and marry his only son to the daughter of him that did it'.[310]

The fifteen-year-old Anne's feelings towards her teenage husband are not recorded, although the Milanese ambassador wrote in February 1467 that although he was only thirteen, he talked enthusiastically about beheadings and war.[311] If Anne could overlook her new husband's unsettling conversations she might even have been keen on the union, gaining the title Princess of Wales and imagining herself Queen of England one day, with Lancastrian heirs of their own.

Any ambitions of queenship were dashed when Edward was killed on 4 May 1471 at the Battle of Tewkesbury. Just weeks earlier, her father and uncle had also fallen at the Battle of Barnet, their blood-stained bodies placed on public view at St Paul's Cathedral in London.

Anne's second husband was already known to her, having lived with the Warwicks when he was a boy. Like high-born women, it was not unusual for boys to be brought up in the homes of similarly wealthy families to learn the duties expected of them in adulthood. But Richard's brother George, Duke of Clarence (already married to Anne's sister, Isabel) tried to derail the wedding, resentful at one day sharing the Warwick fortune with his brother. Eventually the wedding went ahead, Cokayne giving the date of their ceremony as 12 July 1472.[312]

Anne may have been naturally quiet and obedient in character. If she had been outspoken like Catherine Moleyns, or actively involved in preparations for war, the Tudor chroniclers would almost certainly have mentioned it, Anne being Richard III's queen.

Born into the Warwick family shortly after the First Battle of St Albans, Anne's life was always at the centre of the Wars of the Roses. She watched her family march into battle, devise rebellions and conspiracies and escape to exile. Anne learned early that events could be unpredictable and sometimes brutal, as her family were tossed around in the wars' chaos. In 1460 her father was disgraced. In 1461 he was one of the most powerful men in the kingdom. Just ten years later he was lying dead, naked except for a loincloth for the Londoners to see outside St Pauls and declared a traitor. Even the nation's anointed queen, Margaret of Anjou, was now imprisoned, Henry VI likely murdered in the Tower of London.

Some of Anne's decisions seem to point towards a need for security. After the disastrous marriage arranged for her by her father, Anne might have considered that a union with someone she knew would be better than another stranger she might otherwise have been matched with. Richard was a wealthy and experienced military leader and loyal to his brother Edward during his reign. The sources hint at Richard as more serious and withdrawn than the charming, outgoing Edward, a trait that again might have appealed to her. Strickland believed Anne had been forced into her marriage with Richard, but the match offered her stability and wealth as well as royal influence.[313] In 1471, Anne's position as the daughter of a traitor and the widow of a Lancastrian prince was far from secure.

Anne was crowned with her husband on 6 July 1483. As she processed to Westminster Abbey, accompanied by gentlewomen, countesses, and duchesses, she would have waved gently and smiled to crowds gathered along London's streets. From hints in sources, it appears that Anne was a diligent queen, travelling with Richard to the north and presiding over the Feast of the Nativity, according to Croyland, where 'far too much attention was given to dancing and gaiety'.[314] She was also a founder and patron of the University of Cambridge, and according to Mancini, took custody of her nephew Edward of Warwick after the Duke of Clarence's death.[315] Sarah Gristwood in *Blood Sisters* has also stated that a message sent from Anne to the city of York in 1475–76 suggests that she was able to act on her husband's behalf.[316] That she offered her assistance also demonstrates she felt confidently able to step in and provide it when needed. John Rous describes her as 'marvellously conveyed by all the corners and parts of the wheel of fortune and ... exalted again ... over all other ladies of this noble realm'. He wrote that in person she was amiable, beautiful and virtuous.[317]

1484 would prove a tragic year for Anne, bringing the sudden death of her and Richard's only son, Edward, at Middleham in Yorkshire. The royal couple were in Nottingham when they heard the news, the *Croyland Chronicler* stating that they were 'in a state almost bordering on madness, by reason of their sudden grief'.[318] Anne died the following year.

Anne stands, depicted on the Rous Roll alongside her husband. He holds in one hand his upright sword and in the other an orb. Decked out in armour and crowned, at his feet rests his famous symbol, a boar. Anne is clothed in a regal gown and cloak both furred with ermine and also wears a crown. An orb and sceptre rest in each of her hands and her hair is long and loose, tucked behind her right ear. A bear, the symbol of the earls of Warwick, looks up from her feet. Either side of her, a hand emerges from a cloud, presenting her with two more smaller crowns, perhaps alluding to her other titles as Princess of Wales and Duchess of Gloucester. The Rous Roll was written to celebrate the history of the Warwick family, and here, for once, Anne is centre stage.

We may not have reams of evidence about Anne Neville's life, but she still deserves to be remembered as an important character and integral part of the wars. She endured grief and turmoil within her family, losing both her father and sister Isabel. She would have seen her mother fight for her lands. Quiet and cautious, her character seems restrained, ordered and driven by a desire for security, although from the few glimpses we have of her, she appears to have conducted herself professionally in her positions as duchess and queen. In her short life Anne held the titles Princess of Wales, Duchess of Gloucester and Queen of England. She was just 28 years old when she died on 16 March 1485.

Bridget Plantagenet 'The Nun Princess'

Bridget, the youngest daughter of Elizabeth Woodville and Edward IV, was born in early November 1480 at Eltham. But Bridget was never destined for life in a royal palace. At just ten years old, she was led through the doors of Dartford Priory in Kent, to embark on a religious and solitary life.

The reason for Bridget's entry into Dartford is unclear. It's possible that, with an already large brood of princes and princesses to take on royal roles and form foreign alliances, Edward and Elizabeth decided on a religious life for their youngest. It's possible too of course, that from a young age Bridget expressed a personal desire to enter the church. Alison Weir has pointed out her parents' unusual choice of religious name for the baby princess, a devotional life potentially always having been on the cards for her.[319]

Bridget's entry into Dartford Priory is featured in Mary Russell Mitford's early-nineteenth century poem *The Young Novice*. The narrative is highly romantic, as might be expected from a literary work of this period. However, Mitford does follow an interesting line of thought. Could Elizabeth Woodville have been motivated towards a secluded life for her youngest child, away from the plots, schemes and political games she had seen during the height of the Wars of the Roses while queen?

The poem has Elizabeth handing her daughter over to the prioress, asking her to 'shelter her from the dark perils that hang over our house, from open foes and treacherous friends'. She also speaks of the need to protect her daughter from 'stern ambition' and 'cunning cruelty'.[320]

By 1490 Elizabeth had seen enough of the wars for the protective instinct Mitford describes to kick in. Her first husband was killed in battle, her father and brother were executed, and her mother was accused of witchcraft. Ambition had divided her husband's brothers and led, ultimately, to their deaths. Her two sons were missing, presumed dead. Twice she had fled to sanctuary fearing repercussions from her enemies, one of them her own brother-in-law. Bridget may also have had hazy memories of this second flight, being just a toddler at the time. Later, as news of royal imposters, rebellions and executions trickled into the priory's gates, she might have felt grateful for her life within its secluded walls.

Bridget seems to have stayed at Dartford for most of her life. Not much more is known about her, but an entry in her sister Elizabeth's Privy Purse Accounts shows that she paid towards some of Bridget's living costs in 1502, suggesting they kept in touch.[321]

Bridget's life may have been short, but it wasn't uneventful. As a child, she had lost her father and was whisked into sanctuary with her mother and siblings. Although still young, she would have been aware of her uncle's accession to the throne and the disappearance of her two brothers, Edward and Richard. The reasons for her entry into a religious life are uncertain, but it is conceivable that the impact of the wars may have played a part in her parents' decision. For Bridget, the woman Strickland called 'the nun princess', life was filled not with ambassadors' visits and the blessing of royal beds but a devotion to God and friendships within the priory's community.[322]

CHAPTER EIGHT
RELIGIOUS SANCTUARY

We don't tend to think of religious houses being affected by the Wars of the Roses, but while those in the secular world needed to maintain continuity, those in the religious world did too. Monks and nuns still needed to confirm charters, manage legal disputes and conduct the business of worship. Some of these, women included, found themselves involved in events directly related to the Wars of the Roses.

The *Croyland Chronicler* wrote that 'in every society, whether chapter, college or convent … this unhappy plague of division affected an entrance'.[323] The wars affected those living in convents, abbeys, and monasteries in different ways. Gathering to solemnly chant prayers for the war's dead, they also oversaw some of their burials. They conducted processions in hope of peace and offered those who found themselves on the losing side of the conflict a place of safety from the charged political atmosphere outside their walls. One abbey became entangled in a high-profile, politically motivated allegation of witchcraft. Another abbess would be vital to the outcome of the wars in 1485. And one woman quietened her prayers as the sound of trumpets, shouts and gunshots muffled through the abbey's glass windows.

Women in secular society too, sought help from religious houses as they found themselves vulnerable after the war's losses. Anne Beauchamp, Countess of Warwick, wrote from Beaulieu Abbey in the New Forest to try to secure her lands from a furious Edward IV. Margaret Hungerford was lodged with the nuns at Amesbury Abbey in Wiltshire, under arrest for her family's support of the Lancastrian cause. While there, these women found a temporary place of protection where they could attempt to negotiate with their enemies.

Other women entered priories or convents on a more permanent basis. Elizabeth, the wife of John Talbot, Second Earl of Shrewsbury, entered Shrewsbury Abbey on 19 July 1460, just nine days after the death of her husband and his brother at the Battle of Northampton.[324] Margaret Ingleby also entered a religious life after her husband Richard Welles Lord Willoughby was beheaded near Stamford, following his son's involvement in the Lincolnshire Rebellion of 1470.[325] After the shock of their husbands' brutal deaths from the wars, it's not surprising that women like Margaret and Elizabeth looked towards a quieter, more reflective life, away from the wars' spotlight. Of course, for Margaret, whose son had openly waged war against the king, it also provided a neutral location to wait cautiously for the dust to settle. Women who lived through the wars interacted with monasteries, priories and abbeys in search of space, prayer, negotiation, physical safety or simply to grieve and establish new connections. The *Croyland Chronicler* was certainly right, as they too, became embroiled in events of the Wars of the Roses.

Katherine de la Pole

The futures of Jasper and Edmund Tudor would be crucial to the outcome of the wars and the Tudor accession in 1485. They were the sons of Owen Tudor, the man who, after his death, received the attention of the 'mad woman' we have seen in Hereford's marketplace. A servant in the household of the then-widowed queen of Henry V, Catharine Valois, they began a relationship and eventually married. They had two sons, Jasper and Edmund.

Edmund married Margaret Beaufort, who gave birth to their son Henry when she was just thirteen years of age. This boy was Henry Tudor and would eventually become king. Jasper Tudor, Henry's uncle, would be crucial to Henry's success, taking him from the care of Anne Herbert on his journey to the throne.

However back in 1440, no one could have foreseen Tudor roses, a seventh King Henry or the historical significance of a field just outside Leicester. Back then, Jasper and Edmund were small boys in the care of the abbess of Barking Abbey, Katherine de la Pole.

The ancient building at Barking was said to have been founded in the year AD 666 with alterations throughout the medieval period; it was destroyed in the sixteenth and seventeenth centuries.[326] As abbess, Katherine seems to have been tenacious and efficient. She appears in various grants and petitions but also seems to have attracted the anger of locals. In one dispute over access to abbey grounds in February 1450, Robert Osbern and his servants were accused of having 'shouldered her against the wall where she fell to the ground' and assaulted her servants.[327] These attacks were thankfully rare, and Katherine's business was usually overseeing the other sisters of the house, necessary paperwork and of course, devotion.

It was against this backdrop that the two young Tudor brothers were guided by Katherine through the abbey gates and shown to their lodgings. She would have been responsible not only for the boys' food and other living arrangements but also their education. Henry VI's biographer John Blacman wrote that the king provided his half-brothers with 'most strict and safe guardianship, putting them in the care of virtuous and worthy priests, both for teaching and for right living and conversation, lest the untamed practices of youth should grow rank if they lacked any to prune them'.[328] If Henry's main concern was to give the Tudors a devout, strict, and moral upbringing, then Katherine must have demonstrated these characteristics for him to put them in her care. She requested £53 12 shillings for Jasper's and Edmund's maintenance, the equivalent of around £34,465 today.[329] Katherine wouldn't know it, but by safeguarding the boys at this young age, she would play an indirect role in bringing the Tudors to power.

However, Katherine's role in the Wars of the Roses wasn't restricted to raising the father and uncle of the future king. She is also mentioned on a pardon roll of rebels associated with Jack Cade's uprising in July 1450.[330] Could Katherine have been actively rebelling against the king? Her recently murdered brother was the influential William de la Pole, Duke of Suffolk. She also had her own status to uphold as a devout role model in the community. The trace of Katherine in the records shows a dependable, strict and capable woman which is at odds with any riotous behaviour and so any notion that she joined the rebellion seems doubtful. The pardon not only includes Katherine, but her tenants and servants too. It's plausible that some of them had taken part in the rebellion, and Katherine was being pardoned in case accusations of involvement were ever levelled at her personally. Alice Raw, in *Gender and Protest in Late Medieval England*, a discussion of women involved in late medieval revolts, mentions the point of view of Isobel Harvey; that Katherine's pardon may have been an administrative exercise to provide security against attacks from Suffolk's enemies.[331] Harvey's view places Katherine in the wider political context of the Wars of the Roses through her brother and his opponents.

Katherine is not often discussed in the context of the wars, and if she is, it's as an aside, as guardian of the young Tudor brothers. But she is an example of how a woman at the head of a religious establishment became involved in not just the wars' politics but also its associated rebellion. She carried out the daily duties of abbess defending the abbey's rights, taking legal action and at least once enduring a personal attack. She secured the upbringing of Jasper and Edmund Tudor, one going on to father the king who would engineer an end to the conflict in 1485. The death of her brother, whose headless body was thrown onto the Dover sands in May 1450 must have affected her emotionally, and perhaps led to fears for her own safety as his sister. Katherine died, in the position of abbess of Barking, in around April 1473 and was succeeded in the role by one of the nuns of the abbey, Dame Elizabeth Lexham.[332]

A Religious Life and The Wars of the Roses

Inside religious buildings all over the country, prayers were said for the souls of those who had been lost to the wars. In 1465 chaplains were asked to hold service for Edward IV, his mother and brothers and the souls of the Duke of York, Edmund, Earl of Rutland and 'all the faithful departed and especially those who shed their blood for his right'.[333] Margerey Swinfen, prioress at Whistones Priory in Worcestershire also prayed for 'the soul of the noble prince of blessed memory Richard, late Duke of York' in 1476 and held mass three times a year for the king, queen and their children. Reflecting a nation exhausted with civil war, she agreed to hold a procession with her nuns every Friday for 'the tranquillity and peace of this realm of England'.[334]

Several nuns and abbesses came from high-born families, but not all of them. A brass in St Peter and Paul Church in Dagenham depicts Sir Thomas Urswyk and his wife with four sons and nine daughters; the eldest daughter is wearing a nun's habit. Urswyk eased Edward IV's entry into London in 1471 by dismissively ordering armed Lancastrian supporters to 'go home to dinner', according to John Warkworth.[335] Sadly, nothing more is known of his daughter.

The fear of attacks on nuns and monks' communities during the wars was real. As the Lancastrian army headed south after their victory at the Battle of Wakefield in 1460, the Croyland monk wrote of the 'utmost dread' that they would descend on them with their 'unbridled and frantic rage'. He describes how treasure was buried in the earth and valuables were hidden inside the abbey walls. The men, he wrote, rushed into 'churches and the other sanctuaries of God and most nefariously plundered them of their chalices, books and vestments'. It didn't help either, grumbled the anxious monk, that residents fled their villages for safety with valuables of their own. 'By bringing with them whatever treasures they considered of value, they rendered the place a still greater object of suspicion', he wrote.[336]

It's not surprising that they were worried about their valuables. Religious buildings were perceived to contain huge amounts of treasure. Towering above their towns and cities, the visitor Schaseck

Windsor Castle. Foreign visitors were amazed at the expensive fabrics and silks adorning Edward IV's court here, Alice Claver's work likely among them. (Jo Romero)

Left: Groat of Henry VI 1422–27. Henry's unstable rule was one of the causes of the Wars of the Roses. (The Met Museum)

Right: Alice Chaucer's effigy in St Mary's Church, Ewelme, Oxfordshire. As Duchess of Suffolk, her legacy lives on in Ewelme today. (Jo Romero, kind permission the Rector, Churchwardens and PCC of St Mary the Virgin, Ewelme)

Above: A late eighteenth-century depiction of Middleham Castle, the site of the alleged Yorkist plotting with which Alice Montacute was charged in 1459 (British Library, Flickr. Online Collection)

Left: Depiction of a knight and a lady by Master E. S. in around 1460. Women's support of their husbands during the wars is well documented, however, the idealized romantic image here gives no hint of the challenges they faced. (National Gallery of Art, Washington)

Salisbury Cathedral, an eighteenth-century depiction. Burial place of Lady Margaret Hungerford, whose son and husband supported the House of Lancaster. Her tomb has sadly been lost. (British Library, Flickr. Online Collection)

Joan Canynges, wife to Mayor of Bristol and wealthy merchant William Canynges. Edward IV was hosted at the Canynges' home soon after his coronation. Her effigy lies in St Mary Redcliffe Church. (Jo Romero, kind permission St Mary Redcliffe Parish Office)

Isabella More, wife to William More has her brass preserved in St Michael's Church, Tilehurst, Berkshire. The secret knowledge of wives to those close to the king and queen during the conflict is rarely discussed. (Jo Romero, kind permission the Rector of St Michael's Church)

London before 1666. This view of the city would have been close to that known by Elizabeth Venour, Alice Claver, Joan Judde and many other forgotten women of the Wars. (Yale Center for British Art)

Mary Going to The Temple depicts four female saints and a female donor and her daughters. Fifteenth century. Nuns, abbesses, prioresses and women donors played a part in events in the undercurrent of the Wars of the Roses. (The Barnes Foundation).

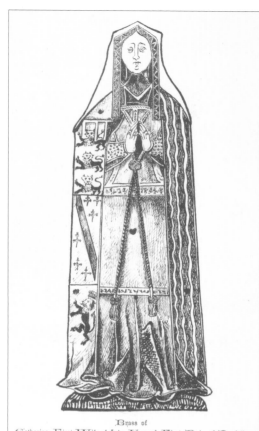

Brass of Catherine, First Wife of John Howard, First Duke of Norfolk,
IN STOKE-BY-NAYLAND CHURCH.

Catherine Moleyns, a drawing of her brass. The outspoken first wife of John Howard. She voiced frustration at the Pastons' property disputes with key characters of the wars. (British Library, Flickr. Online Collection)

Opposite page (bottom right): Playing card depicting the Queen of Horns, Netherlands, c. 1475. Although the clothing portrayed here might be exaggerated, the daily backdrop of duchesses, countesses, and wives of knights during the Wars of the Roses was more colourful than some modern period dramas might have us believe. (The Met Museum)

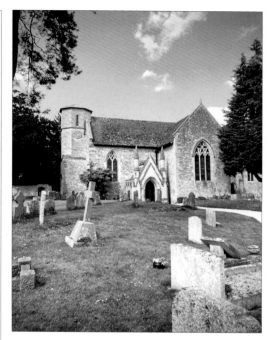

Fyfield Church, Oxfordshire. Resting place of Katherine Gordon, wife of the Yorkist pretender Perkin Warbeck. (Jo Romero)

Reading Abbey Church Ruins. The site of Elizabeth Woodville's introduction as Edward IV's wife in September 1464 during the Wars of the Roses. Elizabeth Clerk, the wife of a local draper, lived nearby. (Jo Romero)

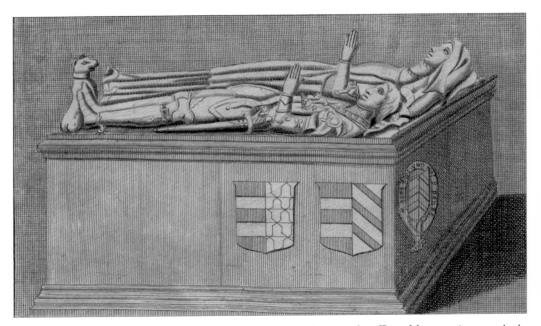

An early nineteenth-century drawing of Margaret Harcourt's effigy. Margaret appealed for compensation after the death of her husband, Robert, in one of the many private feuds that simmered in the unrest of the conflict.
(British Library. Flickr, Online Collection).

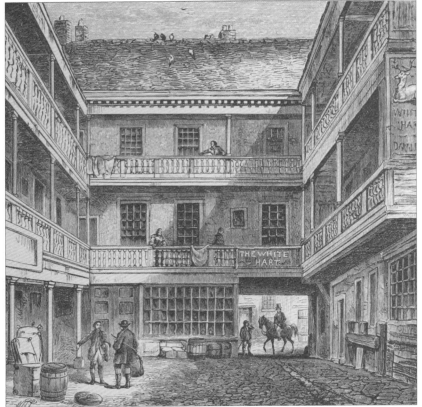

A late nineteenth-century drawing of The White Hart Inn, Southwark, where the wife of the house identified the body of Jack Cade in 1450. (British Library, Flickr. Online Collection)

Above: Monument to Owen Tudor, Hereford Market Place. Near to this spot in 1461 a 'Mad Woman' attended to Tudor's decapitated head. (Jo Romero)

Top right: An eighteenth-century portrayal of Edward IV's mistress, 'Jane' Shore. Her real name was Elizabeth, and she was said to have wielded political and social influence over the king. She was punished and humiliated after his death. (The Met Museum)

A fifteenth-century depiction of the birth of Mary, from the Life of the Virgin. Midwives, nurses, gentlewomen, and servants all played their part in birthing and caring for a new generation of heirs that hoped to secure an end to the wars. (The Met Museum)

A Cook and his Wife by Albrecht Dürer, c. 1496-97. The experiences of women at the lower end of the social scale are not often examined in relation to the Wars of the Roses, however, many were affected by it, some even impacting national events. (The National Gallery of Art, Washington)

breathlessly observed England's beautiful churches and monasteries and the expensive ornaments and relics inside.[337] In 1473 the prioress of Armathwaite Priory in Cumberland complained that her buildings and enclosures had been destroyed by Scottish raids and their relics, jewels and charters stolen or burned.[338] With the heightened unrest, military activity and lawlessness from the wars, nuns often felt just like the anxious monk of Croyland.

Abbeys might have glinted with gold and silver, but they were often in need of money, repairs being a constant demand on finances. Lacock Abbey suffered a lightning storm in 1447 that damaged the bell tower, bell, bakery, brewery and 'two great barns with corn therein'.[339] In 1468 the nuns of St Mary, Winchester, appealed to the king because they were 'so burdened with the repairs of their house and church'.[340] The Patent Rolls of the period show several other establishments struggling to make ends meet, many described as poverty stricken. As well as repairs, legal disputes, administration fees and living costs for the sisters all added to their long list of expenses.

Part of an abbey's income came from gifts left in wills, donated by concerned worshippers to help top up the establishment's purse. Margaret Howard, Duchess of Norfolk, donated twenty-six shillings and eight pence to the nuns of Bruisyard in Suffolk in her will, the equivalent of just under £900 today.[341] The chapel at Warwick received a slightly more political gift in 1480. The will of Lady Elizabeth Latimer bequeathed 'a pair of goodly vestments of white damask, powdered with bears and ragged staves of gold' to be made and delivered to the chapel.[342] Elizabeth was one of the daughters of the 13th Earl of Warwick, Richard Beauchamp, the bear and ragged staff being the Warwick family emblem.

Joan Keteryche 'to fall and perish'

In 1459 Joan Keteryche, the new abbess of Denny Abbey, was putting affairs in order. It was a job that had led to a mental and physical breakdown of the previous abbess, Katherine Sybyle. According to Joan, Katherine was 'so wearied and broken with thought that she is overthrown with daily sickness'. To cope with debts and escalating costs, the nuns had been forced to mortgage their jewels, intended 'to stir us and provoke others to worship God'.[343]

Denny, originally founded as a community of Benedictine monks in 1160, was established as a nunnery in 1339 by Mary de Pol, Countess of Pembroke.[344] An engraving of the building in Cambridgeshire survives from 1730, after the abbey's dissolution, and shows a single-storey stone building with a shallow, pointed roof. There are decorated, arched windows and a boundary wall with a small gateway. Outbuildings can be seen within the fields surrounding the abbey.[345] Joan's leather shoes would have tapped softly on the abbey's tiled floor as she prepared to write to a man she thought might be able to solve their money worries, Norfolk lawyer John Paston.

Paston was dealing with the will of his client, Sir John Falstolf, a wealthy knight who held an impressive portfolio of land and properties which included the coveted Caister Castle. Falstolf's death in 1459 sparked a high-profile battle for these lucrative estates, with dukes and duchesses circling for a share. Abbess Joan Keteryche, picking up her quill, was about to join them.

Joan's letter to Paston survives and was printed in William Keatinge Clay's *History of the Parish of Waterbeach* in 1859. From the beginning, Joan's tone is humble. She refers to herself as 'full simple and young of age' and details the unfortunate luck the nuns have endured, none of it of their doing. She writes of the breakdown of the previous abbess, fees and ongoing money troubles. But she is also strongly persuasive. She asks Paston to 'hear graciously our humble petition' or 'suffer our devout place to fall and perish'. She speaks of the nuns being a 'long time wrongfully oppressed' and that the abbey buildings are 'so far decayed … that we may not well repair them again'. Her tenants, too, have suffered.

She then pulls on Paston's religious conscience. It was while she was at prayer, 'at my complaint making to God' that she was 'put in mind of the goods that be in your hands'. Paston, by the end of the letter, would be under no illusion. Joan's letter was placed directly on Paston's desk, in answer to her prayers. She puts forward a proposition. She asks him to think of them as a 'new foundation' and promises to pray for 'the soul of that worthy knight Sir John Falstolf'.[346]

The job of an abbess to raise funds for the survival and maintenance of her abbey and its community was essential. They could find themselves challenged in legal proceedings which only worsened their financial hardship, as well as generating considerable stress and frustration. But while some, like Denny's previous abbess, crumbled under pressure, others fought back with words that reflected the violence of the age. Isabel de Stanley, a prioress of King's Mead Priory in Derby had been in dispute with the abbot of Burton for twenty-one years. During Henry VII's reign, outraged at the 'churls' that had come to sue her, she declared they should 'be nailed with arrows, for I am a gentlewoman come of the greatest of Lancashire and Cheshire and that they shall know right well'.[347]

Joan seems to have taken a slightly softer approach. Unfortunately, there is no evidence she secured a share of Falstolf's estate. However, she continued as Denny's abbess, her successor Margaret Assheby was elected in 1480.[348]

Abbesses were not always timid, retiring women who quietly accepted their fate. Joan's story is one of those that shows us a different side. She stepped up to take over from the previous abbess, a position she knew to be fraught with anxieties. She wrote to a man she believed could help save Denny's dwindling fortunes, and thus demonstrated leadership and initiative in attempting to secure the funding needed for the running of their house. Squaring up to the likes of Paston and the powerful dukes of Suffolk and Norfolk, Joan shows us that abbesses and prioresses could be confident and persuasive in the fight for their communities.

The Nuns of Sewardsley Priory 'malicious intent'

In early 1470, as Joan Keteryche administered her abbey's finances at Denny, nearly seventy miles away business of a more sensitive and superstitious nature was being heard at Westminster. Jacquetta, Duchess of Bedford, the queen's mother, had been accused of witchcraft.

The allegations were recorded in the Calendar of Patent Rolls. They came from Thomas Wake, who, arriving at Warwick Castle, presented 'an image of lead made like a man of arms of the length of a man's finger broken in the middle and made fast with wire', insisting that it had been made by the duchess. Another man, Northamptonshire parish clerk John Daunger, also claimed Jacquetta had made images representing the king and queen. The implication was that she was, or had once been, engaged in witchcraft. This wire and lead structure, Wake said, had been shown to 'diverse neighbours' in the villages of Shutlanger and Stoke Bruerne. The spooky figure had also been handed round to visitors in the leafy grounds of Sewardsley Priory.[349]

Very little of Sewardsley's medieval building survives today. By the end of the fifteenth century, it had already faced a difficult past, one investigation in 1434 mentions the prioress and nuns 'giving their minds to debauchery, committing in damnable wise, in public … acts of adultery, incest, sacrilege and fornication'.[350] Alice Basynge, the prioress in service at the time, resigned. There were financial troubles, too. In 1459 there was a move to have the priory merged with the more successful Delapré Abbey in Northampton to offset the smaller establishment's poorer financial situation.[351] The last thing that Sewardsley needed then, was to have its reputation muddied even further with links to sorcery and witchcraft.

The nuns at Sewardsley, unwrapping the wire figures and showing them to curious locals, were probably an innocent party, following instructions from a higher authority. But the circumstances surrounding the events here point to something more sinister; a wider, politically driven slander against Jacquetta Woodville.

There are several hints at a conspiracy of some sort. First, the timing is convenient, coinciding with other events that aimed to restore the Lancastrian Henry VI to the throne in 1469–1470. It nestles in the timeline alongside incidents such as the Lincolnshire Rebellion of 1470 and Edward IV's capture by Warwick the previous year. Warwick's dislike of the Woodvilles was well-documented, with Richard and John Woodville executed on his orders in 1469. Could this have been a planned tactic to discredit and remove the Woodville matriarch? The memory of Eleanor Cobham, Duchess of Gloucester, was not far from people's minds. She was accused of employing the services of the 'Witch of Eye' in 1441 and was removed to a nunnery. It was probably hoped that Jacquetta would share the same fate.

The other wire figures mentioned, which the account states were 'one for the king and one for the queen' seemed to have the aim of bringing their union into disrepute. Any link to the royal couple and sorcery would have rattled their image and possibly, depending on the form it took, their legitimacy. That this item had the potential to attack the king himself is probably the reason Daunger, in the end, refused to say anything when pressed further, and 'neither could nor would be entreated' on the subject.[352]

Why the offending item was placed specifically at Sewardsley and the other locations isn't mentioned. However, the three locations are very close to one another, Stoke Bruerne is just a mile from Sewardsley, and Shutlanger is around half a mile from the priory. The records state that a number of people had viewed the object and from these sites, visitors would be well placed to spread the word of Jacquetta's apparent sorcery into the nearby villages and towns. In the end, Jacquetta strongly denied the charges, insisting she had been the subject of 'a slander of witchcraft throughout a great part of the realm'.[353] She was cleared of these allegations in

February 1470, and insisted her innocence be put on record.

The nuns at Sewardsley were a small part of this more than likely political attack on the duchess. But in showing this potentially malicious figure they publicly undermined one of the key women of the Wars of the Roses. At Sewardsley the sisters' involvement in the wars would be subtle. For the nuns at nearby Delapré, it would be far more explosive.

Gonnora Dowtton 'in the meadows beside the nunnery'

Just eight miles to the north of Sewardsley lay the religious settlement at Delapré, near the river Nene. Gonnora Dowtton was a nun at the abbey, elected abbess after the death of Amice Sywel. Gonnora had taken up the post by 23 March 1459, when she is confirmed in the title in the Calendar of Patent Rolls.[354]

Life for Gonnora involved daily prayer, abbey administration, and personal religious contemplation. As abbess, she was involved in any legalities as well as answering to the bishop or other members of local government on abbey business. As a Cluniac she was expected to sleep in the same room as the other nuns and keep an eye on their general conduct.[355] Prayers were said throughout the day, from early in the morning until the evening. After this last scheduled prayer, the nuns would retire to bed.

It may have been during one of these prayers on 10 July 1460 that Gonnora paused as muffled cries filtered through the abbey's stone walls. She would have noticed the pitching of tents and digging of trenches over the last few days. It was here, close to the abbey, that the Lancastrians chose to set their standard for the Battle of Northampton; the author of the *Davies Chronicle* gives Henry's position as 'in the meadows beside the nunnery, armed and arrayed with guns, with the river at his back'.[356] Messengers on horseback rode to and from the Lancastrian and Yorkist camps in a last attempt to make peace, as armies readied themselves on the field.

Negotiations failed and soldiers clashed with arrows, swords and axes. The day would prove disastrous for the Lancastrians. Heavy rain soaked the king's gunpowder so their guns could not be fired.[357] When Henry's men tried to escape the field, many of them waded in panic, and full armour, into the muddy banks of the river Nene and drowned. The trumpets declaring the end of battle, Henry VI was captured by the Earl of Warwick and Edward Earl of March (the future Edward IV).

Although the chronicles do not name Gonnora, the aftermath of the battle would have been a busy time for her. John Leland asserts that some of the dead were buried at the abbey as well as at the nearby St John's Hospital, however no archaeological evidence has so far been able to confirm this.[358] If the burials did occur, Gonnora as abbess would have overseen them and perhaps offered prayers as bodies were tumbled into the earth. The *Davies Chronicle* states that the king and his Yorkist captors stayed at Northampton for three days before travelling to London.[359]

Gonnora held the position of abbess at Delapré for twenty years. She died in 1481, the licence for her replacement appeared in the Patent Rolls on 5 July that year.[360] Gonnora's role, reactions or even her presence at the battle were not recorded by chroniclers but it is unlikely her contribution was entirely passive. Abbesses were used to administering complex estates of abbey lands and tenants. It is difficult to believe that as leader of this community, she would not have offered practical or spiritual assistance to those on her doorstep, alive or dead. Gonnora's close proximity to the fighting also demonstrates just how close the battles of the Wars of the Roses came to those we would probably least expect.

Religious establishments, whether run by nuns or monks, were an important source of spiritual and practical aid during the Wars of the Roses. They offered sanctuary and respite and provided a home for those who continued their lives in religious devotion. They safeguarded heirs, dodged rebellion and fought for the financial future of their communities. They also inadvertently became entangled in slanderous accusations and the discrediting of a senior member of the House of York. The experience of one religious community would involve bloodshed, arrows and the clash of swords. The *Croyland Chronicler* was certainly right. There is real, tangible evidence that what he called 'the unhappy plague of division' rippled from palaces, parliaments and battlefields into the nation's convents, abbeys and priories.

CHAPTER NINE
oVERCOMING ADVERSITY

May 1471. Chertsey, Surrey. Blanche Heriot clings desperately to the cold, metal clapper of the curfew bell at the top of St Peter's church tower. Losing her balance, she is repeatedly thrashed by the force of the bellringer's rope into the bell's curved metal wall. As the movement subsides, she hears distant shouts of celebration. She staggers from the tower, bruised and bloody, having saved the life of her loved one, Neville Audeley.

Neville was a Lancastrian soldier who had recently fought at the Battle of Tewkesbury and was on the run from the newly reinstalled Edward IV. He fled to sanctuary and was held prisoner by Yorkist guards. Negotiating for more time, a royal pardon was sent for, and it was agreed that Audeley would face death if there was no response from the king by the strike of the curfew bell. As the hour grew closer, Blanche ran to the bell tower, clung to the clapper and delayed the ringing of the bell long enough for the messenger to bring Audeley's royal pardon from over the bridge.

An impassioned tale of courage and defiance, Blanche's story is preserved in legend and remembered with a statue that stands today in Chertsey. Her tale embodies strength, quick-thinking and bravery. It is, however, very difficult to know if Blanche, or her heroic actions, ever existed. There is no surviving record of the event before the mid-nineteenth century, when Albert Smith wrote the short story *A Legend of Old Chertsey Church*, published in 1852. It is not known if he created the story himself or, as inferred in the title, penned it from an old tale preserved by word of mouth for generations.

Whether Blanche existed in life, as a legend or somewhere in between, the spirit and resilience she symbolizes does survive in the historical record, through the experiences of many others like her who fought to dispute losses of land, titles, cash or inheritance as a result of the Wars of the Roses. But they had another fight on their hands too, the medieval attitude toward women.

In an imagined address to Jasper Tudor, Bernard André has Margaret Beaufort tell her brother-in-law that 'everyone knows quite well that women are weak, imprudent and unstable'.[361] Vergil's Richard, Duke of Gloucester, passes off Elizabeth Woodville's fear for her sons in sanctuary as a 'womanish disease'.[362] Not much had changed by the seventeenth century, when the clearly Tudor-influenced Richard Baker justified Anne Neville's marriage to Richard, Duke of Gloucester, by explaining that 'women's affections are eccentric to common apprehensions whereof the two poles are passion and inconstancy'.[363]

One fifteenth-century text, *How the Wise Man Taught His Son*, did champion a woman's capabilities, advising that a man should choose a prudent wife. A wife with qualities such as wisdom and judgement, it stated, 'will do you more good service in time of need'.[364]

It was in time of need that women petitioned, alongside and often on behalf of their men, to try and grasp back attainted property and titles during the wars, with varying success. Some women found themselves accused of treason and faced political backlash from the enemies of their husbands. Others navigated relationships torn apart by opposing loyalties. Perhaps a line in the medieval ballad *The Nut Brown Maid* sums it up best, the maid promising that although she has been part of the couple's 'joy and bliss … I must also part of your woe, endure as reason is'.[365]

Anne Beauchamp, Countess of Warwick 'dreading only trouble'

In the spring of 1471 at Beaulieu Abbey, Anne, Countess of Warwick, scratched her inked quill into parchment and addressed a letter to King Edward IV.

The countess had been at the centre of politics from the beginning of the Wars of the Roses. Her husband, Richard Neville, Earl of Warwick, held his prestigious title in her right, and played a central part in the conflict supporting at first York and then Lancaster. His final act was an attempt to restore Henry VI to the throne, fighting at the Battle of Barnet against Edward's forces on 14 April 1471, where he was killed. As his body was carted to London for public display, Anne, fearful of reprisals from an enraged king, bolted into the safety of sanctuary at Beaulieu Abbey and began her own battle for her future.

She writes assertively, calling herself, perhaps somewhat hopefully considering the recent actions of the earl, 'the king's true liege woman'. Lodging at Beaulieu and 'dreading only trouble' after her husband's death, she wrote within five days of arriving to negotiate for her safety with the king. She sent appeals to Elizabeth Woodville, Cecily Neville, Elizabeth of York, Jacquetta Duchess of Bedford, and 'to my lords the king's brethren, to my ladies and the king's sisters ... and to other ladies noble of this realm'. Defiant, Anne promises the king that despite not receiving any replies she 'will continue, as she owes to do' to fight for her 'livelihood and rightful inheritance'.[366]

Anne's words were gently challenging and politely firm. Warwick's lands had been forfeited, but Anne is clear that she is fighting for her own portion, the lands she had inherited at birth and those to which she was 'rightfully born by lineal succession'. Asking Edward to 'ponder and weigh in your consciences' she signed off the letter, folded it and passed it to a waiting messenger.[367] Her admission that she had addressed previous letters not only to the king but many other people of influence at court only demonstrates her anxiety, spending tense days at Beaulieu waiting for a reply.

Edward did ponder Anne's situation, but he was in no hurry to act. Eventually, in 1473, Anne was allowed to leave Beaulieu accompanied by Sir James Tyrrell, but a letter from Sir John Paston in June of that year revealed darkly that 'some men say that the Duke of Clarence is not agreed'.[368]

Anne would have learned that she was at the centre of a squabble between her son-in-law George, Duke of Clarence, who had married her daughter Isabel, and Richard, Duke of Gloucester, who was intending to marry her other daughter Anne. Both men, brothers of the king, had their eye on Anne's wealth. In the summer of 1474 Edward passed an act giving both George and Richard, 'all possessions belonging to the said Countess as if she were naturally dead'.[369]

However, Anne was very much still alive. She outlived both her daughters, Isabel died in 1476 and Anne in early 1485. After the accession of Henry VII, she was restored on paper to all her possessions but transferred them almost immediately back to the crown. Wood points out that Henry then acquired 118 manors from the countess, allowing her the revenues of just one, Sutton in Warwickshire, for her livelihood. She died in 1493.[370]

Anne is portrayed on the Rous Roll gesturing to her husband who stands beside her. He wears armour, complete with a helmet and holds a sword and shield. She wears a veiled butterfly headdress and close-fitting gown, a jewelled collar around her neck. Rous states she was 'by true inheritance Countess of Warwick, which good lady had in her days great tribulation for her lord's sake'.[371] Created during Anne's lifetime, the author of the roll John Rous, who lived in Warwick, may have known the family.[372] Describing her character as patient, devout and ready to help where she could, he gives us a more intimate glance at what may have been Anne's personality beneath the outward challenges of the wars. He also praises her as being an example to 'all others that were vexed with any adversity'.[373]

Anne lived at the centre of the conflict and must, at times, have had anxieties over her husband and two daughters. Edward's calculated and dismissive treatment of her estates in 1473 may have even come from vengefulness that he could no longer take out on Warwick himself. Anne lost lands and estates that were hers by birth. The *Croyland Chronicler* was at least sympathetic to her. 'Little or nothing was left at the disposal of the real lady and heiress, the Countess of Warwick,' he wrote, 'to whom for the whole of her life the most noble inheritance of the Warwicks and the Despencers properly belonged'.[374]

Lady Margaret Hungerford and Botreaux 'seasons of trouble'

Regaining forfeited estates from the crown required determination, persuasion and confidence. But it could also end up costing large amounts of money. In the contemporary ballad *A Lyteel Geste of Robyn Hode*, a parent considers the financial hardship that resulted in families' survival during the wars. He tells of his son 'that should have been my heir' but after killing a knight the father had to 'save him in his right, my goods be set and sold'.[375]

Legal action, travel, lodgings, and fines all took up vital cash reserves in regaining confiscated lands or titles taken by vengeful kings as punishment for backing the wrong side during the wars. The sources show that it was women, as well as men, that bore this burden, the results of which could be very severe.

Robert Lord Hungerford died in May 1459. He was a loyal Lancastrian and soldier and was buried in a tomb in the Lady Chapel of Salisbury Cathedral. John Leland visited in the sixteenth century, noting that Robert lay with his wife, her monument 'in the middle of the same chapel in a high tomb'.[376] The peaceful poise of the two stone effigies in front of Leland that day offered no hint of the suffering they had experienced in their lifetimes.

Margaret Hungerford, Robert's wife, was daughter to William Lord Botreaux and his wife Elizabeth. The early-nineteenth century historian Richard Hoare carried out a great deal of research on Margaret while looking into the history of Heytesbury in Wiltshire, where she lived. She married Robert in around 1420 and brought lucrative estates to the marriage including those in Wiltshire, Hampshire, Cornwall, and Somerset.[377] On the death of her father in 1462 she inherited the title of Baroness Botreaux and spent her days at her family home in Heytesbury with its moat, orchards, and woodlands.[378]

At England's fracture into civil war, Robert remained loyal to the Lancastrian cause, as did his son, also named Robert. Both served in Henry VI's French wars, the younger Robert captured and imprisoned in July 1453 in Chatillon. On his return to England, he caught the attention of the suspicious Edward IV, fought in the Lancastrian army at Towton in 1461, and was attainted. He fought again at the Battle of Hexham in Northumberland in May 1464, where he was captured and executed. His son Thomas was beheaded as a traitor in 1469.[379]

One of the families that suffered greatly from the political bloodshed of the Wars of the Roses, the Hungerfords would face a considerable financial loss too. During his active fighting for Lancaster, Robert had continually looked to his wealthy mother Margaret for financial support. Almost a decade after his death, Margaret drafted her will, noticing the diminished size of her estate which had been dipped into to pay fines, expenses and other costs. Blaming the 'necessity of fortune and misadventure that hath happened in these seasons of trouble time late passed', she felt it necessary to attach a receipt of her expenses to the will, hoping her heirs will see she 'governed me always honestly' and won't have 'occasion to grudge'.[380]

That Margaret was so adamant her heirs understand she had not frittered away vast sums of money in extravagant living reveals that a measured and methodical approach to finances was important to her. There is a hint of her shock when in 1476 she added up the huge amount of money she had spent, noting purchases of lodgings, clothing and 'ambling horses to please his friends with' as well as Robert's travel costs and a large ransom on leaving prison in France. Margaret laid out the costs too, for her grandson Thomas to be 'arrayed and accompanied for the war' and paid her son's creditors. She also mentions a loan she had taken out from several merchants, one of them Anne Hoo's husband, Geoffrey Boleyn.[381]

Margaret also details the 'great suits' she put before the king and her arrest on Edward's orders, when she was forcibly lodged at

Amesbury Abbey. This was badly timed as her stay at Amesbury coincided with a fire that destroyed her bed, hangings, plate, money and other possessions. Her purse was again duly opened to pay to have these living quarters rebuilt.[382] In all, the historian Hoare calculated, Margaret spent the massive sum of over 26,000 marks.[383]

Margaret's readiness to part with cash for her son's cause might suggest that she was supportive of his actions and hoped for a Lancastrian restoration. Her husband had, after all, fought for the same cause. But she left a wary message for Robert's son and heir Walter in her will. If he stayed 'faithful and true to our Sovereign Lord King Edward and his heirs' he would receive a long list of manors. If not, he would receive none.[384] After witnessing the effects of fighting, ransoming and punishments unleashed on her family during the wars, Margaret clearly did not want history to repeat itself and take whatever was left.

Margaret died in around 1477 and was solemnly buried with her husband in Salisbury Cathedral. Her husband's effigy survives today, wearing armour and a collar bearing the Lancastrian 'SS' symbol. However, there is no longer any trace of Margaret's monument that Leland had observed in the sixteenth century.

An exhausting account of preservation on behalf of her family, Margaret's efforts were necessary after the financial and social punishments imposed on her family for their part in the wars. She suffered grief, losing loved ones from three generations, outliving her husband, son and grandson. Margaret paid expenses, ransoms and was herself imprisoned. Reading her will, there is a definite sense of disbelief, as well as some shame and a regret, that she had not left enough for her younger heirs. Her estate on her death might not have been its original size but she still left a sizeable income and took full accountability for her expenditure in support of the wars. Perhaps what endures most about Margaret's story is the concern she had for her family, working relentlessly to ensure future heirs could inherit a livelihood, and trying cautiously to manage their political safety from beyond the grave. For Margaret, the future generation was at the forefront of her thoughts, and she demonstrated a relentless passion for its security.

Alice Chaucer, Duchess of Suffolk 'subtle counsel'

In the Oxfordshire countryside, the village of Ewelme nestles at the base of a valley, a patchwork of tiled roofs, cottages and tall brick chimneys, the grey, crenelated tower of the church of St Mary rises up into the sky. In the mid-fifteenth century, this sleepy village was the home of Alice Chaucer.

Alice was born in around 1404, the daughter of Thomas Chaucer and his wife Matilda, her grandfather was the celebrated poet Geoffrey, author of *The Canterbury Tales*. Her father seems to have been in favour at the courts of Richard II, Henry IV and Henry V, receiving a grant in 1399 of £10 for 'good and agreeable service'. He is also recorded at Agincourt with 'twelve men at arms and thirty-seven archers'.[385] Alice would have been around ten years old when she waved goodbye to her father as he left for France.

She would marry three times. The first was an arrangement during Alice's childhood to Sir John Phelip. Phelip's death in 1415 widowed Alice at the age of eleven.[386] She then married Thomas Montacute, Earl of Salisbury. One of the leading statesmen of the realm, he served in France early in the reign of Henry VI, dying at the Siege of Orléans when a nearby window was shattered during battle, ripping off his jaw, in 1428.

Her final marriage, taking place in her late twenties, was to William de la Pole, then the Earl of Suffolk and close advisor of Henry VI. It was around this time that Alice was granted the prestigious Order of the Garter. Her Garter ribbon was carved, likely at her request, onto the wrist of the effigy that would later adorn her tomb, demonstrating her life-long pride in having been granted this honour. Although de la Pole was a close advisor to the king, like Margaret Harcourt, Alice would have earned this acknowledgement through her own actions. It was relatively rare for women to be granted this honour, especially non-royals.

The Suffolks set to work founding an almshouse next to the church at Ewelme, the red-bricked building is still in use today. With her husband in a prominent role at court, Alice settled into a position as gentlewoman to Margaret of Anjou, and with her husband, was one of those who escorted the future queen to England. She would have been one of the queen's entourage described by Bale in 'most joyful and costly devise that ever was seen' in 1445.[387] William's elevation to duke would have been celebrated by the couple in 1448, as they rose in royal favour.[388] Alice's relationship with Margaret of Anjou seems to have been a good one and Strickland saw her as the driving force between the queen's relationships with the Suffolks and with the Beauforts.[389] By the late 1440s Alice had an adoring husband, her own wealth, and a front seat at the glamorous Lancastrian royal court.

Things started to fall apart for the Suffolks by the end of 1449. Discontent had spread among the commons and within parliament, raising doubts about Suffolk's suitability as one of Henry's key advisors. He was accused, at parliament in November of that year, of double dealing with the French, revealing English secrets and provoking war. He was also blamed for the loss of Anjou along with 'various serious offences, misprisions, faithless acts and false deceits'.[390] Hall relates that Suffolk 'was called in every man's mouth a traitor, a murderer, a robber of the king's treasure and worthy to be put to most cruel punishment'.[391]

Suffolk's cruel punishment was in fact waiting, bobbing gently off the Dover coast in a vessel named *Nicholas of the Tower*. Having been ordered by Henry into exile in 1450, Suffolk boarded a boat and headed to sea. He hadn't got far before he was intercepted and captured by the crew of *The Nicholas*, given a mock trial and executed with a rusty sword. His lifeless body was found on the sands of Dover.

Before leaving, Suffolk had written a letter to his son. He asks that he 'be bounden by the commandment of God, to do, to love, to worship your lady and mother; and also that you obey always her commandments, and to believe her counsels and advices in all your works, the [sic] which dread not but shall be best and truest to you. And if any other body would steer you to the contrary, to flee the counsel in any wise, for you shall find it naught and evil'.[392] Suffolk clearly trusted his wife, and their relationship, as far as we can tell, was a good one. Leland visited Ewelme around sixty years after Alice's death and tended to speak to locals when forming his assessments of people and places. He said that it was 'for love of her and the commodity of her lands' that was the reason the couple settled in Oxfordshire and Berkshire, 'where his wife's lands lay'.[393]

It didn't take long for the murdered duke's enemies to circle Alice. Her behaviour was declared 'improper' in parliament, and they insisted she be removed from the king's presence on pain of losing her lands. In answering, the king pointed out that he chose to have morally upstanding people in his presence and saw no reason for her, or the others that were accused, to be removed.[394] That her influence with the king was discussed in parliament only underlines the powerful character Alice must have had.

What happened next demonstrates Alice's skill for political versatility. Despite serving in the Lancastrian household and lending 3,500 marks to Henry VI for his wars in France, Alice deftly switched to the Yorkist cause, arranging a marriage between her son John and Elizabeth, daughter of the Duke of York.[395] The couple later appear in many letters of the Paston correspondence over legal rights to lands. In 1472 Alice and her royal mistress Margaret would find their roles reversed, as the Lancastrian queen was held at Wallingford Castle before her return to France, overseen by Alice. Wallingford too, was close, just under four miles from Alice's home at Ewelme.

Alice has been criticized for switching her allegiance, perhaps most scathingly by nineteenth-century historian Henry Alfred

Napier. Napier saw Alice as ambitious, immoral and 'undeserving ... of her late husband's love ... for she acted directly contrary to the excellent advice he had given their son, ever to continue faithful to King Henry'. He adds that 'the murderers of his father were now his mother's firm friends and allies' and sums Alice up by saying that of her 'own individual merits and character, there is little to excite admiration'.[396]

This is a harsh, unfair judgement of Alice. It is easy to see why she would defect to the Yorkists after the hapless administration of Henry VI's rule and their mishandling of not only the events leading to Suffolk's murder, but the growing unrest and uncertainty in the realm. While grieving and uncertain of her own safety, she must have felt frustration with Henry's government and hoped for change.

As for Napier's claim that 'there is little to excite admiration', this is also grossly unjustified. As well as an astute politician, mother and duchess, Alice and her husband heavily rebuilt the church of St Mary at Ewelme, and their adjoining almshouses are still lived in by residents of the village today. She took an active part in the property disputes of her son, most notably with the Pastons in Norfolk, who often remark on her business in their correspondence. Margaret Paston gave a clear indication of the power of Alice's negotiation skills when she warned her son, 'if you should be at my Lady of Suffolk, it were necessary to have Playter there with you ... for she is subtle and hath subtle counsel with her'.[397]

Towards the end of her life, Alice retreated to her manor at Ewelme, where she had once lived with William de la Pole. Her son John had inherited the title of Duke of Suffolk from his father, and he was now brother-in-law to the king. A deed surviving from 1470–1471 shows that she made a gift to her son and his wife Elizabeth of all her gold and silver plate, beds of cloth of gold, silk, arras and tapestry work except the older ones that 'daily serve me'.[398] Not only does this give us a clue into her luxurious surroundings but also suggests that in later life she felt these outward shows of wealth less necessary. This is also borne out by her choice to include a cadaver monument in her tomb at Ewelme. Entombed, Alice is portrayed twice, above she lies fully dressed in her gown with Garter ribbon, a coronet on her head. Beneath, she is portrayed in death, covered loosely with a shroud. It's possible that in the years before she died, she was beginning to reject the trappings of wealth and luxury preferring to follow a more devout, simple life.

However she felt at the end, Alice's life was certainly full and eventful. By the time she was in her late forties she had been widowed three times, all husbands suffering sudden or violent deaths. Facing the possibility of royal banishment, she resolved to work towards the future of her son. There are traces of her strong personality in the sources, as well as her capacity for shrewd, quick-thinking. Alice died in 1475 at her home at Ewelme at around the age of seventy-one. William de la Pole is a central figure of the early Wars of the Roses; however his wife is rarely mentioned. We should remember the adversities that Alice overcame, her influence with powerful figures such as Henry VI, Margaret of Anjou and the Duke of York, along with the valuable legacies she left behind at Ewelme.

Ladies of the Garter during the Wars

Alice Chaucer wasn't the only woman during the wars to have been awarded the ancient Order of the Garter. The Order, established by Edward III in the fourteenth century, aimed to recreate the idea of the legendary Knights of the Round Table, rewarding those who had demonstrated exceptional loyalty or service to the crown.

It was relatively rare for a knight to be awarded the Garter, and even rarer for a woman to receive it. Elias Ashmole, who wrote *A History of the Most Noble Order of the Garter* in the seventeenth century stated that it was bestowed for 'the performance of some virtuous or heroic action, directed for the public good', although he later discusses its statutes promoting friendship, peace, loyalty and constancy.[399] All these qualities could well be demonstrated by a fifteenth-century woman, but traits such as virtue, constancy and loyalty may have been especially rewarded in the context of wives' support for their husbands despite the adversity they faced.

It was traditional to receive a Garter on the Feast of St George at Windsor Castle. Women such as Alice Chaucer, Elizabeth Woodville, Margaret Harcourt and Margaret Beaufort would have bowed low and reverently to the king, watched by nobles, ambassadors and other courtiers. For men, the garter was buckled around their lower leg, but women received it fastened around their arm, for convenience and ease of display.[400] In her effigy Alice Chaucer wears hers on her lower forearm, Margaret Harcourt wears hers nearer her elbow. It was a rare honour, and these women may have worn the Garter when attending important or state occasions.

Due to the attitude toward women in medieval times one assumes that women who received the Order of the Garter did so purely out of royal respect or recognition for the bravery of their influential husbands. However not all wives of husbands who received the Garter were invested themselves. It thus seems more likely that they attracted the recognition of the crown in some way as reward for their own actions. Specific reasons for investitures are often not found, and it would be unwise for us, 600 years later, to speculate on these. However, there is an implication, because of its rarity, that these women fulfilled some remarkable and exceptional service to the king, and their country, during one of its most turbulent periods in history.

Katherine Gordon 'unknown, destitute and helpless'

Off the coast of Ayr in Scotland in the summer of 1497, the pretender Perkin Warbeck boarded a ship to assert his claimed Yorkist birthright to the English throne. A fair-haired woman sat beside him as the cool waves broke gently against the bow of the ship. As the sails billowed above and the ship lurched with a creak into the Scottish sea, Katherine Gordon, Perkin's new bride, cast a glance back at her homeland.

Katherine was the daughter of George Gordon, Earl of Huntly. She is often described as a cousin of the Scottish king, James IV, but Nathen Amin in *Henry VII and the Tudor Pretenders* has pointed out that they were related by marriage rather than blood.[401] Katherine and Warbeck married in 1496, on the orders of James IV.

A love letter from Warbeck to Katherine survives, written shortly before their wedding. In it, he praises Katherine's sparkling eyes, fair hair and her 'fine forehead'. He may have been in love with her, but there's no escaping that the match was primarily of political benefit to Warbeck. He can't resist praising the 'nobility of your lineage and the loftiness of your rank' in what was supposedly a pre-wedding declaration of true love.[402] Bernard André also states that the marriage was arranged to establish an alliance between Warbeck and the Scottish.[403]

Warbeck claimed that he was the lost Richard, Duke of York, son of Edward IV and Elizabeth Woodville. But did Katherine believe him? There was no reason she wouldn't. Warbeck had won the backing of the Scottish king, along with that of Richard's aunt, Margaret of Burgundy. She had probably never seen the real Richard, and Warbeck's claims, substantiated with powerful support, must have seemed compelling. As she boarded the ship and watched the Scottish coast fade into the distance, she probably imagined her own coronation at her husband's side in just a few weeks.

Warbeck's plan failed dramatically. He lacked wider support in England and James withdrew his backing, telling him, according to Hall, 'to depart out of the realm'.[404] Katherine was taken to St Michael's Mount in Cornwall while Warbeck made for the sanctuary of Beaulieu Abbey in the New Forest. He was eventually arrested and brought to Henry VII. Katherine too, was found and brought 'straight like a bond woman and captive to the king'.[405]

Historians have acknowledged Katherine's natural beauty and noble birth as reasons for Henry's gentle treatment of her after her capture. Holinshed says it was her 'beauty and amiable countenance' that impressed him, while Grafton states she was 'so goodly a young woman'.[406] But surely Katherine deserves more credit than this. Bernard André, who was in a position to have known Katherine at court, described her appearing humble and afraid at her meeting with the king.[407] Conducting herself with remorse and humility rather than arrogance or defiance helped secure Henry's trust and underlined her role as innocent in Warbeck's campaign. Moved by her plea, Henry had Katherine taken to serve in the queen's household.

Despite Henry's reassuring words Katherine must have spent the long ride to Winchester in a state of unease. She was potentially an accessory to an attempted invasion, having accompanied her husband on his journey from Scotland. She was away from family and friends who could vouch for her and must have felt very alone in those first few hours or days. If she did feel anxiety, she needn't have worried. Katherine was welcomed by Elizabeth of York and served her until the queen's death in 1503.

Katherine did have the opportunity to meet with her husband at least one more time. André wrote an account of the meeting, although it's unlikely he was there to see it. It's possible that he heard the account from others at court. Perkin was said to have apologized to his wife before a tearful Katherine lashed out at him. 'Are these the royal sceptres you promised us?' she cried, calling herself 'unknown, destitute and helpless'.[408] Katherine's shock at her husband's confession does suggest that Perkin had never revealed his true identity to her in private.

From now on, Katherine used her unmarried surnames of either Gordon or Huntly at court, which would have helped create more distance between her and the royal imposter. She married three times after Warbeck's death, first to James Strangeways from Fyfield, and then, after his death, to the Welsh knight Sir Matthew Cradock of

Cardiff. Cradock paid for an elaborate double tomb effigy for him and Katherine at St Mary's Church, Swansea and the couple may have lived at Place House where Cradock's arms were carved into the gateway. The house was in ruins by 1840.[409]

Katherine's effigy was badly damaged in an air-raid attack on Swansea during the Second World War. Luckily, a Victorian visitor made a sketch of the tomb showing Sir Matthew in armour beside Katherine, who wears a long gown and a hood with long sides. A collar links around her neck and a tusked boar lies at her feet. John Montgomery Traherne, writing in 1840, noted that the tomb appeared to have once been painted in bright colours but didn't record the specific colours that he saw.[410] In his will, Sir Matthew bequeathed Katherine lands and money and the jewels 'she had of her own the day she and I were married'. These included a gold chain, a cross of gold studded with diamonds and pearls, and a large gold pomander, which would have been filled with herbs or dried petals and lifted to the nose for fragrance. It would also have left a sweet scent as she walked, her long gown swishing with each step. Other jewels are mentioned that sparkled with garnet, ruby and sapphire. Similar to Elizabeth Fitzherbert, she also owned a piece of jewellery that contained the likeness of the Virgin Mary, a brooch.[411]

After Sir Matthew's death in 1531 Katherine was married, for the last time, to Christopher Ashton. It seems that Christopher had helped her manage a long illness as she describes herself as 'sick in body and of perfect and whole mind' in her will, where she acknowledges her husband's 'gentle sufferance'. She bequeathed clothing to her 'diligent servant Phillipa Hulls' who also witnessed her will, and requested her burial take place in Fyfield's parish church, in Oxfordshire. As executrix to her second and third husbands' wills, she urges Christopher to continue to honour their wishes after her death. Katherine died just a month after making her will, in November 1537, and so may have known at the time of writing that death was near.[412]

It could have all gone so wrong for Katherine, captured by the king's men as the wife of a royal imposter. There is evidence of some wives being complicit in their husband's protests and rebellions during the Wars of the Roses, but there is no trace of Katherine's involvement in Warbeck's campaign, other than as a spectator and political trophy. As far as we know, Henry VII never suspected her of any involvement, although he did keep a watchful eye over her at court. His kindness to her following her capture has been explained away by her beauty, but Katherine deserves credit for choosing to act with humility and remorse. After Warbeck's death in 1499 she put the episode behind her, disassociating herself with the pretender up until her own death. Katherine risked disgrace and charges of treason but reversed her fortune with cleverness, tact, loyalty and quiet resilience.

'All stain of attaint' Women Petitioners

There are other examples in the records of women fighting for livelihoods and pardons despite adversities experienced because of the wars.

Elizabeth Lutterell, the widow of Sir James Lutterell, complained that although her husband had been attainted and his lands forfeited, 'certain officers of the king do not permit her to enjoy her jointure, although she is a loyal subject'.[413] A similar case occurred in May 1476, when Elizabeth Baynton of Faulston in Wiltshire acknowledged that her husband Robert had been attainted of high treason for having 'levied war against the king' but argued for her inheritance after his death.[414] Robert Whittingham was one of the Lancastrians attainted in Edward IV's first parliament in 1461. In 1472 Margaret Versey, his daughter and heir, successfully won back some of her inheritance along with written confirmation of her freedom 'from all stain of attaint'.[415]

It was one thing to point out the law. It was another thing to try and obtain a pardon for injustices committed. Alice Berworth of Kent, however, successfully managed to persuade Henry VI to grant her husband John a pardon for 'all treasons, felonies, robberies, appeals, trespasses' in 1455, while Yorkshire woman Elizabeth Sotehill argued for the reversal of the attainder against her brother and her cousin, Anthony and Walter Nuttyl, who had fought on the side of Lancaster before Edward IV's accession and had both been attainted.[416]

PART THREE:
A Call to Arms

CHAPTER TEN
THE ORGANIZER: MARGARET PASTON

So far we have seen the many ways in which the Wars of the Roses affected the men and women who lived through it. Some found themselves inadvertently in the thick of battle while others switched sides and secured advantageous marriages for their children. Many women ran the household in the absence of their husbands, paying bills, organizing servants and overseeing building work.

These organizational skills could easily be transferred to support the war effort more directly. From co-ordinating the procurement of weapons and resources, communicating news and overseeing building reinforcements, women turned their comfortable country homes into military fortifications. In some cases, we see clear evidence of women preparing for rebellion or war. In others, there are only hints. For example, Margaret Gaynesford, gentlewoman to Elizabeth Woodville, absented herself from court at the same time as her husband Nicholas, who was implicated in the Buckingham Rebellion of 1483. Is Margaret's absence significant, mirroring that of her husband's? While it does seem to suggest a political cohesion between the couple, without more evidence on their individual movements we can't be sure.

The willingness of women to support local and national resistance might be explained by the medieval attitude towards marriage. In the fifteenth-century etiquette manual *The Book of the Knight of the Tower*, it was stated that 'every good woman do the commandment of her husband, be it evil or well, for if he bid her thing that she ought not to do, it is his shame'.[417] Later it states that a wife 'oweth to support him over all and to save and keep him ... since God hath knit them together by bond of marriage'.[418]

Women still risked punishment though serious penalties were rarely handed out to them. Some, who were deeply involved in major conspiracies, were treated surprisingly leniently. Stow explained that despite suspecting Margaret Beaufort of supporting her son Henry Tudor's campaign overseas, Richard III considered 'the enterprise of a woman ... reputed of no regard'.[419] Katherine Gordon, wife of pretender Perkin Warbeck, was welcomed into the royal household.

Whether out of duty or passion, many women were essential to their husbands' efforts in the wider campaigns of the war. They crucially kept lines of communication open, shared news and sent valued supplies. They negotiated with household staff, collected debts and sent money, horses and weapons for their political cause. Some found themselves imprisoned, while others scribbled hasty letters of warning based on new intelligence they had received.

Some of their letters have survived, but it is certain that many more have been lost over time. Chroniclers are largely silent on women's active involvement in rebellion and warfare due to the secret nature of these communications and plans. Much of this business too, would have been carried out verbally, or letters destroyed on receipt to avoid suspicion or incrimination.

Margaret Paston, the 'woman of letters' whose correspondence reveals so much about fifteenth-century life, leads this chapter. We'll see how she co-ordinated her family, stocked up for a siege and still had time to make a shopping list. And there are others we will discover, playing their own distinct roles underneath the national and visible narrative of the wars.

Margaret Paston 'your enemies begin to wax right bold'

In Norwich, 9 July 1468, Margaret Paston picked up a quill. Dipping it in the glossy ink, she writes to her son Sir John, with the latest news, family business, and a gentle reminder that he hasn't let her know how he is. When the ink is dry, she folds it and hands it to a messenger.

The Paston Letters, a collection of letters and notes written between and concerning members of the Paston family in Norfolk, reveal so much about fifteenth-century society and politics. Margaret, the wife of Norfolk lawyer John Paston, emerges as one of the key figures in the letters sharing news, advice and often the odd telling off to her children for not writing to her more regularly.

In 1448, the Pastons were plunged into a dispute with Lord Moleyns over their manor, Gresham Castle. With the Moleyns' servants occupying the house by force, Margaret wrote to her husband with recommendations for defence. Asking him to send crossbows and windlasses, she told him 'Your houses here be so low that there may be none man shoot out with no long bow, though we had never so much need'. Before signing off, she reminds him to buy sugar, almonds, and some material to make their children's gowns. There is even a tip on where he can get a good price: 'ye shall have best cheap and best choice of Hay's wife as it is told me'.[420]

Later, Margaret faced more attacks on her home at Hellesdon and the Paston manor of Drayton. Their claim to the properties was contested by the Duke of Suffolk, John de la Pole, with the support of his mother, Alice Chaucer, and his wife, Elizabeth. Margaret wrote to her husband in October 1465 to tell him how the house had been left damaged and the local church raided by Suffolk's servants. Margaret told John how she kept more than thirty people with them 'for salvation of us and the place' and was convinced it was this that had stopped the duke attacking them further.[421]

More trouble for the Pastons came over the contested Caister Castle, claimed by the Duke of Norfolk, John Mowbray, and seized in 1469. It was defended by John, the younger of the brothers, with some local supporters and servants. Sir John, the older brother, was in London trying to gain support from the king but had no luck. Margaret, now widowed, wrote to him that his brother and his men 'stand in great jeopardy at Caister, and lack victuals'. Men had been killed or wounded and the place was 'sore broken with guns'. She sent an impassioned plea for help, sending him 'the greatest rebuke' that he had not achieved a resolution or come to help his brother.[422]

While acting as a central hub of communication for the family, Margaret also demonstrates her sensitivity to the suspicious and often paranoid times. In one letter, which Fenn places in around 1460–1461, she keeps specific details and names vague, finishing the letter with a series of lines across the seal, to show the recipient whether the letter had been intercepted and opened.[423] If Fenn's dating is accurate, the letter was written around the time of a spate of battles including Mortimer's Cross, the Second Battle of St Albans and Towton. Edward IV was proclaimed king in March 1461 and Henry VI, Queen Margaret and Prince Edward were on the run. Margaret's evident caution in handling her correspondence during this period reflects the visible uncertainty of the times.

She also wrote with sound advice for her family in these worrying times. In July 1468 she wrote to Sir John, telling him 'your enemies begin to wax right bold, and they putteth your friends both in great fear and doubt, therefore purvey that they may have some comfort', adding ominously, 'for if we lose our friends it shall be hard in this troublesome world to get them again'.[424]

Letters from and concerning other members of the Paston family are vitally important to historians in understanding how the Wars of the Roses affected the lives of those living through it. But Margaret's presence is clear throughout, not only as a business assistant and household controller, but as a woman who rallied her family around her to physically defend a siege and other attacks on their property. Her letters also show she was sensitive to the difficult and uncertain times in which she lived.

Margaret de Vere, Countess of Oxford 'send me in all haste'

Margaret Neville, whether she chose it or not, was embroiled in the Wars of the Roses from a young age. Her father, the Earl of Salisbury, was one of those attainted in the 'Devil's Parliament' at Coventry in 1459, along with her mother Alice Montacute, Countess of Salisbury. Her brother was the Earl of Warwick, a figure whose story is interwoven with so many of the husbands and wives we have already discussed. No doubt Margaret would have overheard hushed conversations and the unravelling of battle plans at the family home.

Margaret married John de Vere, Earl of Oxford, the son of Elizabeth de Vere we have seen signing over her estates to Richard, Duke of Gloucester. John's father and brother had been loyal to the House of Lancaster and John would become known as a faithful supporter of Margaret of Anjou and Henry VI, and later of Henry Tudor's claim to the throne. He was present at Henry VI's reclamation of power in 1470 and held the sword for the king's procession. Eventually he was rounded up by an exasperated Edward and imprisoned at Hammes Castle in Calais, from where he would later escape. John was attainted in 1474.[425]

But while John de Vere was escaping from castles and gallantly fighting for Henry VI, where was his wife? She wasn't sitting idly at home; she was playing a major role supporting her husband's adventures.

In a letter to Sir John Paston on 18 July 1469–1470 de Vere asks him to buy some horse's harness and secretly 'devise as it were for yourself', assuring him that 'my wife will deliver you silver, and yet she must borrow it'.[426] Margaret was by now, if not earlier, John's eyes, ears, and hands at home. It suggests too that Margaret was in on the Lancastrian plans. Wives do not hand over silver, especially borrowed silver, to anyone that knocks asking for it. John's faith in Margaret's abilities is clear. At the time of his writing, he knew Margaret did not have the silver in her possession, but he went ahead with the plans in no doubt that she would obtain it.

In April 1471 John wrote to Margaret. He writes that he is 'in great heaviness' but is safe, having found himself 'suddenly departed from my men'. He asks her to send him, 'in all haste all the ready money that ye can make; and as many of my men as can come well horsed, and that they come in divers parcels'. He asks her to send the horses with steel saddles and have them covered in leather. 'Also ye shall send to my mother and let her [know] of this letter and pray her of her blessing, and bid her send me my casket by this token; that she hath the key thereof, but it is broken. Also ye shall send to the Prior of Thetford, and bid him send me the sum of gold that he said that I should have'.[427]

Margaret would have spurred immediately into action, rounding up cash and calling in the gold promised to John by the prior. She is to gather men and horses and must take care to send them in small groups. John clearly didn't want to raise suspicion by having a large group of men in Oxford livery riding through the countryside towards their lord, who was in hiding. Finally, she is to let her mother-in-law, Elizabeth, know that John is safe and ask her to send him his casket. She was to do all this without raising suspicion. John's last sentence in the letter reveals that Margaret knew of her husband's plans and had been in on the conspiracy. He reassures her to 'be of good cheer ... for I shall bring my purpose about'.[428] Margaret must have known of her husband's purpose. The following month the Lancastrian army would fight the Yorkist forces at Tewksbury.

As Oxford's wife, Margaret had full knowledge of their household, servants and which of their friends could be trusted. She would immediately have known the people that could help and where they could be found. Oxford himself could not send for troops. The letter physically hints at the danger of its contents, signed with an intentionally illegible signature and no names included of the sender or the addressee. We have already seen Margaret Paston anxious in sending potentially treasonous messages that might be intercepted, something John de Vere was certainly aware of too.

The Battle of Tewkesbury, which took place on 4 May 1471, would be a decisive blow for the Lancastrian party. By the end of the battle all the main adherents of the regime were either dead or demoralized. The Earl of Warwick, and Edward, Prince of Wales, were both dead. Henry VI, imprisoned in the Tower of London, would soon follow them. Margaret of Anjou was captured and would soon be ransomed to France. John went into hiding but was later imprisoned at Hammes.

John's absence throughout the 1470s and early 1480s had a severe financial effect on Margaret. We have already seen that she was borrowing silver to support her husband and used her needlework skills to try to raise a light income. Fabyan wrote that she had nothing 'to live upon, but as the people of their charities would give to her, or what she might get with her needle or other such cunning as she exercised'.[429]

There were emotional effects, too. Despite her husband's soft words that she not feel dejected, Margaret must have been lonely, and the Paston Letters hint at this. Sir John Paston wrote in June 1477, while Oxford was imprisoned at Hammes, 'the good Lady hath need of help and counsel how that she shall do'.[430] Her situation had not improved by 1482 when she was granted a pension of £100 per year by Edward IV 'on account of her poverty'.[431]

Predictably, it was Henry Tudor's accession that changed the lives of the Oxfords. The attainder against him was reversed and he received his mother's inheritance too, in November 1485.[432] But despite this restoration of calm, Margaret couldn't help dabbling in a spot of Medieval policing. A letter survives, written by Margaret to John Paston, Sheriff of Norfolk and Suffolk. She urges him, in May 1496, to watch out for the staunch Yorkist Francis Lovell, rumoured to be returning to England. She asks him to watch in 'ports and creeks', adding with a raised eyebrow 'and what pleasure you may do to the king's grace in this matter, I am sure is not to you unknown'.[433]

The traces of Margaret in the sources suggest she was politically aware and as fiercely loyal to the Lancastrian cause as her husband. Her brother, the Earl of Warwick was, after all, one of its principal leaders in the late 1460s until his death in 1471. Despite the risk to herself, Margaret was involved not only in the procuring and sending of war supplies and cash, but her husband's letters hint at her knowledge of his plans and conspiracies. It is unlikely Margaret was the only woman who served this role during the Wars of the Roses. There were almost certainly many more like her, whispering to servants and packing up chests with cash, sending them to husbands and fathers across the country. Despite emotional and financial hardship Margaret demonstrated bravery and faith.

Alice Montacute 'traitorously conspired'

Margaret de Vere was certainly a force to be reckoned with. But there is another woman, equally brave and resourceful, who was not only accused of working against the king during the Wars of the Roses but was attainted and declared a traitor. Margaret's mother, Alice Montacute.

Alice was the only daughter of Thomas Montacute, Earl of Salisbury, and his first wife Eleanor. A notable and famous soldier, Thomas fought in France for both Henry V and Henry VI before his tragic death at the Siege of Orléans. Cokayne stated he lived for three days before dying from his injuries on 3 November 1428.[434] The legend of Thomas' heroism lived on into the Tudor age and beyond, with Vergil describing him as 'a man always of most ready wit, and mature judgement', while Baker proclaimed his name 'sufficient charm to daunt a whole French army'.[435]

Alice was Thomas' only heir, inheriting the title Countess of Salisbury when she was twenty-two years old. As the birth of her son Richard (the future 'Kingmaker') occurred on 22 November of that year, Alice would have been heavily pregnant on hearing news of her father's tragic death less than three weeks earlier.[436]

Richard Neville, Alice's husband, now held the title Earl of Salisbury in Alice's right. He would prove a key figure of the wars, both politically and militarily, backing the side of his brother-in-law, the Duke of York. It was through this marriage, as well as through Alice's own personal connections, that she was closely associated with many of the wars' key figures, many of them women. Her stepmother from her father's second marriage was Alice Chaucer, the bold Duchess of Suffolk we have already seen at Ewelme. Her sister-in-law was Cecily Neville, Duchess of York. Her eldest son Richard married Anne Beauchamp and became the 16th Earl of Warwick. Alice was at the very centre of the Yorkist party.

In the winter of 1459 Henry VI presided over Parliament held in Coventry, listening carefully as the Yorkists' 'most diabolical inhumanity and wretched envy' was condemned. York and his adherents, it was argued, had been given enough chances to submit themselves to the king. It was now time for decisive and firm action.[437]

This 'Devil's Parliament' attainted York, Salisbury, and Warwick, among others, who had 'traitorously waged war' against the king and queen. Among the names scrawled into the record was a woman's: Alice Montacute, Countess of Salisbury.

The precise nature of Alice's involvement is not specified in the parliament records. On 1 August 1459, while at Middleham in Yorkshire, she was said to have 'falsely and traitorously schemed and plotted the death and final destruction' of the king. Alice, they insisted, had 'worked upon, abetted, instigated, prompted and provoked' the Duke of York and his earls to commit acts against the king at Blore and Ludford. Two other men were also attainted on the same charge but had carried out their conspiracy in London four weeks' previously. Now personally attainted of high treason, Alice's lands and title were forfeited to the crown.[438]

The attainder of a woman was unusual, and Henry must have

had damning evidence against Alice to single her out in this way. The wording of the charge suggests her involvement was tactical and organizational, and she may have been gathering supporters in Yorkshire or helping with strategy, perhaps inspired by old conversations with her war-hero father. However, the wording and the punishment certainly imply she played a prominent role, and Alice may well have been a driving force behind the Yorkist insurrection.

As shocking as Alice's involvement might seem to us modern readers, her attainder barely raised an eyebrow in contemporary sources. John Bocking shared the news with William Yelverton, John Paston and Henry Filongley; Alice's name, listed among the others, elicits no particular shock or surprise.[439] This suggests that it was indeed an expectation that wives would assist and follow the loyalties of their husbands, despite risking heavy punishments.

It didn't take long for the king to start dividing up the Salisburys' forfeited lands, the Patent Rolls of the following months reveal a long list of gifts and grants from their estate, along with offices previously held by the earl. In February 1460 Henry granted one of their London properties to his groom of the bakery, John Eton, while Thomas Roos collected rents from some of their Yorkshire lands from March.[440]

Despite their attainders, Richard continued to fight for York, and there is no reason to suggest that Alice was no longer at her husband's side. However, the fight would eventually cost him his life. He was beheaded after the Battle of Wakefield on 31 December 1460.[441] On the accession of York's son Edward IV in the following year, Alice was granted permission to enter her lands, but died soon after, in her mid-fifties.[442] She was buried at Bisham in Berkshire.

Isabel Berkeley 'all things shall be well'

Underneath the national events of the Wars of the Roses ran local feuds. Isabel Berkeley might not have known it as she stood at the altar on her wedding day, but like many other women of the wars, she would discover that she had married into one.

Isabel married James Berkeley in around 1424. Their home, Berkeley Castle in Gloucestershire, was a stone fortress with high walls that had been passed down through her husband's family for generations.[443]

Her husband was involved in bitter hostilities with Margaret and John Talbot, the Countess and Earl of Shrewsbury. They had claimed some of the Berkeley lands and manors through Margaret's descent, leading to violent attacks from both sides as they wrestled for control.

James was outspoken and temperamental, having once angrily snapped at one of Talbot's messengers serving him a subpoena that he should eat the wax and parchment it was written on.[444] John Talbot was also proud, having served in the French wars of both Henry V and Henry VI. He was known to be so terrifying, wrote Baker, that mothers of crying children would look up and whisper 'Lord Talbot comes' to stop their sobbing.[445] John's wife Margaret also played an active part in the dispute, the Berkeleys later condemned both her and John's 'subtle and damnable imaginations'.[446]

James, John and Margaret then, were all strong personalities that clashed in the growing unrest and political divisions of the early 1450s. However, Isabel's approach to the dispute was much more subtle.

A letter survives in the *Berkeley Manuscripts*, which were collated and examined in the nineteenth century. Isabel had set off for London while James was at Berkeley protecting the family home. From there she wrote to her husband, warning him of 'false counsel', and what she considered Shrewsbury's motives. 'He will not meddle with you openly no manner wise', she wrote, 'but to be with great falsedom, that he can bring about to beguile you, or else he causeth that ye have too few people about you. Then he will set on you'. Isabel's letter shows she had full knowledge of the dispute and had already formed her own opinions about Shrewsbury and his tactics. She pleads for James to send money or else she will have to 'come home on my feet' and urges him to speak with her before doing anything, writing '[entreat] not without me, and then all things shall be well'.[447]

This last point is crucial. Isabel was a key advisor to Berkeley during the feud. Her letter is reassuring but firm, and she presses her husband not to do anything before speaking with her. With James' hot temper, she was probably anxious that any passionate intervention on his part might make the matter worse.

Cokayne believes that Isabel was on her way to appeal to Henry VI about the Talbots, but never made it. In 1452, aware of Berkeley's reliance on his business-minded, efficient wife, they captured her and had her imprisoned at Gloucester. Isabel never left her prison and died in September of that year. It's not known whether her death was caused by neglect, violence, illness, or natural causes. She was buried in Gloucester's Greyfriar's Church.[448]

Dame Jane Harcourt of Bosworth 'jakkes, swordes and billes'

So far, we have seen women conspiring behind the scenes during the wars, sending for supplies and advising on tactics and approach. But there is also evidence that women provided weapons for warfare.

Dame Jane Harcourt was born Jane Francis, the daughter of a Derbyshire knight and married Sir Thomas Harcourt in the early 1400s. A Justice of the Peace for Staffordshire, Thomas and Jane lived at Ellenhall, a small village with a twelfth-century parish church where the couple worshipped and baptized their children. On Thomas' death in July 1420 Jane remarried, to Sir Robert Strelley.[449] By 1448 she was a widow for the second time and put her energy into the causes of her son.

Like the Berkeleys and the Talbots, Jane's son, Robert Harcourt, had entered a feud. His enemy was the Stafford family, and in the summer of 1448 both families clashed violently in Coventry's High Street. We have already seen Margaret, Robert's wife, petitioning for assistance after Robert was eventually killed by one of the Staffords at the Lancastrian surge of power in 1471.

The investigation into the skirmish at Coventry stated that Harcourt's servants had 'designed the death of Sir Humphrey Stafford and of Richard Stafford, his eldest son'. They 'had insulted, beaten and wounded Sir Humphrey and murdered Richard Stafford and William Sharpe his servant'. Robert himself was accused of swinging a two-handed sword and striking Richard on the head, 'causing a mortal wound'.[450] Richard died, his father Humphrey was left badly injured, but alive.

Significantly, Robert's mother, Jane, was noted in the Plea Rolls for her part in the fray. The charges stated that sixty men were armed with 'salades, jakkes, swordes and billes by the procurement of Lady Jane Harcourt of Bosworth, widow'. It also specifies the use of other weapons, such as swords, short poleaxes and daggers, which might also have been organized by her.[451]

Jane's actions in procuring Harcourt's small arsenal of weapons overturns the traditional image of the middle-aged medieval widow at home, living a tranquil and isolated life. Jane actively supported her son's cause and would have known where and how to buy the weapons and have them sent to her son. She also must have had the funds to pay for them. Jane's involvement in her son's legal battles may also support the idea that she considered them justified, but there is no evidence of her thoughts.

Were there other women who conspired and supplied weapons for battles, skirmishes, and private feuds? The collective examples of Margaret Paston, Margaret de Vere, Alice Montacute, Isabel Berkeley, and Jane Harcourt strongly suggest there were. These women provide evidence of women's involvement in both the national and local struggles of the period. With the sharing of communication, organizing military supplies, weapons, horses, saddles, men and cash they also reveal the wide range of duties these women were responsible for in the undercurrent of the Wars of the Roses. There were certainly many more, whose evidence has not survived. Etiquette manuals of the period may well have urged wives and mothers to show obedience, loyalty, and duty toward their family, but it's clear that this sense of duty was carried out not only in the home but engaged in the war efforts too.

CHAPTER ELEVEN
THE DEFENDER: ALICE KNYVET

We have already seen the besieged Margaret Paston overseeing fortifications, sending messages and reporting back on casualties. But there is even more evidence that places women at the centre of violence during this period.

Medieval queens naturally deputized for their husbands while they were absent, even in times of war. Although they didn't take part in the actual fighting, they oversaw and rallied troops, ordering executions of enemies in the aftermath. Margaret of Anjou was a prominent force during the Wars of the Roses, and later Henry VIII's young wife, Catherine of Aragon, would famously oversee events at the Battle of Flodden in 1513.

But it wasn't just the royals who rose in military defence. Nicholaa de la Haye famously defended Lincoln Castle against a French attack in 1217, assisted by Sir William Marshall, and Joan of Arc commanded French soldiers against the English earlier in Henry VI's reign.

Christine de Pisan encouraged women to take up arms if needed. She wrote that a woman 'ought to have the heart of a man ... know how to use weapons and be familiar with everything that pertains to them, so that she may be ready to command her men if the need arises'.[452] Similarly, in the ballad *The Nut Brown Maid*, a woman assures a gentleman of her love, agreeing to 'short my hair, a bow to bear, to shoot in time of need'.[453]

Alice Knyvet 'I shall defend me'

A group of Edward IV's men, including Sir William Chamberlain, John Twyer and Gilbert Debynham shielded their eyes against the autumn sun, squinting up at the entrance to Buckenham Castle, Norfolk. They had been ordered, in a commission of October 1461 to take the castle into the king's hands and evict John and William Knyvet, who, it was believed, had entered the castle unlawfully. The castle had been taken by Henry VI following an enquiry and now Edward IV wanted it back. They stood by, as ordered, to 'arrest and imprison any who resist'. Facing them, at the far end of the raised drawbridge and at the head of a small force of armed men, was Alice Knyvet.[454]

Nineteenth-century historian Jonathan Barrett identified Alice as the daughter of William Lynne of Norfolk. She married John Knyvet, and they had a son, William, perhaps named after her father. It may be this William that is referred to in the king's commission, being then twenty-one years of age. The family's Lancastrian sympathies lasted into the reign of Richard III, the king attainting William for his support of Henry Tudor in 1483.[455] From the wording in the document, neither John nor William were present at Buckenham Castle, Alice was alone.

The events at Buckenham are preserved in an account in the Calendar of Patent Rolls. Arriving at the castle's outer ward, the men found the drawbridge raised over the moat to prevent their entry. Alice appeared in a tower armed with 'slings, paveises, faggots, timber and other armaments of war', accompanied by around fifty people including William Toby of Old Buckenham, a local gentleman. According to the account, those with Alice were also armed with swords, bows and arrows.

Addressing the men who had come to evict her and her family, Alice stood firm. 'Maister Twyer', she shouted from across the sparkling moat, 'ye be a justice of the peace and I require you to keep the peace, for I will not leave the possession of this castle to die therefore'. Issuing a warning, she continued. 'And if ye begin to break the peace or make any war to get the place of me I shall defend me, for lever I had in such wise to die than to be slain when my husband comes home, for he charged me to keep it.'[456]

The men did not engage Alice in battle, probably because they were there in a legal capacity rather than a military one and because they may have expected Alice to quietly hand over the keys. But even though Alice did not have to physically fight on this occasion to defend her home, she was certainly ready and willing to, and had rallied locals to her aid.

The matter seems to have been concluded between Edward and the Knyvets peacefully. In December 1461 another entry in the Patent Rolls records a licence for John to enter Buckenham castle and his manors, along with a pardon for him, Alice and William.[457]

Alice leads our chapter as an example of a woman who took up arms to defend her property during the Wars of the Roses. She handled the situation with boldness and practicality, raising the drawbridge before their approach to prevent them entering and securing the support of servants and locals to join her. However, Alice was far from the only woman who took up arms to defend her home and estates, some finding themselves at the very centre of the wars' military action.

Elizabeth Blount 'speedily they armed themselves to defence'

Over in Calais, the grand castle in the village of Hammes was the home of Elizabeth Blount, wife of James, the Constable of the fortress. Built in stone with a deep moat, towers and imposing curtain walls, it defended the English held Pale of Calais.[458] The area was prone to flooding, with 'diverse lands and tenements' damaged by rising water.[459] Elizabeth would have known the village well, its taverns and shops as well some of its residents, including Robert Radclyf acting as Hammes' bailiff and John de Vere, Earl of Oxford, who had been imprisoned in the castle since 1474.[460] Elizabeth's peaceful life in Calais would be interrupted however, in the autumn of 1484, by a hail of arrows and gunshot.

The Lancastrian Earl of Oxford had spent the last decade at Hammes under guard on the orders of Edward IV. A relentless campaigner for the return of Lancastrian rule, Edward thought him safely out of the way there while his wife Margaret struggled to make ends meet in England. But by 1484 Oxford had managed to convince the castle's keeper, James Blount, to join him in the Lancastrian cause and champion Henry Tudor's claim to the throne. After many discussions, James and the earl left Elizabeth with a force of armed men for her safety and joined Henry in Brittany.[461]

Word soon reached Richard III that Hammes had defected to Tudor. He ordered a force of Calais soldiers to seize the castle and bring it back under royal authority. Elizabeth and her men, alarmed at the sight of the advancing troops, made immediate preparations and, according to Thomas More, 'speedily they armed themselves to defence'.[462] A message was sent urgently to Henry, pleading for assistance against Richard's army. On receiving the news Henry sent Oxford to her aid.

John de Vere, Thomas Brandon, and a force of 'valiant men' managed to slip inside the castle. From here, they overcame Richard's army, and a deal was offered. If Elizabeth gave up the fortress, they would be allowed to leave safely with all their possessions and goods. More writes that 'the Earl of Oxford hearing this, which came only to save his friends from hurt, and namely James Blunt's [sic] wife, was contented with this condition'. Oxford then returned to Paris, to Tudor.[463] The following January, Elizabeth's name headed a pardon granted to soldiers of Hammes by Richard III. James continued to serve as lieutenant of the castle into the reign of Henry VII and fought at the Battle of Stoke against Lambert Simnel's supporters in 1487.[464]

Elizabeth must have been terrified at the sight of the advancing soldiers, knowing that James had defected to support Henry Tudor against the reigning Yorkist king, Richard III. Margaret Paston once wrote that 'I cannot well guide nor rule soldiers, and also they set not by a woman as they should set by a man'.[465] If Elizabeth had encountered any problems in ruling her force, there is no trace of it.

Like the warden of the Fleet we have already met, Elizabeth Venour, Elizabeth Blount was a woman involved in local justice and, like Venour, would likely have had daily contact with prisoners, including the Earl of Oxford himself. The Siege of Hammes is sometimes mentioned in histories of the wars, but it is not often that we stop to think of Elizabeth and her experience at its centre.

Elizabeth Treffry 'repelled the French'

The town of Fowey in Cornwall, according to sixteenth-century visitor John Leland, was framed by strong defensive walls and gates. It held a weekly market, and the homes were built mostly of stone. There was also a church, and a chapel dedicated to St Catherine.[466]

The town Leland saw wouldn't have changed much since the 1450s, when Elizabeth Treffry made the short walk from her home to the harbour. The Cornish seas 'sparkled with ships' noted the Elizabethan visitor Richard Carew, observing the abundance of merchant activity in the area.[467] There was a peculiar phenomenon, residents told him, of a whirlpool in the nearby Dozmery Pool. When a faggot (a bundle of wood) was thrown in at Dozmery it resurfaced some distance away, at Fowey.[468] Dangerous currents sucked and swirled underneath Fowey harbour, but on the surface lurked a different danger: pirates.

Fowey sustained a number of attacks over the centuries, including one in 1457 which was, according to Carew, 'encouraged by the civil wars' and in retaliation for English attacks on French ships.[469] Scrambling from their vessels they waded into the town, their attention drawn to a grand house overlooking the harbour. Inside, at a window, surveying the chaos below, was Elizabeth Treffry.

A Fowey resident in the mid-sixteenth century leaned close to Leland and revealed the tale. 'The French-men diverse times assailed this town, and last notably about Henry the Sixth's time: when the wife of Thomas Treffry the second with her men repelled the French out of her house in her husband's absence'.[470] According to legend, Elizabeth ordered her men to strip lead from the roof, melt it down and pour it onto the attackers from above.

There is some confusion over the date of the attack. Carew places it in 1457. Some modern sources date it to 1475. The earlier date coincides with the kingdom's heightened unrest including a French raid on Sandwich. Carew and Leland agree on dates and there is nothing to suggest that their sources, likely the children of men and women who had witnessed the raid themselves, had made it up.

After the attack Elizabeth's husband Thomas ordered the building to be fortified, Leland writing that he 'built a right fair and strong embattled tower in his house, and embattling all the walls of the house in a manner made it a castle'.[471] Carew called it 'a fair and ancient house... castle-wise builded and sufficiently flanked'.[472] The house was later altered in the eighteenth and nineteenth centuries and still stands today.

The attack on Place House is rarely mentioned in histories of the wars and has survived mostly through verbal legend. However, it did inspire romantic literary works of the Victorian period. The 1884 poem *The Lady of Place* by Henry Sewell Stokes commemorates Treffry, while another written in 1895, speaks of her, 'who defended an old castle in Cornwall, against the French, for hours and hours. Her husband was away, so she was in command, and all her household obeyed her' and refers to the boiling down of lead from the roof to be used in the attack.[473]

Elizabeth Treffry's story was preserved by word of mouth, with the Tudor residents of Fowey keen to tell curious visitors all about her. There are references to the family in court documents in the Patent Rolls relating to merchant activity and local government in Cornwall, but nothing can be established from the sources about Elizabeth's individual actions during Fowey's raid. Taking place at the beginning of the Wars of the Roses and after its first battle at St Albans, it also occurred during the unsteady leadership of Henry VI, amid uneasy tensions with the French. Elizabeth's legend also raises questions about the use of orally preserved stories in our histories. Despite all this however, her actions are completely plausible, and add weight to the idea that a woman commanded men and defended homes and villages against military attack. Elizabeth's existence may have been blurred by legend, but it should still be noted in a discussion of women defending their homes and living through the Wars of the Roses.

Margaret Talbot, Countess of Shrewsbury 'great multitude of people, warlike arrayed'

Berkeley Castle, before dawn. James, Lord Berkeley, is sleeping in his feather bed, his four sons slumbering lazily in their rooms. Suddenly woken by a clamouring of armed men, they are roughly grabbed and jostled into one of the chambers of the castle. As the wooden door slams shut, James, groggily blinking his eyes in confusion, knows exactly who he thinks is responsible: Margaret Talbot.

Margaret's sketch on the Rous Roll shows her wearing an embellished headdress, the thin veil jutting out behind her head. A close-fitting gown hugs her frame, and she wears a mantle around her shoulders, furred at the breast. The daughter of Richard Beauchamp and his first wife Elizabeth Berkeley, she was confident, orderly, and pious. John Rous notes that no one was allowed to blaspheme or swear in her household, on punishment of a diet of only bread and water for the rest of that day. Fitting her status, Margaret secured a suitably well-off marriage, to John Talbot, Earl of Shrewsbury, the couple recited their vows at Warwick Castle.[474]

We have already seen the Berkeley-Shrewsbury dispute in the tale of Isabel Berkeley, who wrote to her husband from London, urging him to beware of Talbot. But according to a complaint later issued by John's son William, it was also Talbot's countess that the family needed to be wary of.

William Berkeley complained, in a Chancery document that survives in *The Berkeley Manuscripts*, that Margaret and her husband had aimed 'to deceive and utterly destroy' his father, himself and his brothers. They accused the Shrewsburys of bribing a castle servant named Rice Tewe to allow them into the fortress, where they imprisoned the Berkeleys for eleven weeks, 'by the commandment of the said Countess'.[475]

Margaret was also accused of obtaining 'certain Indentures of Covenants' from the captive Berkeleys by force which they gave, fearing for their lives. On 4 November 1451 she had, said William, taken them to the Greyfriars in Bristol and made them swear to these agreements in front of the mayor and constable 'with great multitude of people, warlike arrayed'. Berkeley adds, the Shrewsburys then took court action, 'at that time being in so great favour with the king'.[476]

Margaret denied this. The Berkeley manors were hers by right, she insisted, the property of her grandfather, Thomas Lord Berkeley. Margaret insisted it was the Berkeleys who had destroyed Shrewsbury property, including their manor house at Wotton and threatening one of her tenants with a brand iron. Her men had gone to the castle, but only because the Berkeleys were 'misgoverned'. After this admission of intimidation, she insisted they had done so 'without any hurt or misdoing to any person'. Additionally, the Berkeleys had 'freely offered' their property to the Shrewsburys, 'in recompense of the riot beating down and defacing the Manor of Wotton'.[477]

Margaret's insistence of her right to the Berkeley lands would directly influence events after her death. The Battle of Nibley Green, a less well-known battle of the Wars of the Roses, was fought in 1470 by the families' descendants. Her grandson Thomas Talbot, Viscount Lisle, renewed hostilities with William Berkeley, challenging him to a battle in a field just outside the village of North Nibley in Gloucestershire. John Leland recounted this battle when he visited the scene in the sixteenth century. They met at a meadow, when 'Berkeley's archers suddenly shot sore, and the Lord Lisle lifting up the visor of his helmet was by an archer of the Forest of Dean shot in at the mouth and out of the neck'. Lisle's men ran from the scene.[478]

Margaret died a widow in 1467, John Talbot was killed fighting in France in 1453. An assertive and bold woman, if the Berkeleys' account of her is to be believed, she was not afraid of intimidation. She orchestrated the raid and capture of James and his sons and bribed his servant. Throughout the proceedings, it is Margaret's influence that is repeatedly highlighted, as well as her husband's. Margaret might not have wielded a sword or commanded troops, but she was prepared to take physical action to defend and enforce her rights.

Ellen Gethin 'Ellen the Terrible'

Ellen Gethin's story exists somewhere between reality and legend and involves loss, revenge and murder. She is celebrated today as a feisty woman of the wars who avenged the death of her brother by shooting his murderer with an arrow aimed at his heart. But Ellen Gethin was not just a legend, she was a woman who endured her own losses as a result of the Wars of the Roses.

The Victorian historian William Valentine Lloyd identified Ellen as the daughter of David of Llinwent in Radnorshire and his wife Tanglwyst. She married Thomas Vaughan of Hergest, the son of Gwladys Gam and Sir Roger Vaughan.[479] Their home at Hergest Court was a stone and timber building just a twenty-minute walk from the nearby parish church, St Mary's in Kington. Thomas was named in a 1457 pardon issued by Henry VI, but later fought in the Yorkist army at the Battle of Edgecote in 1469.[480] At the close of this battle Ellen would become one of the wars' many widows, with Thomas either killed in fighting or executed with his two half-brothers William and Richard Herbert. On Ellen's death she was buried with her husband at Kington.

However, the details of Ellen's association with the infamous murder are less clear. A number of Victorian authors refer to a manuscript containing the details, quoted by Samuel Lewis in his *Topographical Dictionary of Wales* published in 1834. Although Lewis helpfully transcribes the part of the document relating to Ellen, he does not identify its source. It states that 'Ellen Gethin (or the terrible) of Hergest, a devilish woman, was cousin-german to John hir ab Philip Vychan, who was killed by the said Ellen at St David's church, for that he before killed her brother, David Vaughan, at Llynwent in Llanbister, Radnorshire'.[481]

There is another clue. The Welsh poet Lewis Glyn Cothi includes a note to Ellen in one of his poems, writing of the hope that her husband's death will be avenged by his three sons.[482] Although acts of revenge are mentioned in other poems and ballads during the period, it is just possible that Cothi, who wrote a number of poems for the family, intended this as a subtle reference to Ellen's own legendary act of vengeance.

The often-quoted legend of Ellen Gethin depicts her with a bow and arrow, shooting her cousin in the chest. While the account referenced by Lloyd does not specify Ellen's murder weapon, a bow and arrow does seem the most likely as there is plenty of evidence that medieval women knew how to use them, particularly when hunting. Fourteenth and fifteenth-century manuscripts often depict women holding a bow in hunting scenes and Mancini also noted Englishwomen's experience in archery in the context of the hunt.[483] Author Juliana Berners, writing her *Treatise of Fishing with an Angle* in the fifteenth century knew firsthand the hard work of the hunt. She writes of 'sweating full sore', and how a man whistles for his hawk 'until he be right evil a thirst'.[484]

Ellen's use of a bow and arrow in this instance resulted in murder. It echoes the earlier tale of Agnes Hotot, preserved in a manuscript in around 1395, who, armed with lance and fully armoured, defeated her father's opponent in his place.[485] *The Nut Brown Maid* also promised to use force if required, offering to 'withstand, with bow in hand' against her loved one's enemies.[486]

Ellen Gethin may have been the mysterious avenger of medieval history. While she lived, events were primarily shared and preserved by word of mouth and so the lack of indisputable written contemporary evidence for her deed is not confirmation that it could never have happened. At the very least, Ellen Gethin was a woman who lived through the Wars of the Roses and lost her husband and two brothers-in-law to war. Thomas and Ellen are buried together at Kington Church in Herefordshire, their effigies lie side by side. Ellen's headdress covers her hair and ornamental clasps secure a cloak around her shoulders. Thomas is depicted in armour with a lion at his feet.

Women Rebels 'lying in wait, ill treating, slaying and spoiling'

We have seen women at the centre of sieges, making a show of armed strength and indulging in capture, intimidation, and coercion. Many of those we have encountered in this chapter were involved in local conflicts that were exacerbated by the civil wars, foreign tensions and the weak rule of Henry VI. Elizabeth Blount played a significant role at a major siege, the events of which would be crucial to the collapse of Richard III's government and support.

But what about other events of the wars, such as the many rebellions that took place from the early 1450s? We have seen women negotiating with rebels and witnessing bloodshed first hand. However, they were not only victims. Records show that it wasn't just men marching through streets and lanes causing devastation and fear but women, too.

In July 1450, Henry VI's court writer scrawled over a thousand names into the historical record, which survive today in the Calendar of Patent Rolls. Offering a 'general pardon' for their involvement in Cade's Rebellion that summer, it lists those who 'in great number in diverse places of the realm and specially in Kent and the places adjacent of their own presumption gathered together against the statutes of the realm to the contempt of the king's estate'.[487] Of these names, 134 of them are women.

The scribe diligently recorded their names and occupations and included people from all walks of medieval life. Alice Deraunt, the wife of a gentleman named William Deraunt, is pardoned along with wives of merchants, tailors, taverners, bakers, labourers, and yeomen. Emma Pryk from Hadley was a merchant's wife. On the roll, they are mingled with goldsmiths, constables, ferrymen, butchers, and mariners.

There were widows too, including Joan, who is marked as 'late the wife of John Kent' and 'Alice, late the wife of William Broun'. Joan Stayn is mentioned in her own right. Some are pardoned with their family, such as Isabel Richere who is recorded with her husband John and a 'John Richere the younger' likely to be their son. Margery Appleton was listed with her husband Roger, her son (also named Roger), a yeoman called Thomas Herry 'and all other men and servants of Roger, Margery and Roger'. They all lived in Dartford.[488]

In Payn's account of entering Cade's headquarters in London, where he was taken to a tent 'and one axe and one block was brought forth to have smitten off mine head', he doesn't mention seeing any women among the rebels.[489] But statistically, as shown by the pardons and chronicles, he was more likely to have come across men in the group. As the block was dropped in front of him, the glint of an axe drawing closer, it's fair to say too, that Payn's attention wouldn't have been on the crowd.

Although their names are preserved in the pardons, women's precise involvement in the rebellion is not. We have seen how abbess Katherine de la Pole's entry may have been a paperwork exercise rather than a pardon for any violent action, and this may be true for others listed. It's unlikely however that this applies to all 134 women. They appear with husbands, sons and servants and represent a cross section of medieval society. There is no reason to suggest that women were any less angry at the growing political unease or were less stirred by Cade's words than the men in their lives. It's possible too, that some were accompanying families in a non-violent role. Either way their appearance among the rebels' names should not be dismissed.

There were other reports of riots and 'illegal gatherings' with investigations, arrests and subsequent pardons carried out up and down the country. Lucy Lanam was among those arrested in Southampton in 1452 until 'good behaviour towards the king and the people' could be demonstrated.[490] Agnes Mainfold was another suspected of riotous behaviour in 'various parts of the realm' in 1458.[491] In 1459, the year Yorkists and Lancastrians clashed at Blore Heath, Henry VI issued a pardon to Agnes Warman, Joan Brett, and Joan Chapman, three women out of a group of seventy-nine who had been charged with 'lying in wait, ill treating, slaying and spoiling' in 'various parts of the realm'.[492]

It wasn't just Henry VI who had to put up with rebels. The pardons granted in the aftermath of the rebellions in Cumberland and Yorkshire in 1470 included those for Joan Musgrave, Joan Robynson, Alice Bereworth and Elizabeth Appilby.[493] Joan Musgrave again appears at Edward IV's reinstatement in 1471, the king calling on her and others to be arrested and their goods seized.[494]

In the north there was the added threat of Scottish raids. In June 1477 the citizens of Yorkshire complained to the king that women were among groups of those burning buildings in the West Riding of the county.[495] The king called for the perpetrators to be arrested and imprisoned.

Alice Walron 'opprobrious words'

As disillusionment with Henry VI's reign grew, his subjects could no longer conceal their frustration. In August 1459 a clerk recorded a serious complaint of 'opprobrious words' being spoken against the king by Henry Walron, bailiff of Bawtry in South Yorkshire, and his wife Alice.[496] Officials were sent to Yorkshire to investigate, imprisoning Alice and her husband in Coventry jail. Three months later we find Henry confirmed once again in his role of bailiff.[497]

Henry VI had succeeded the throne at just nine months old. His father Henry V was celebrated for his decisive rule, gaining influence and power in France. He died in 1422, having reigned for just nine years. As a consequence, Henry VI would need to rely on advisors to rule for him for most of his early reign; their jostling over royal control destabilized the crown and its authority. As Henry matured, it became clear that he lacked the decisiveness and strong character to keep these ambitious nobles in check. He also suffered with severe mental health issues, which Bale described as a 'frenzy, and his wit and reason withdrawn'.[498] Unsympathetic to the situation, Henry's inability to rule effectively was ridiculed by the common people. Written in around 1450, the poem, ominously titled *A Warning to King Henry*, spoke of 'Truth and poor men been oppressed/And mischief is nothing redressed/So poor a king was never seen/Nor richer lords all bidden/The commons may no more'.[499]

Alice and Henry weren't the only ones frustrated with their king. In 1444 Thomas Kerver, a Reading man, narrowly escaped execution having complained about his capabilities, and on 24 March 1450 John Ramsey, a vintner's servant, was hanged, drawn and quartered for saying that 'London shall put the king from his crown'.[500] Gervas Cole had already found himself, like the Walrons, contemplating his fate in Coventry gaol in 1447 charged with criticizing the king.[501] With harsh penalties for speaking out, Alice and Henry would have had every reason to worry, as they awaited their fate in Coventry.

PART FOUR:
Cogs in the Machines of Power

CHAPTER TWELVE
TRADE AND INDUSTRY

Away from rebellions, murders, and sieges there was a more subtle side to the contribution of women during the Wars of the Roses. We have seen how they continued to work as merchants, in law enforcement and acted as ambassadors and assistants for their husbands in local government. Many were personally affected by the wars while earning a living. But there is evidence that through their trades, women directly supported the war effort itself, supplying clothing, practical objects, and articles of war.

Alice Claver 'fully befits a most mighty kingdom'

In 1445, Queen Margaret paraded through the city of London towards Westminster, sparkling in a litter of white cloth of gold. Robert Bale recorded that she was in 'as costeous array as ever was seen afore'.[502] In 1482 the Croyland monk saw Edward IV wearing a robe 'lined with the most costly furs and rolled over the shoulders as to give that prince a new and distinguished air to beholders'.[503] Elizabeth of York, at her coronation procession in November 1487 was 'royally apparelled', glittering in 'a kirtle of white cloth of gold of damask, and a mantle of the same suit furred with ermines, fastened before her breast with a great lace curiously wrought in gold and silk, and rich knoppes of gold at the end tasselled'.[504] Bloodline was important during the wars, but ancestry aside, kings and queens needed to look the part too.

Behind all the posturing and processions was a network of men and women who supplied fabrics to the royal court and senior lords and ladies of the realm. They included cloth merchants, embroiderers, furriers, silk women, drapers, dyers and laundresses. Without them there would be none of the crucial 'theatre' of royalty. The textile industry was enmeshed with the outward appearance of the wars, as men and women of rank processed with trappers, tassels and canopies. Armies marched under stitched standards and flags; the emblems of their lords embroidered onto their clothing. Copes sparkling with gold threads were worn by archbishops at coronations, weddings and baptisms. The *Croyland Chronicler* wrote that the appearance of Edward IV's court 'fully befits a most mighty kingdom'.[505] The shimmer of fine silks and golden tassels all gave the outward impression that England was a strong, composed and impressive nation. In reality, it was tearing itself apart.

Clothing also set the king apart from the commoners. Sir John Fortescue, a Lancastrian supporter who wrote *The Governance of England* in the 1460s stressed the political importance of a monarch's attire. He warned 'when such a rebel hath more riches than his sovereign lord, for the people will go with him that best may sustain and reward him'.[506] Expensive finery marked a king's place in the social order, putting even his mightiest subjects in their place.

Alice Claver knew all this too well. On a cloudy afternoon in 1480, against the backdrop of London's rumbling carts and the chiming of church bells, she gently wrapped up a parcel bound for the king.

Edward IV's Wardrobe Accounts of 1480 give us a detailed insight into the king's clothing and the people that supplied it. Alice Claver is repeatedly mentioned, providing sewing silk, ribbons and silk for laces. She supplied a 'fringe of gold of venus' along with fringes of yellow, green, red, white and blue. Some were finished with gold, others decorated with images, including one item with the Yorkist symbol of roses and suns and the addition of crowns. On one occasion, Alice was commissioned to create 'laces and tassels for the garnishing of the king's books'. Right down to Edward's private library, no expense was spared to create the ambience of kingship.[507]

Priscilla Lowry, in *Secrets of Silk*, identified Alice's workplace in London's Soper Lane area along with a number of other silk women who formed part of a close network within her community.[508] Frank Warner found that there were many women supplying the royal court, including the finishing touches for Henry VII's ceremonial robes. Cecyly Walcot supplied ribbons of damask gold and 'venys gold' for Henry's gloves, with Kateryn Walshe supplying similar decorations.[509] David MacGibbon, in *Elizabeth Woodville: A Life*, identified Elyn Longwith, a London silk woman supplying materials to decorate Elizabeth Woodville's 'chairs, saddle and pillion' at her coronation.[510]

A small section of the Privy Purse Accounts for Edward's daughter Elizabeth, during her time as queen, survives. In February 1503 Elizabeth of York paid for Mistress Lokke to supply 'frontlets, bonnets and other stuff of her occupation', as well as her transport to and from the court. Agnes Bretayn provided her with nine pounds and eleven ounces of gold of venus while Mistress Bourne kitted the queen out with laces, ribbons and sarcenet for her girdles.[511] All this luxury even lulled the queen to sleep at night, as she slumbered in bedsheets of 'crimson satin, embroidered with crowns of gold, the Queen's arms and other devices ... garnished with fringe of silk, and gold, and blue and russet'.[512] Work was also commissioned on a 'rich bed' for the queen in December 1502, embroidered by several men and women. Among them was Margrette Stokes, who was paid five shillings fourpence (the equivalent of around £175 today) for two weeks' board and wages.[513]

Textiles could work political magic overseas. In 1472 Lord Gruuthuse marvelled at the silk hangings, linen cloth and expensive floor carpets at Windsor Castle. He noted with enthusiasm the luxurious Rennes sheets on the bed, decorated in cloth of gold, furred with ermine.[514] Edward and Elizabeth were well aware that Gruuthuse would relate these luxuries, along with appropriate awe, to the Burgundian court back home, sealing Edward 's reputation as a powerful monarch of infinite resources and wealth.

Whenever the royal family donned a tasselled cloak or snuggled up in heavy blankets, the work of silk women and embroiderers was not far behind. They were skilled workers and businesswomen, working diligently through the wars. Women like Alice, and others in her community, are not often examined in the context of the Wars of the Roses but were responsible for helping to create the illusion of majesty in public and in private. Their work shone at coronations and processions in outward displays of the king's ancient birthright, established his place in the social order and conveyed the perception that he had unlimited resources and strength at his disposal.

Alice Shapster 'sworn to keep the chamber counsel'

The closets of kings and queens may have bulged with expensive fabrics but how did they keep them clean? Royal bedsheets, napkins and tablecloths were not only of the best quality, they had to be unblemished and sweet-smelling, too. This was the job of the laundress.

Washing clothes was mostly women's work in medieval England, although men were also contracted at court to wash the king's linen. Henry VI had a yeoman, two grooms and a page in his office of laundry.[515] Edward IV's Ordinances list his grooms, who were 'safely to keep and tenderly to wash and preserve diligently the stuff for the king's proper person'. They washed bedding, towels, robes, tablecloths and napkins, and kept a steady stock of soap on hand for the job. Separate provision was made for the queen, the Ordinances state that if she was in the household, 'then there be women launderers', who should be 'sworn to keep the chamber counsel'.[516]

Edward did however pay Alice Shapster for making and washing a batch of laundry that included twenty-four shirts and stomachers, five dozen handkerchiefs and various large bedsheets.[517] His daughter

Elizabeth of York paid for her laundress Agnes Dean to travel from Berkeley Herons to Windsor in September 1502, covering the costs of food for her horse.[518]

Henrietta Leyser, in *Medieval Women, A Social History of Women in England 450-1500*, has discussed the links between washerwomen and gossip, and stated that they met not only to wash the shirts and tablecloths of their lords but to exchange news.[519] This would have been of benefit during the wars, keeping communities up to date with ever-changing situations. But with such a sensitive job, care was taken that the king's laundry was not the subject of gossip. Alice Shapster would have sworn an oath of privacy and Edward IV warned that no 'stranger' should touch or otherwise set hands upon his linen. During the reign of his grandson, Henry VIII, his laundress Anne Harris was ordered to 'discreetly pursue' his laundry.[520] A dribble of sauce or a smear of grease shattered the mystery and majesty of kingship, making him as human as his poorest subjects. In the case of the queen, her laundry could reveal more intimate details, such as whether she was menstruating, potentially leading to gossip about a royal pregnancy before the household had chosen to make an announcement. Any traces of a long-term illness left on fabrics could undermine the perceived state of the king's health and his relative ability to rule. During the Wars of the Roses, with so many well-born figures hovering around the throne, keeping any doubts around a monarch's health away from public scrutiny was vital. The role of a laundress was an important one, and it required sensitivity, respect and dignity. From the palace's bedsheets to the treatment of the royal napkins, there was a conscious need for the mystery of royalty, and the household's control over it, to be preserved.

Purveyors of War 'six longbows and a long gown of velvet'

The women providing their services to the crown were an invisible but crucial part of maintaining the majesty of kingship and asserting the king's status over his subjects. This is especially important during the rebellions and insurrections of the wars. However, there are other women who assisted much more directly with the war effort.

In the 1460s Edward was gearing up for war with Scotland as a result, according to Fabyan, of the support they had recently shown to Margaret of Anjou.[521] John Howard, the future Duke of Norfolk, was commissioned on 29 May 1462 to amass a fleet of shipmasters and mariners for the ships *The Mary Talbot* and *The Mary Thompson*. On 22 March 1463 he was tasked with rounding up 'men at arms and other able bodied men ... in thousands, hundreds and twenties as may be convenient to the sea coast'.[522]

John Howard's account books from around this period indicate the scale and variety of suppliers needed to raise a medieval fleet for war, some of them women. A 'Belkin's wife' was paid for 'meat for salting of flesh' while equipping *The Mary Talbot* in 1463 and the wives of Deve and Edward for herring in 1466. In the same year Marget Forde was paid 'for the freight of an anchor from London' and 'Hervyis wyffe' provided a cloth to carry a sail.[523]

It's likely these wives were involved in assisting with their husband's trades, although some widows may have been working in their own right. However, with this in mind, questions can be raised over the contributions made by the many wives of bowyers, saddlers, ironmongers and blacksmiths that appear in fifteenth-century records of this period. Unfortunately, there is little evidence of wives' individual participation. However, one woman's interaction was much more overt. An entry in Howard's accounts in July 1472 records a woman taking delivery of longbows. 'This day my Lord sent to Mason's wife, [Christopher] Cresford standing by, six longbows and a long gown of velvet, furred with shanks'.[524]

'Cakes and pears'

Surviving royal accounts show that locals were quick to spot an opportunity for a sale when the royal family was in residence. ...ther for profit or to boost the morale of a troubled king and ...we find several women delivering produce to the doors of ...palaces.

...ary VII's Privy Purse Expenses reveal that he rewarded ...nging Aqua Vitae' and in July 1498 paid a 'Benson ...ht for my lorde of York and for my lady Margaret'. ...son's wife was paid the handsome sum of ...round £4,500 today. However, what she ...y and Margaret wasn't recorded. Other ...rries and cherries, flowers, and in ...Perkin Warbeck was imprisoned ...ose'.[525] In May 1502, the wife ...cods to Elizabeth of York, ...akes and pears. Others

...rs in a business ...They may also ...duce to the ...hey were ...eens, ...les,

ed
eted
enry
lished
old and
f women
une. With
ven virgins,
umably also
dialogue and
and sword.[528]
the king but to
ll as mythical and
endary kings from
nqueror accompanied the man
Normandy', the man
ward's welfare in a land
s treated to displays of St
n and a 'king and queen on

miserly, solemn king, enjoyed
es rewarding performers with
he gave the huge sum of £30
damsel that danceth'. There were
urt. Henry's accounts' book paid
King and Quene' in August 1495
woman that singeth with a fidell'.[530]

s
rom

enjoying the performance, he fled the room in embarrassment at their nudity.[527] We can imagine the awkward and confused faces of these women as the king staggered from the room, his robes swirling behind him as he ran.

There was a better outcome in 1432 when the ten-year-old Henr[y] processed into London on 21 February after having been crown[ed] in France. Robert Withington discusses the pageants that gre[eted] the young ruler in *English Pageantry: A Historical Outline*. As H[enry] entered the city, allegorical performances reinforced and estab[lished] his right to the English and French thrones. As cloths of g[old and] silk fluttered in the wind, Henry's eyes settled on a group o[f women] swathed in costumes, dressed as Nature, Grace and For[tune. Near] them were fourteen more women; seven maidens and se[ven] 'pure and clean'. As they bowed and gestured, pre[sumably] trembling in the cold February streets, they recited [and] sang to confirm Henry's right to his crown, sceptre[.528]

These pageants were designed not only to flatte[r but to] communicate his undeniable right to rule. As we[ll as] allegorical figures, this also took the form of le[gendary] history. When Edward IV entered Bristol in 14[61,] an actor playing the part of William the Co[nqueror greeted him] by his lords. 'I am thy forefather William o[f] bellowed theatrically, promising to see to E[dward,] 'many years hast thou lacked'. Edward wa[s also shown St] George vanquishing the legendary drago[n with a maiden] high in a castle'.[529]

Henry VII, despite his reputation as a [miser, paid for] a number of entertainments, sometim[es] extravagant sums. In September 149[ ] (around £20,000 today) 'to the youn[g] other talents in the early Tudor c[ourt] 'the woman that sange before th[e] and the following November, 'a[

Both women and men entertained the kings and queens of the Wars of the Roses, providing some lightness to the otherwise tense business of administering government. For just a few minutes or hours their thoughts were diverted towards dancing, singing or music. Pageants too, not only provided a warm welcome from towns and cities but communicated the birthright of the ruling family through allegory and historical figures. Their appearance in this respect is subtle, but they were a soothing distraction at a time of intense political pressure.

The Flirtatious Widow

In the mid-1470s Edward IV, in heavy furs and glinting with jewels, was on the prowl for cash to raise a war against the French, in alliance with the Duke of Burgundy, intent on punishing them for their earlier support of the House of Lancaster. Edward may have considered he had the grounds and motivation for a foreign war, but he lacked the finance. A tax was imposed on his subjects, ironically called a Benevolence. 'Many grudged thereat', wrote Stow cheekily, 'and called it a Malevolence'.[531] The king rode around the country visiting wealthy subjects to lay out his reasons for war and to receive their financial support.

One woman, Richard Baker calls her 'an old rich widow', was only too pleased to see the tall, charming king beaming at her door. Welcoming him in, she listened intently as he gently outlined his wish to avenge France's wrongdoings and asked what she could give to support him. 'By my troth, said she', presumably with a modest smile and a flutter of the eyelashes, 'for thy lovely countenance thou shalt have even twenty pounds'. The shocked king had expected half that amount. He thanked her and gave her a kiss. 'Which wrought so with the old widow that she presently swore he should have twenty pounds more, and paid it willingly'.[532]

Playful as she was, there is of course no further evidence of this woman's identity. Fabyan claimed Edward raised cash for his war by using 'the people in such fair manner', suggesting she was not alone in receiving Edward's charming affections.[533] Widows like this lady would have been among the many subjects who helped raise money for Edward's war, although in the end the matter was concluded without battle.

CHAPTER THIRTEEN
COMPANIONSHIP

Whenever we see depictions of royal or noble women in medieval sources their ladies in waiting are not far behind. They worked as trusted companions to mistresses, giving advice or much needed company during the Wars of the Roses. There are also a number of examples where women went further and worked in secret, undercover roles or steered their mistress towards a particular cause.

These women fulfilled ceremonial duties, too, providing a luxurious backdrop to weddings, pageants, coronations, and other court functions. Richly clothed in silks and velvets and sparkling with diamonds and sapphires, their presence sent a clear message to spectators. Queens of the Wars of the Roses were powerful and supported by the wealthiest families of the realm. A throng of duchesses and countesses gave a serene dignity to the occasion, as well as a sense of loyal subservience.

Margaret Gaynesford 'well and richly beseen'

Margaret Gaynesford's striking brass can be seen on the wall of Carshalton Church in Surrey. She kneels with her husband Nicholas and their eight children, Nicholas in armour and Margaret wearing a billowing butterfly headdress and red gown, a result of unusual enamelling decoration on the brass. They wear matching collars of suns and roses, a sign of their loyalty to the House of York.

Margaret's husband Nicholas was summoned in July 1460 to round up those 'spoiling, beating, maiming and slaying' in Sussex.[534] From Edward's accession in 1461 he appears more often and in a wide variety of commissions. Nicholas was made Porter of the Castle of Odiham and the Gaynesfords benefited from the receipt of lands previously belonging to attainted Lancastrians John, Lord Clifford and John Penicock.[535]

The couple had roles within the royal court, too. Nicholas served in Edward's household as Esquire of the Body and by 1464 he is named as his usher, becoming Queen Elizabeth's usher in 1476.[536] It's here that he may have regularly bumped into his wife who was also serving in the queen's household as one of her gentlewomen. The Gaynesfords were keen to have these roles immortalized on their brass, the inscription telling us that they both served not only Edward IV and Elizabeth Woodville but also Henry VII and Elizabeth of York.

Both enjoyed close proximity to the king and queen and may have maintained good personal relationships with them, demonstrated by their length of service. As esquire, Nicholas would have been one of those who dressed the king and ensured he had everything he needed, day or night. It was written in the Ordinances that this role was especially entrusted, and that 'their business is in many secrets'.[537] Henry VII expected his esquires to keep watch at his door until he had gone to bed and to be present when he woke.[538] Margaret would have attended her royal mistresses in a similar role, providing companionship as well as performing public and ceremonial functions.

We have already touched upon the gap in the Gaynesfords' service during the reign of Richard III and his consort Anne Neville. Nicholas was implicated in the Buckingham Rebellion of 1483 with Margaret also absent from court at this time. As we have hinted at, this may suggest she was supportive of her husband's actions, but there is no further evidence for this. She may simply have had a special fondness for Elizabeth Woodville, or Anne might not have invited her to court. Nicholas was pardoned by a cautious Richard III in 1484, and he gained a full pardon from Henry VII in 1485.[539]

Both Nicholas and Margaret had prominent roles at Elizabeth of York's 1487 coronation. Leland describes Nicholas riding in procession with men dressed in 'gowns of crimson velvet, having mantels of ermine ... and on their heads hats of red cloth of gold ermines'. Margaret is recorded as one of the gentlewomen attending the queen that same day. She may have been one of the ladies who entered the procession 'riding upon goodly palfreys well and richly beseen, with great beads and chains of gold about their necks in marvellous great number'.[540]

Margaret Gaynesford, decked out in sparkling jewels and riding in procession towards Westminster Abbey was a gentlewoman to two queens, reinforcing her power as she attended ceremonial occasions. There are questions over the break in her service, but we may never now know the reason for this. She was clearly proud of the service she gave, insisting it be commemorated on their family monument.

The Art of Ceremony 'ladies of the highest rank in England'

Margaret Gaynesford, along with Elizabeth of York's other gentlewomen, would have inspired gasps from the public as they gave a dignified sparkle to administrative or religious events. However, their presence also implied power, as they reflected their own wealth and political strength onto their king and queen. A queen with a trail of commanding, high-born ladies processing behind her implied that she and her husband had the nobility's consent to reign and strengthened their position. At a time when questions were raised over the power of the crown's authority, this was a subtle but vital part of royal showmanship.

The queen's 'churching' or 'purification ceremony' was one of these occasions. It marked her official re-entry into public life after giving birth. Ancient and symbolic, gentlewomen were of course present. Strickland notes a writ of summons sent to 'ladies of the highest rank in England', for the churching of Margaret of Anjou on 18 November 1453, adding that duchesses, countesses, a viscountess and seventeen baronesses were present.[541]

Elizabeth Woodville was at the centre of an equally luxurious churching after the birth of her daughter Elizabeth in February

1465. The ceremony was witnessed by the Bohemian visitor Gabriel Tetzel, who told of trumpeters, pipers, string players, heralds and a choir accompanying the queen back into public life. Like Gruuthuse at Windsor Castle, his presence at the event suggests the royal couple were keen for the opulence and ancient ceremony of the English court to be discussed in European circles. Tetzel remembered the 'courtly reverence' the dukes paid to the queen 'such as I have never seen elsewhere'. He also noted the presence of 'daughters of influential men' along with eight duchesses and thirty countesses, adding 'nor have I ever seen such exceedingly beautiful maidens'.[542]

But it wasn't enough for gentlewomen to just look the part, they were expected to play it, too. Formal events such as churchings came with ancient rituals designed to promote loyalty and subservience, reinforcing each woman's place in rank. Even senior royals were to observe these customs. Tetzel related how the queen sat on an embellished golden seat while her mother Jacquetta Woodville knelt, stood and kept her distance from her.[543]

A similar mark of respect was shown to Anne Neville at her coronation with Richard III in July 1483. An observer noted that at the dinner, Anne sat to the left of her husband. She was flanked by two gentlewomen. 'On the right hand of the Queen standing my Lady of Nottingham and on the left hand standing the Lady of Surrey holding the cloth of estate over her head when she both eat or drink'. Eventually the ladies were permitted to leave Anne and join the feasting.[544]

Royal weddings were another event that required the attendance of gentlewomen, and it is likely they offered moral support to their mistress during what was likely a stressful or anxious day. Their generic, anonymous features can be seen in paintings and stained-glass windows marking the occasion. One eighteenth-century sketch in the Wellcome Collection of a now lost stained-glass window is believed to show Margaret of Anjou and Henry VI standing either side of a priest at their ceremony. Behind Margaret, three ladies are carefully depicted wearing red gowns, mirroring the three men lined up on Henry's side. Similarly, a fifteenth-century image of the wedding of Edward IV and Elizabeth Woodville also shows three gentlewomen standing demurely and attentively beside the royal bride. Their wedding was conducted in secret with only a few people present. However, that they are depicted in public works of art shows the expectation that they would be present to give their support, symbolism and help calm any last-minute nerves.

A gentlewoman's role at court then was as symbolic as it was practical. Their presence was visually stunning but also implied that they gave the ruling monarch their blessing. Some of the most powerful nobles in the realm bowed, knelt, and solemnly processed behind their king or queen showing, at least on the outside, that they gave their approval to their rule.

But these were difficult times and the Wars of the Roses tested loyalties, relationships between gentlewomen and their queens were no exception. In a world which Sir John Paston described as 'right queasy', roles and statuses could change suddenly.[545] Margaret of Anjou would have agreed with John's assessment as she found herself overseen by Alice Chaucer, once her gentlewoman, at Wallingford Castle in the early 1470s as conditions for her ransom to France were negotiated. Similarly, she would have heard of the rise of the Woodvilles in the Yorkist court and remembered the service given to her by Jacquetta Woodville, once one of her ladies. Cecily Neville and Anne Beauchamp were with the queen too and would later become central figures in the opposing Yorkist party as their husbands fought to unseat her and her royal husband from the throne. Thomas More states that Elizabeth Woodville served in the household of Margaret of Anjou; if this was the case, this lady in waiting would succeed her as queen.[546] Finally, it is often also remarked that Margaret Beaufort, Henry Tudor's mother, carried the train of Anne Neville's robes at her coronation. Smiling and processing elegantly behind her, Margaret was crucial in her son's acquisition of Richard's throne just two years later.[547]

However, even in the turbulent period of the wars, there is evidence that women's relationships with their gentlewomen were strong. The Household Ordinances of Cecily Neville reveal that her gentlewomen provided much needed company and a calming influence over the ageing duchess, with time allocated for her to spend time with them after supper.[548] Ending the day with some of her most trusted ladies would have helped the duchess relax before retiring to her chamber.

The companionship provided by loyal gentlewomen stretched to the battlefield too. John Warkworth stated that Margaret of Anjou's trusted lady Katherine Vaux was with her in the tragic aftermath of the Battle of Tewkesbury, along with Anne Neville and the Countess of Devonshire.[549]

With these close relationships, it's not surprising that gentlewomen were called upon to influence the actions of their mistresses or their families, in attempting both local and national change.

Jane Rodon 'The most special labourer'

Jane Rodon was a gentlewoman to Elizabeth, Duchess of Norfolk. She appears in the Paston Letters in September 1472 in a letter from John Paston to his older brother Sir John, as they try to secure support in the Norfolk household during their property dispute with the duke, John Mowbray. The brothers had asked Jane to put in a good word for them with her mistress, Elizabeth. John the younger, referring to Jane, writes to his brother to 'also in no wise forget not in all haste to get some goodly ring at the price of twenty shillings, or some pretty flower of the same price, and not under, to give to Jane Rodon; for she hath been the most special labourer in your matter, and hath promised her good will forth; and she doth all with her mistress'.[550]

If Jane Rodon could be persuaded to drop positive words about the Pastons' cause in daily conversations with her mistress, we can imagine similar situations developing across the realm. Not only were they in a perfect position to influence property disputes but, it appears, they were able to help sway significant allegiances towards the crown.

The Mystery Woman of the Duchess of Clarence 'employed in this secret'

In 1470 one lady was sent on a covert peace mission to Calais. Here, the Duke of Clarence and the Earl of Warwick were plotting to reinstate Henry VI to the throne of England. Claiming to be a gentlewoman with letters for Isabel Neville Duchess of Clarence, she was absent-mindedly waved through into the duke's chambers. It was here that she carried out her mission: to win the duke back to his brother Edward's side in the wars.

The gentlewoman's name has not been recorded. However, she 'managed the affair that was committed to her charge with so much cunning and dexterity', wrote Commines, 'that she prevailed with the Duke of Clarence to promise to come over to the king's party as soon as he was in England'. He describes her as 'no fool, nor loquacious' and 'carried on her intrigues till she had effected the ruin of the Earl of Warwick and all his faction'.[551] What she said to the duke isn't known, but she may have cast doubt in his mind about Warwick's intentions following Henry VI's retaking of power. Commines certainly acknowledges her ability, as a woman, to visit without arousing suspicion.[552] Baker also found Clarence's servant had this advantage, as women were 'fit agents of state … that can transact a business in covert, which if men should attempt, they would soon be discovered'.[553]

The gentlewoman completed her mission and on Clarence's return to England he was reunited with his brothers Edward and Richard. Her job proved decisive for the York victory at the Battle of Barnet in 1471, Commines noting that Clarence's defection earned the Yorkist side 12,000 men, a 'mighty strengthening' to King Edward.[554]

Apart from her identity, another question remains: who sent her? In 1470 a number of people wanted Clarence back on the side of York. His sisters Margaret of Burgundy and Anne Duchess of Exeter have already been mentioned in their endeavours to reunite the brothers. Their mother, Cecily Neville, must also have been eager to see them together after this period of instability. Edward IV too, must have wanted his brother (and his 12,000 men) back on his side and was probably the best person to brief the gentlewoman on how to handle Clarence and what to say to win his trust.

Gentlewomen had also been deployed to ease political and military tensions in 1461. Stow wrote that the Londoners, on hearing of the approach of Margaret of Anjou's forces, refused them entry into the city, afraid they would commit violence upon the citizens. He writes that Jacquetta, Duchess of Bedford, and the Lady Scales were sent to negotiate with Margaret.[555] 'It was well advised to send women to entreat a woman', writes Baker on the subject, 'for by this means they prevailed'.[556]

The job of a gentlewoman demanded a high level of personal commitment as they gave political and personal support to their mistress and often to their wider family. Those that proved loyal would be rewarded, sometimes years after they had left service. For example, Edward IV rewarded Alice Russel in 1462 with lands and manors worth £10 a year 'for her true heart to the king and his father' granting the same amount in the following year to Alice Mortymer, an elderly family servant.[557]

These rewards demonstrate a gratitude to the families for their many years of service, some living out their old age with financial assistance from the crown. Other servants would not be so lucky.

Ankarette Twynhoe 'a venomous drink'

In the early spring afternoon of 12 April 1477 Ankarette Twynhoe was at her home in Somerset. She lived in some comfort, her husband identified in a document in 1455 as 'William Twynnyo, nobleman, lord of the place of Keyford'.[558] They were still married in 1470, when they are mentioned together in a land transfer but by 1477 she is named a widow.[559] Ankarette, a grandmother said to have had a 'good disposition' had served in the household of Isabel Neville, Duchess of Clarence at Warwick Castle. She had been recently attending to her after the birth of a son in early October 1476.

The Duke of Clarence kept a tight order over his and his duchess' servants. They were to 'be of worshipful, honest, and virtuous conversation' and to avoid 'seditious language, variances, dissentions, debates and frays'. There was to be no eating in rooms other than in the dining hall, and a bell was rung on holy days to signal when it was time for prayer. Isabel was in charge of setting the salary for her ladies and gentlewomen, them taking 'such fees, rewards and clothing as shall please the Duchess'.[560] The household that Ankarette knew would have been a busy one with gentlewomen, chamberers, a treasurer, chaplain, grooms and pages all providing daily assistance to Isabel.[561]

Tragically, soon after the birth Isabel died, perhaps as the result of complications from the delivery, a bacterial or viral infection or a longer-term illness. Ankarette returned to her home in Keyford.

Suddenly, two men, with a large band of 'divers riotous persons' stormed into Ankarette's home and bundled her onto a horse. They took her first to Bath, through Cirencester, and then to Warwick, where she was imprisoned. There, the shocked and frightened Ankarette had her jewels, money and possessions stripped from her. Her concerned daughter Edith, along with Edith's husband Thomas, raced through the countryside to her mother, to be told by the Duke of Clarence 'as though he had used king's power' to stay away and lodge at nearby Stratford upon Avon.

George, Duke of Clarence, had come to believe that Ankarette had poisoned his wife. The dishevelled widow was brought to the Guildhall in Warwick on the Tuesday morning, where she was accused of having, on 10 October 1476, 'given to the said Isabel a venomous drink of ale mixed with poison.' Ankarette was sentenced to be 'led from the bar there to the gaol of Warwick and from thence should be drawn through the town to the gallows of Myton and hanged till she were dead'.[562]

The account of Ankarette's arrest and hasty trial can be found in a petition for a pardon from her grandson Roger, heard in the presence of the king at Westminster in February 1478. In it, the jurors asked for forgiveness, having passed the verdict due to the 'imaginations of the said duke and his great might'.[563]

Ankarette was hanged. Her formal accusation, trial and judgement had taken just three hours.

She was almost certainly innocent of the charges against her. No physical evidence in support of the allegations was mentioned in the trial, and Isabel's death occurred in December, too long after the supposed date of the poisoning in October. The jurors' later request for a pardon for themselves demonstrates they had clearly struggled with making their judgement, terrified of a backlash from Clarence.

Clarence was never known for his compassion or trustworthiness. The sources in fact suggest a somewhat easily influenced, volatile and highly ambitious personality. He had switched sides in the wars twice, once to Warwick and then to his brother Edward. Stow wrote that he accused Edward of being illegitimate, belittled the king's judgement and reminded the people of his own claim to the throne should his brother die without heirs.[564] Polydore Vergil put it mildly when he wrote that 'the duke was not very constant'.[565] Strickland suggests that Clarence's erratic behaviour during the Twynhoe affair can be explained by feelings of grief over his wife's death, acting without self-control 'in order to drown the pains of thought'.[566] However, the duke had already demonstrated a changing and volatile temperament long before Isabel's death.

Ankarette's case, although she would never know it, turned out to be one of the reasons for Clarence's eventual downfall. Plotting, switching, and proclaiming his own right to the throne, he had also now contrived the death of a woman in a forced trial, with no respect for the king's legal process. Despite being Edward's brother, Clarence had overstepped the mark. The duke was attainted and sentenced to execution, legend has it, by drowning in a bucket of Malmesey wine on 18 February 1478.

On 20 February 1478, ten months after Ankarette's death and just two days after Clarence's, Edward IV listened intently to her case. John Twynhoe's petition asked that 'as the premises were done by the command of the said duke' that the justices and sheriffs in the case should be pardoned, as well as the 'record, process, verdict and judgement' of Ankarette be made void. Edward conceded.[567]

Edward's pardon and Clarence's fate may have eased the consciences of those present at Ankarette's proceedings, but for the Somerset grandmother who unwittingly ended her life at the end of the hangman's rope, it came far too late.

Mistresses and Lovers

Companionship during the Wars of the Roses took many forms, and it wasn't just servants and gentlewomen that enjoyed associations with their sovereigns. There is some evidence that royal mistresses, far from being giddy or insignificant, were able to exert influence and raise their status at court. For one of the wars' kings, an old relationship would re-emerge, casting doubt over the legitimacy of his descendants. Another woman's name would be brought from the past to discredit and bring down a powerful duke. Not only will we look at the mistresses and lovers of the wars' statesmen and kings, but also the different monarchs' attitudes to women.

Henry VI 'wholly and sincerely'

Through the side-switching and political games of the Wars of the

Roses, there is one theme that emerges as constant. Henry VI, in the sources that refer to him, was a religious, sensitive and gentle king. There is no evidence that he took mistresses outside of his marriage to Margaret of Anjou. In fact, according to his biographer John Blacman, he actively shunned nudity or lust in and away from the court. Blacman remembered how, as a boy, the king would keep watch through windows to ensure no women were being smuggled into the palace buildings. He was horrified at the nakedness of men washing as he travelled through Bath, and we have already seen him run from the 'bared bosoms' of dancing women.[568] On the plus side though, Henry's enemies were unable to use lust or sinful living to blacken his reputation, Stow writes that 'suspicion of unchaste life never touched him' and Blacman insists he 'kept his marriage vow wholly and sincerely'.[569] In 1450, Henry would find that one of his prominent advisors had not been so chaste.

Malyne de Cay 'sinful living'

In the summer of 1429 in Normandy, a nun was entangled in a passionate clinch with the Earl of Suffolk, William de la Pole. Her name would later be used to discredit him in a chain of events that ultimately led to his fall and eventual murder at the beginning of May 1450.

De la Pole, then Earl of Suffolk, but later created duke, was serving in France in 1429 with the English army. A manuscript detailing several charges against him specifies one in particular that is often overlooked. One night, states the document, he 'lay in bed with a nun whom he took out of holy profession and defouled whose name was Malyne de Cay, by whom he gat a daughter, now married to Stonor of Oxfordshire'. The following day he was captured by the French, the author blames his distraction from duty on his 'sinful living'.[570]

We don't know the context of William's relationship, if there was one, with Malyne de Cay. Certainly, the one-sided nature of the allegations, that he 'took' her from her religious orders, serve the purpose of William's enemies in making him appear hostile and disrespectful, especially regarding a woman of religion. Whatever their history, de la Pole's enemies used it to add weight to the existing complaints against him, and in 1449 their case was set. He had lost English lands in France, ingratiated himself with enemies and enriched himself through his influence over the king. Now the story of his selfish defiling of a nun from a religious house in Normandy sealed his reputation as self-centred, lecherous and careless, even with women of God.

Very little is known of Malyne, and her appearance in the records exists only to shame and discredit a man whose enemies wanted him removed from power more than twenty years after the event had occurred. We do not have Malyne's own version of the story, which would have added context and balance to the account, nor do we know if she was at all involved in revealing the details of their affair, if there indeed was one. One of the wars' forgotten women, it is surprising she is not discussed more widely, her name being used to help bring down the Duke of Suffolk is one of the significant preludes to the Wars of the Roses.

The Women of Edward IV

Edward IV couldn't have been more different than his predecessor, Henry VI. He engaged confidently in politics, dressed extravagantly and was a capable soldier in battle. We have seen how the flirtatious widow generously helped to fund his war with France, and it seems his love of women was well known during his lifetime. The *Croyland Chronicle* stated that he was 'a man of such corpulence, and so fond of boon companionship, vanities, debauchery, extravagance and sensual enjoyments'; while Vergil wrote, a little more reservedly, that the king 'readily cast an eye upon young ladies'.[571] Commines wrote that Edward's dealings with influential ladies of the realm may have gained him some political support as 'the ladies of quality, and rich citizen's wives with whom he had formerly intrigued, forced their husbands and relations to declare themselves on his side'.[572]

Of all the kings of the Wars of the Roses Edward is best known for his taking of mistresses and was said to have had at least two secret weddings. But could a mistress have exercised influence over her royal lover, changing the course of events during the wars? She certainly had the ear of the king and could have provided moral support in their intimate moments. It's time to untangle the women that surrounded Edward and examine their function within the wider Wars of the Roses.

Eleanor Butler 'feigned marriage'

Back in the fifteenth century, a verbal agreement of marriage was as legally binding as one committed to paper. It was not unknown, for a couple fuelled with lust, to promise themselves in marriage to one another before consummating the match, making them formally betrothed and unable to take another husband or wife. If the ceremony did go ahead, it was conducted with witnesses and could not simply be undone without a formal divorce. If the couple separated, they were still legally married and could not take another spouse.

In the parliament of January 1484, the gathered nobles were reminded of the Titulus Regus, or 'Royal Title', that had been drawn up to legitimize Richard III's claim as the only surviving heir to the throne. The children of Edward IV were declared illegitimate on the basis that at the time of his 'feigned' marriage to the queen, Edward had already been 'married and troth-plighted to one Dame Eleanor Butler'.[573]

Eleanor was married to Sir Thomas Butler, the son of the Lancastrian supporting Ralph Butler, Baron of Sudeley.[574] However, Richard argued that she had previously been formally betrothed to

Edward, who was, back then, Earl of March. This of course meant that his marriage to Elizabeth Woodville in 1464 was illegal and any children born from the marriage illegitimate.

This was undoubtedly a convenient assumption for Richard to make, as it meant, as the sole heir to the throne, he could legitimately take the crown. If the marriage did take place, then Edward seems not to have foreseen any difficulties arising later, and it seems Eleanor too was silent on the matter. She died in around 1468.[575] However, Commines states as a fact that the Bishop of Bath married Edward and a secret bride. Although he does not record her identity, he may be referring to Eleanor when he says that he 'had promised her marriage, upon condition that he might lie with her'.[576]

Whatever the truth, like Malyne de Cay, Eleanor's name was used as a political tool to slash Edward IV's bloodline and legitimize that of his uncle, Richard. It is convenient that anyone who could dispute the wedding was, by 1483, dead, including Edward and Eleanor.

Elizabeth Lucy 'such kindness'

The earliest mention of Elizabeth Lucy's existence, along with her association with Edward, comes from Thomas More in his *History of King Richard III*, written in the early-sixteenth century.[577] George Buck, writing over a hundred years after More, examined her in a little more detail. He identified her as the daughter of a Southampton man named Wyatt, 'a mean gentleman, if he was one'. Buck further names her husband, a man with the surname Lucy, who he says, was as 'mean' as her father.[578] The word 'mean' in medieval society tended to describe someone of lower status or poorer background rather than someone with a cruel or malicious temperament. Although More gives Elizabeth the title 'dame', Buck certainly believed she was of lower rank.

Stow records Elizabeth Lucy's conversation with Edward's mother Cecily Neville. Cecily had 'openly objected' to her son's marriage to Elizabeth Woodville, and summoned Lucy to answer whether he was in fact Lucy's 'husband before God'. Affirming to the duchess that 'they were never ensured', Elizabeth said the king 'spoke so loving words unto her that she verily hoped he would have married her, and that if it had not been for such kind words, she would never have showed such kindness to him to let him so kindly get her with child'.[579]

Edward fathered at least one illegitimate child with Lucy. Baker identifies their son as Arthur Plantagenet, created Lord Lisle during the reign of Henry VIII and hints at an illegitimate daughter named Elizabeth.[580] If Baker's identification of two illegitimate children born to the king by Elizabeth is correct, then their relationship might have been longer-term.

Very little else is known about Elizabeth Lucy. If Buck is right in his identification of her father, she would have been raised among the coasts and forests of rural Hampshire, possibly in Southampton's busy port itself. During her time at Edward's court, however, she would have been well placed to see some of the powerful characters of the wars, and some of its major events. Sadly, without more evidence it is impossible to ascertain what influence, if any, Elizabeth had on the king or his court.

Elizabeth 'Jane' Shore 'unshameful and mischievous woman'

One of the more well-known of Edward IV's mistresses, Elizabeth Shore, was commonly recorded by chroniclers as either 'Shore's wife' or by the first name Jane. Born Elizabeth Lambert, she is named by her birth name in a request for a divorce from her husband William in the mid-1470s.[581] More says that she was attractive, intelligent and well educated. He wrote that men weren't enthralled so much with her beauty as much as they were by 'her pleasant behaviour'. He continues, 'for a proper wit had she, and could both read well and write, merry in company, ready and quick of answer, neither mute nor full of babble, sometime taunting without displeasure, and not without disport'.[582] More wrote extensively about Elizabeth, perhaps to highlight Richard III's later treatment of her for a pro-Tudor audience. However, he was writing while she was still alive and had been told about her by others who knew her.

No contemporary image of Elizabeth survives, although the words of the Elizabethan poet Michael Drayton might reveal more about her appearance. He recorded his impressions of a portrait he believed was Elizabeth, which has since been lost. In the picture Drayton saw, he described her as having dark blonde hair, a rounded face and grey eyes, depicted by the artist with a 'cheerful' expression and seated on a chair.[583]

Edward and Elizabeth had an interesting connection and Edward seems to have encouraged Elizabeth to offer her advice to him. 'Where the king took displeasure', writes More, 'she would mitigate and appease his mind: where men were out of favour, she would bring them in his grace. For many that had highly offended she obtained pardon. Of great forfeitures she got men remission'.[584] More is tantalizingly silent on the identities of the men she helped, but this lack of evidence is to be expected, with arrangements between Elizabeth and the petitioners at court almost certainly made secretly and verbally.

Enjoying influence over Edward along with his protection, Elizabeth held a place at the king's side. But like so many of his associates, her fortunes changed after his death. She was linked to William Hastings before his fall from power in June 1483, and received the anger of Richard, then Duke of Gloucester, who Stow says sent men into her house and seized up to 3,000 marks worth of goods and sent her to prison. Accusing her of witchcraft he also publicly shamed her for her unchaste living, branding her an 'unshameful and mischievous woman'.[585] The word 'mischievous' is interesting here for its connotations of subtle workings or assertion of power, possibly a reference to More's suggestion that she held influence over the late king. Elizabeth was made to walk through London in her kirtle, a long undergarment, processing before a cross while holding a candle. Despite curious stares, she walked with such dignity and solemnity that More said the Londoners 'pitied they more her penance than rejoiced therein'.[586]

With no evidence that he chased down any of his brother's other mistresses, Richard's sole focus on Elizabeth underlines her prominent role at Edward's court. It's also possible of course that Richard may have believed Edward had revealed secrets to Elizabeth that could be damaging to him. She would then need to be discredited before she spoke out. Richard Baker later wondered wryly whether Elizabeth 'might complain why she should do penance for offending lightly against only the Seventh Commandment, and King Richard do none for offending heavily against all the ten', adding dryly that 'perhaps he had gotten some good fellow to be his Confessor'.[587]

Elizabeth was walking through London's streets in 1513 when More portrayed her as a shadow of the woman she once was. He describes her as 'in the more beggarly condition, unfriended and worn out of acquaintance' and 'old, lean, withered and dried up'.[588] This is harsh. Apart from being in 1513 an elderly woman, the stress and uncertainty of the wars would have taken their toll on Elizabeth emotionally as well as physically. She endured anxiety, distress and grief, learning of the executions of men she knew from court and the upheaval of the 1480s. She must have been anxious for her future, facing imprisonment and humiliation. It's no surprise that she kept a low profile after 1483.

More urges us to remember Elizabeth and the difference she made to Edward's court.[589] An eighteenth-century depiction of Elizabeth shows her bare-breasted and heavily jewelled with her hair tightly braided on top of her head. She smiles slightly as she gazes softly towards us. But is this the image she would have wanted history to remember her by? Well educated, literate and with a sharp wit and intelligence all the evidence points to her being more than just

Edward's mistress. Soothing his anger, she appealed to him for the good of others, and she later paid the price for her closeness to the king. A three-dimensional woman of the Wars of the Roses, Elizabeth, or 'Jane' Shore deserves to be remembered as far more than just 'Edward's favourite mistress'.

We have seen the many ways women carried out duties in companionship underneath the main political and military action of the Wars of the Roses. As ladies in waiting and gentlewomen they reflected the king's and queen's status, majesty and legitimacy and impressed ambassadors and spectators at prestigious ceremonies. Working subtly, they influenced decisions and allegiances. As mistresses they unknowingly contributed to falls in power, negotiated on behalf of others and provided what must have been a welcome distraction from the dynastic struggles of the period.

CHAPTER FOURTEEN
BIRTHING A NEW DYNASTY

Although the marriage of Henry VII and Elizabeth of York was said to have united 'the two bloods of high renown', it was the result of their union that sealed it.[590] The baby slumbering in his wooden cot was the undisputed legitimate heir, his veins gently throbbing with the blood of both Lancaster and York. For all anyone knew, as the country's church bells rang out in celebration, the Wars of the Roses was now over, and Arthur would go on to father his own line of kings and queens.

Producing a steady line of royal heirs was vital to political security, but it was no guarantee. Henry VI and Queen Margaret had only one heir, who died at the Battle of Tewkesbury in 1471. Might Margaret have fought on if there had been other heirs in line to their father's crown? Instead, her hopes for Lancaster ended with the death of her only son. Then again, Edward and Elizabeth had ten children. Neither of his sons were crowned after his death in 1483, but his daughter Elizabeth would be, as Henry VII's wife, in 1487.

A princess might hope to marry a foreign prince, stabilizing overseas support and promoting peace. Margaret of York's marriage to the Duke of Burgundy in 1468 certainly helped Edward while in exile during Henry VI's brief return to the throne in 1470-1471. However, girls were not yet permitted to inherit the crown in their own right. Royal parents eagerly anticipated the birth of boys. In April 1469 Luchino Dallaghiexia cooly reported to the Duke of Milan, in a letter that survives in the Calendar of State Papers, that the newborn Cecily Plantagenet was 'a very handsome daughter, which rejoiced the king and all the nobles exceedingly, though they would have preferred a son'.[591]

Back in Edward IV's early reign, John Fortescue, a Lancastrian supporter of Henry VI who served as Chief Justice of England, argued against the Duke of York's claim to the throne because it descended through two women. York's claim came from his descent from Edward III, through Philippa, daughter of Lionel Duke of Clarence, one of Edward III's sons, and her grand-daughter, York's mother, Anne Mortimer. Fortescue wrote that 'no woman by the law and custom ... may or can inherit the crown thereof, for it is only descendable to heirs males'. The duke therefore had 'no true or rightwise claim or title' to the crown.[592] In the politically charged atmosphere following Edward IV's death, Mancini recorded the Duke of Buckingham insisting that it was 'not the business of women but of men to govern kingdoms'.[593] Even John Leland, writing in the mid-sixteenth century, shook his head sadly at the fate of a Neville lord buried at Branspeth Church in Durham who he said, 'lacked heirs males' which triggered a bitter fight between the next heir and the contender to his estates.[594] The inference here was clear. Legitimate princes ensured a peaceful succession and founded strong dynasties.

By the 1480s, in terms of the crown, this was never more necessary. At his first parliament in 1485, Henry listened as those present hoped soon for the 'propagation of offspring from the stock of kings, to comfort the whole realm'.[595]

If a son was crucial to medieval national security, then so were the women delivering them. Behind queens lying full-bellied in beds, temporarily isolated from the outside world, there was an often-overlooked team of midwives, nurses, wet nurses and rockers taking care of tiny, sleeping babies that would one day grow to be kings, queens, dukes and princes. Many worked in comfort with rich, warm hangings and a group of trusted gentlewomen to assist.

For others, the atmosphere was less certain.

Marjory Cobbe 'The midwife of the king's consort'

Inside the walls of Westminster Abbey on 2 November 1470, Marjory Cobbe unfolded a leather bag of small pots and clean cloths, placing them on a wooden table in a corner of the room. The apartments were dark, the sunlight blocked by coverings hastily draped over windows. The air was musty and warm. A fire crackled softly in a recess in the wall.

Elizabeth Woodville was in sanctuary at Westminster with her mother and children. Edward IV, her messengers told her, had escaped overseas and Henry VI had been led into the city to retake his throne. Elizabeth was in a precarious position as a deposed queen and the wife of the king's enemy. As a Lancastrian government starts the work of securing the realm, Elizabeth awaits the birth of a Yorkist heir.

Marjory straightened her coif and secured her apron around her neck and waist. She stepped toward the queen, propped up in a feather bed with thick pillows and bolster cushions, warm coverings tucked over her swollen belly. Marjory took a small bottle and poured a few drops of sweetly scented olive oil onto her fingertips, warming it between the palms of her hands.

We know very little about Marjory. She appeared in a grant with her husband John in the Calendar of Patent Rolls dated April 1469, and is identified as 'the midwife of the king's consort Elizabeth'. The couple received £10 a year from the issues of Staffordshire.[596] Thus Marjory was already employed by Elizabeth before her entry into sanctuary in 1470. From the timing of her 1469 grant, and its naming of her as Elizabeth's midwife, it's likely that she had assisted in the birth of the princess Cecily earlier that year. By November 1475 Marjory was a widow, recorded as receiving an annual payment of £10 from the issues of the county of Devon.[597]

Marjory safely delivered Elizabeth of a son, named Edward after his father. Both Jacquetta Woodville and Lady Scrope were present and would have given their support during the birth.[598] It was normal for a group of gentlewomen and assistants to help the midwife, their presence not only useful for practical reasons but also in case of unexpected problems during labour. Henrietta

Leyser, in *Medieval Women, A Social History of Women in England 450-1500,* pointed out that witnesses to the midwife's actions would be beneficial if questions were raised as to her conduct.[599] Considering the expectations and anticipation of a royal birth, the presence of other ladies was a further insurance for Marjory.

A birth manual published early in the following century called *The Birth of Mankynde, otherwise The Woman's Booke,* urged the midwife to speak 'sweet words' to the mother in encouragement while administering baths and massaging oils onto the belly and back. Some gentle moving around during labour was encouraged. The text also mentions the use of a special birthing stool with a hole in the centre that could help during labour, and as an experienced midwife, this may have been something Marjory owned.[600] Medieval healthcare was still based on the concept of the four humours and there was no knowledge of bacteria, viral infection, or conditions such as postnatal depression or pre-eclampsia.

Without this modern knowledge some mothers of the Wars of the Roses died, even experienced mothers were among those at risk. Elizabeth of York, whose pregnancies would be considered so crucial to the new Tudor dynasty and the conclusion of the wars, died after the birth of her seventh child in 1503. Because of these risks, families could be large. Cecily Neville bore thirteen children, while a brass commemorating John and Elizabeth Baynard in St Cyriac's Church in Lacock, Wiltshire, depicts them with eighteen. Sir Richard Delabere's brass at Hereford Cathedral illustrates the knight's twenty-one children, born of his two wives.

With so much riding on survival, it was necessary at times to ask for divine intervention. Prayers and chanting were considered crucial, along with the use of holy relics. Items linked to saints representing childbirth were preferred, such as the Virgin Mary. Elizabeth of York's accounts record a monk who delivered 'our Lady girdle' to the queen in December 1502.[601] A study on a surviving medieval birth girdle, published by the Royal Society in 2021, found traces of honey, egg and milk remained, and some of the decorations painted on it had been rubbed off and smudged. This demonstrates its use in active labour. This girdle was made of parchment, but the study also found other girdles made of silk or iron.[602]

Spiritual assistance was also needed in the event of illness or death, either of the mother or the child, after or during the birth. In January 1449 on the Isle of Wight, the residents expressed anxiety that women in labour on the island had died without receiving confession because the chaplain was frequently unavailable.[603]

The birth room was expressly for women only, unless a physician or priest was called in an emergency. One story, related by Fabyan, tells of the birth of Elizabeth and Edward's first child in February 1466. Master Dominic, a royal physician, had predicted the queen would deliver a boy. Impatient to be the first to deliver the news to Edward, in hope of 'great thank and reward of the king', he hovered anxiously outside the chamber waiting for the baby's high-pitched cry. On hearing it, he knocked, asking what sex the child was. A woman opened the wooden door a crack, pressed her face up to his and quipped, 'whatsoever the queen's grace hath here within, sure it is that a fool standeth there without'.[604] No doubt the woman was eager to get back to the important business of caring for the mother and baby in the throng of the birthing room. The child was in fact, a princess, Elizabeth of York.

The Royal Nurses 'The keeping and governance of women'

The hopes of a nation rested on the exhausted newborn sleeping peacefully in the cradle, swaddled with velvet and ermine coverings. Once the midwife left, responsibility for the care of the child transferred to the nurses of the royal household.

The importance the royal family attached to their nurses can be seen in the many rewards they were granted, some profiting from the actions of traitors during the wars. In 1460, Henry VI granted

Joan Sloo, 'nurse of Edward, prince of Wales', forty marks a year 'in the king's hands by the rebellion of Richard Duke of York'.[605] Marion Chamber was Edward Plantagenet's nurse, the son of George, Duke of Clarence, and Isabel Neville. In 1480 she and her husband received proceeds from the boy's lands in Oxfordshire during his minority.[606]

Just like royal servants, the gratitude royals felt for their nurses extended long after the children had grown up and left the nursery. In 1458 Henry VI awarded Margaret Benet, his childhood nurse, 100 shillings a year.[607] We also see nurses acknowledged for their service to both the child and the parent, Edward IV granting Joan Turgys £20 a year 'for her good service to the king's father and to the king while at a tender age'. Similarly, Richard III awarded Joan Malpas with twenty marks annually, 'for her good service to the king in his youth and to his mother the Duchess of York'.[608] Some were rewarded for even longer service. Joan Waryn, wet nurse to Henry V, was still being supported by his son's government in 1426, receiving £20 a year.[609]

However, even royal fledglings had to leave the nursery and take their place in the outside world. The perception of the feminine world of the nursery, in the medieval mind, contrasted sharply with the masculine and intrepid territory of men, as one commission preserved in the Patent Rolls of 1460, during the reign of Henry VI, shows:

'Commission to Alesia, Lady Lovell, reciting her service to Edward Prince of Wales, in his tender days, and discharging her from attendance about his person, because he is now so grown as to be committed to the rules and teachings of men wise and strenuous, to understand the acts and manners of a man befitting such a prince, rather than to stay further under the keeping and governance of women; and because she is oppressed with grave infirmities in body and sight'.[610]

Care was taken to instil the ideals of a strong and vigorous kingship even at a young age. The Household Ordinances of the future Edward V, carefully set out by his parents Edward IV and Elizabeth Woodville in 1473 when the prince was still a toddler, specified that for his education their 'dearest first begotten son' should hear 'such noble stories as behoveth to a prince to understand'.[611] Additionally, to encourage the young boy to be brought up as a solemn and respectable future king, those around him, whether man or woman, were not to swear, brawl or 'use words of ribaldry, and especially in the presence of our said son'.[612]

The behaviour of the men and women around the young prince was monitored, but nurses were given permission to chastise the future monarch while teaching them basic manners and upbringing. Dame Alice Boteler, Henry VI's nurse, was given royal approval to punish the two-year-old king and 'chastise us reasonably from time to time'. At the age of seven he was removed from Alice's care and placed with Richard Beauchamp, the older Earl of Warwick. Warwick's responsibilities echo the sentiment of Alesia Lovell's later commission, with the king under his care to learn literature, language and 'cunning as his age shall suffer him to more comprehend, such as it fitteth so great a prince to be learned of'.[613] Alice may be the 'Lady Butiller' mentioned in a list of New Year's gifts given to the king in 1437. The inventory notes a 'little tablet of gold made in manner of a book and enamelled within on that one side with an image of the Trinity and on that other side with an image of Our Lady and her Son'. Sparkling with garnets and sapphires, it was an expensive and thoughtful gift for the pious Henry and could have been given to the fifteen-year-old king by his old nurse in remembrance of her and to mark the beginning of his adulthood.[614]

In 1494 Henry VII wrote a detailed Household Ordinance, setting out the structure of the household of his sons. These rules would have been used for both Arthur and Henry's upbringing, along with any other future sons born to the royal couple. It allocated staff to the nursery including a governess, chamberers or rockers, yeomen, and grooms. Anyone working there swore 'straight oaths' to the Chamberlain. The nurses and rockers would soothe the prince's cries and place him in a cradle painted with the king's arms, a constant reminder of the special treatment and safeguarding that this tiny, crucially important baby should receive.[615]

Emlyn Hobbes 'our dearest son the Prince'

At Greenwich on 27 May 1491, Henry VII wrote to his Treasurer and the Chamberlains of his Exchequer concerning the wages of certain women looking after Prince Arthur. The four-year-old prince was looked after by 'our dear and well beloved' Dame Elizabeth Darcy, the 'lady mistress' of his household, along with two 'rokkers', Agnes Butler and Emlyn Hobbes. Emlyn and Agnes would have had to make oaths of good conduct and secrecy before being appointed. With Arthur now four years old, their responsibilities would have extended to more than just rocking him to sleep; they probably included overseeing the day-to-day care of the prince as well as tucking him in for the night. Henry's gratitude to them is in any case evident, calling them 'our wellbeloved' and urging the Treasurer to pay them quickly, willing their speedy contention'.[616]

Henry's letter reveals the typical wages a rocker to a Tudor prince could expect to receive. He directs the Treasurer to pay Emlyn and Agnes thirty-three shillings and fourpence each.[617] A letter written by the king in the following month confirms the wages of those in Arthur's sister's household, the eighteen-month-old Princess Margaret. Anne Maylande, Margaret Troughton and her day wife Alice Bwymble, all received the same wages as Emlyn, presumably the going rate for a rocker in the royal household.[618]

The Patent Rolls of February 1487 state that Arthur's nursery was established at Farnham in Surrey.[619] Here Emlyn came into contact with the king and queen when they visited him there with men of his household, including Richard Howell, Marshal of the

Prince's Household, in 1490.[620] Emlyn and the other ladies would also have been closely supervised when feeding the prince, Henry's Ordinances specified that a physician would stand over the nurse 'every meal, and see what meat or drink she give the child'.[621]

The names of Emlyn, and the other ladies working in the royal nurseries, are largely forgotten, but they were crucial for the security of the much-needed Tudor heir. Emlyn fed and cared for Arthur despite lingering threats posed to Henry's throne. As Henry signed the letter to authorize the payment of Emlyn's wages, he had recently defeated the supporters of Lambert Simnel. Soon, he would face another Yorkist-led plan to seize his throne as Perkin Warbeck entered the realm, with his wife Katherine Gordon in tow.

Royal families certainly placed a great deal of effort in employing, overseeing, and setting out the duties of midwives and nurses. Some received generous rewards and benefitted directly from falls in favour that resulted from the Wars of the Roses. Others found themselves in the possession of grants or other revenue as a reward for their long and faithful service. With strict controls over their behaviour, they were to ensure princes remained uncorrupted and listened to stories of brave and valiant kings before being tucked into bed.

Working invisibly underneath the wars' narrative, their position must, at times, have been stressful. Bells rang across the realm to celebrate the birth of a legitimate heir, realizing the nation's hopes after decades of conflict, for a smooth transfer of royal power. But the work was not done yet. Henry VI's accession in 1422, while still a baby, triggered dynastic struggles and fuelled the ambitions of powerful characters who set their sights on the crown. It was essential that Arthur grow to adulthood, learn the business of ruling from his father and have the strength to keep ambitious nobles in check. But first he had to survive into his teenage years, and this responsibility fell to now-forgotten women: midwives, nurses, wet nurses and rockers.

EPILOGUE

In the process of researching this book I found myself reading about Katherine Gordon. A Scottish woman of high birth, she found herself at the centre of an attempted invasion against Henry VII, as the wife of pretender Perkin Warbeck. Establishing herself securely under the Tudors she died in middle age in 1537. The next day I was scrolling through an account of the trial and execution of Ankarette Twynhoe, a relatively obscure grandmother, inadvertently tangled up in the paranoia and ruthlessness of the age. In three hours, she had been formally accused, tried and sentenced to a hasty execution. The experiences of these two women demonstrate how quickly, and unexpectedly, the period could either raise a person to security and safety or throw them to ruin.

The christening of Prince Arthur was, to the Tudors, the dawn of a new age. However, Henry's reign in 1486 was still far from secure. He would face the Yorkist pretenders Lambert Simnel in 1487 and Perkin Warbeck in the 1490s. Yorkist heads would continue to tumble from the executioner's block: the Earl of Warwick, son of George, Duke of Clarence in 1499, and another less well-known pretender Ralph Wulford in the same year. As silk women and laundresses busily produced textiles and hangings for the christening, and nurses rocked Arthur's cradle, the threat to the Yorkist bloodline continued to pose a dormant threat long into the reign of not only Henry, but his son, Henry VIII.

In public and private the realm's seamstresses, weavers, embroiderers and laundresses underscored the reigns of kings and queens that processed through streets. People grumbled in the streets at the fragile, dishevelled Henry VI in 1470, but ambassadors praised the cut of Edward IV's gowns and ability to govern in the same sentence. A show of wealth was a show of power and royal prestige.

Women played a part in the social backbone of the wars too. They acted as ambassadors and assistants for their lawyer and sheriff husbands. They rode away from home on errands and physically defended their homes and estates with weapons, commanding armed men. Others managed businesses impacted by the wars. We have seen how the conflict affected merchants as well, and at least one woman who led some of the wars' characters through the musty corridors of the Fleet.

Women also made up a proportion of the large number of rebels that reacted to unrest while others organized horses and cash and co-ordinated supplies. Some even took the law into their own hands and supplied weapons from the sidelines for family feuds and local skirmishes.

Thousands of women had their own experiences of the Wars of the Roses. They lost loved ones on the battlefield and by execution. Some took sanctuary in religious houses and others took vows of chastity and devotion, praying for the prematurely departed souls of the wars' victims. Rebellion and war even sometimes came to them as they sheltered from hails of arrows and hand to hand combat in their streets and near their homes.

Companionship was provided by women from all strata of medieval society, from noble-born gentlewomen to those providing entertainment to soothe the king's worries for an evening. There were mistresses and lovers, and we have seen how people like Elizabeth 'Jane' Shore may have exerted more influence during the wars than is often claimed. Finally, there were the rockers, midwives and nurses, carefully selected and employed to usher in a new dynasty of, preferably, male heirs.

These women's stories reveal bravery, courage, loyalty and strength, contrasting with the medieval ideal of meekness and submission. At this time, more than ever before, a woman who could issue legal proceedings, question the cost of goods, and physically defend her home if needed, was valuable to her family and wider community. However, the surviving documents suggest that, rather than actively campaigning for equal rights, they were simply fulfilling the duties expected of them. Organizing weapons for a siege, negotiating with rebels for a ransom, or asking their husband to collect almonds on the way home from work, they were a crucial part of the nation's workforce, acting alongside men. The many ways in which they contributed to the social, political, military, and religious structure of the Wars of the Roses, as well as their actions and experiences, should not go unnoticed when discussing its history.

ENDNoTES

Part One, Chapter One: The Consequences of War

1. William Shakespeare, *Henry VI* Part 3, Act 2 Scene 5
2. Fenn, vol. 1, p127
3. Croyland, p419
4. Hall, p205
5. Gregory, p212
6. Stow, p659
7. *Chronicles of the White Rose of York*, plii
8. Vergil, p111
9. Stow, p701
10. Stow, p721 and Strickland, vol. 2, p221
11. Strickland, vol. 2, p289
12. Percy Society, *Early English Poetry,* p40
13. The Home Treasury, *The Ballad of Chevy Chase* p52-53
14. Cokayne, vol. 7, p274
15. Cokayne, vol. 7, p275
16. Percy Society, *Early English Poetry,* p39
17. Percy Society, *Early English Poetry,* pvi
18. Nicholas, *Testamenta Vetusta* vol.1 p304, Fenn vol. 1, p18
19. Baker, p234
20. Stanley, *The House of Stanley,* p142-143
21. Fenn, vol. 2, p1
22. Fenn, vol. 2, p2
23. Fenn, vol. 2, p2
24. Castor, *Blood and Roses,* p283
25. Croyland, p418
26. Cokayne vol. 7, p171
27. Weir, *Lancaster and York,* p136
28. Cokayne, vol. 7, p171
29. Cokayne, vol. 2, p64
30. Higginbotham, Susan. *The Mysterious Margaret Beaufort, Countess of Stafford* (article) www.susanhigginbotham.com/posts/the-mysterious-margaret-beaufort-countess-of-stafford/ [accessed 20 January 2023]
31. Cokayne, vol. 7, p171-172
32. Cokayne, vol. 7, p171
33. Wood, *Letters of Illustrious Ladies* vol. 1, p98
34. Cokayne, vol. 7, p73
35. Stow, p644
36. Wood, *Letters of Illustrious Ladies* vol. 1, p98
37. Stow, p678
38. Stow, p679 and Hall, p245
39. Stow, p679 and Gregory, p211
40. Cokayne, vol. 7, p73. Danielle Burton's help here has also been invaluable,

sharing some of her research on Elizabeth Scales as well as the dispute over the date of her marriage to Anthony Woodville.

41. Stow, p701
42. Cokayne vol. 7, p73
43. Commines, p394
44. Gregory, p193
45. Fenn, vol. 1, p22
46. Noorthouck, 'Cade's Rebellion', pp94-106 (British History Online)
47. Nichols, J.G. *Chronicle of the Rebellion in Lincolnshire* 'Confession of Sir Robert Welles', p21
48. Scofield, vol. 1, p592
49. Holinshed, p513
50. Davis, Norman, *Paston Letters,* p93-94 and also cited in Castor, Helen p152
51. *List of Early Chancery Proceedings*, vol. 1, Bundle 19, p191
52. CCR, 1447-1454, p142
53. CPR, 1452-1461, p342
54. CPR, 1452-1461, p416, p485, p527, p536, p605
55. Flenley, Ralph, *Six Town Chronicles of England*, p149 and CCR 1461-1468, p57
56. Fabyan, Robert, p624
57. Hall, p222
58. Harcourt, Edward William, p67
59. Harcourt, Edward William, p70 and *Collections for a History of Staffordshire* p202-203. There is some debate over the year of Robert's death, some sources dating it to 1471. However, 1470 is the date of death stated on his Inquisition Post Mortem the following year. (p203 *History of Staffordshire*)
60. *Collections for a History of Staffordshire,* p202
61. Stow, p668
62. Gregory, p211
63. William Shakespeare, *Richard III.* Act 5, Scene 5

Chapter Two: Business As Usual

64. CPR 1446-1452, p255
65. Fitzherbert, *The Book of Husbandry* pp95-101
66. Kingsford, Stonor Letters, vol. 1, p110
67. Rickert, Edith, p36
68. Fenn, vol. 1, p34
69. Landry, pp14-25
70. Skeat, Walter, p98
71. Fenn, vol. 2, pp65-66
72. Stonor Letters, vol. 2, p91
73. Stonor Letters, vol. 1, 'Inventory of Jane Stonor: Heirlooms in the chapel and house at Stonor', p145-146
74. Kerry, Rev Charles, *Journal of the Derbyshire Archaeological and Natural History Society*, vol. 20, 1898. 'The Will of Elizabeth Fitzherbert of Norbury', pp32-39
75. Nicolas, *Testamenta Vetusta*, vol. 1, p256 and pp422-423
76. Nicolas, *Testamenta Vetusta*, vol. 1, p295 and 356

77. Nicolas, *Testamenta Vetusta*, vol. 1, p258 and Nichols, *Wills of Eminent Persons,* p2
78. Nicolas, *Testamenta Vetusta*, vol. 1, p330 and p435
79. Fenn, vol. 1, p40
80. Torlesse, p39
81. Christine de Pisan, p115
82. *Southampton Terrier*, p65, 79, 89, 91, 93
83. Leland *Itinerary*, vol. 1, p276-278
84. Davies, J.S., *A History of Southampton*, p73-202
85. Watson, Gemma Louise (2013), "Roger Machado: A Life in Objects", The University of Southampton, Faculty of Humanities, Archaeology, English and History, PhD Thesis, p119-120
86. *Southampton Terrier*, p91
87. Davies, J.S. *A History of Southampton*, p472
88. Davies, J.S. *A History of Southampton*, p470
89. Leland, *Itinerary*, vol. 9-11, p72
90. Stonor Letters, vol. 1, xxvi
91. Stonor Letters, vol. 1, xxvii
92. Stonor Letters, vol. 2, p18
93. Stonor Letters, vol. 2, p14 and 42
94. Stonor Letters, vol. 2, p11
95. Stonor Letters, vol. 2, p18
96. Stonor Letters, vol. 2. p98
97. Collier, p48-49
98. Collier, p98
99. Collier, p184, p186, p206 and p218
100. Christine de Pisan, p112
101. Goldberg, P.J.P., (1995), p15
102. *Testamenta Vetusta* vol. 1, p404
103. Fenn, vol. 1, p185
104. Davis, The Paston Letters, p137
105. Fenn, vol. 1, p39, p196 and vol. 2, p17
106. Fenn, vol. 1, p69, p85
107. Davis, The Paston Letters, p257
108. Stonor Letters, vol. 2, p15
109. Gerard, John, p1354 and Stonor Letters vol. 2, p45
110. Rickert, Edith, p97
111. CPR 1467-1477, p24
112. CPR 1461-1467, p380
113. CPR 1442-1461, p269
114. CPR 1476-1483, p383
115. Penn, Thomas, Audible audiobook, 21:43:28
116. Moore, Joseph S., p27-35
117. Torlesse, p37
118. Cokayne, vol. 6, p44
119. Davis, Paston Letters, p77
120. Davis, Paston Letters, p84, also cited in Castor, p151

121. Castor, p150
122. Botfield, p304
123. Gerard, John, p744-745
124. Botfield, p312
125. Torlesse, p38
126. Pryce, p101
127. Pryce, p114 and C. T. Jefferies, A Guide to St Mary Redcliffe Church, Bristol (C. T. Jefferies, Bristol, 1858) p57 (British Library, Public Domain)
128. Rickart, Robert, p43 and Stow, p691
129. Pryce, p124
130. Christine de Pisan, p129, p131
131. Stow, p700
132. Stonor Letters, vol. 2, p73
133. Dallaway, p209

Chapter Three: The Business of Marriage

134. Stonor Letters, vol. 2, p19
135. Cokayne, vol. 2, p430
136. CPR 1452-1461, p64
137. Clark, p76 and p370
138. For example, see Higginbotham, p83 and K. L. Clark, p279
139. Cokayne, vol. 4, p252-3
140. Stow, p668 and CPR 1452-1461, p410
141. Norton, p22-23
142. Fenn, vol. 2, p20
143. Kingsford, C.L. *Prejudice and Promise in Fifteenth Century England,* p121
144. Deeds 9111-9113, in *A Descriptive Catalogue of Ancient Deeds*: Volume 4, ed. H. C. Maxwell Lyte (London, 1902), pp. 392-401. www.british-history.ac.uk [accessed 25 August 2022].
145. Baker, Richard, p205
146. Milan: 1465', in *Calendar of State Papers and Manuscripts in the Archives and Collections of Milan 1385-1618*, ed. Allen B Hinds (London, 1912), pp. 115-117. British History Online [accessed 18 July 2021] and also pp110-114 www.british-history.ac.uk [accessed 10 March 2022].
147. Cokayne, vol. 6, p213-214
148. CPR 1461-1467, p114
149. *Testamenta Vetusta,* p305
150. Strickland, vol. 2, p414
151. Strickland, vol. 2, p414
152. Strickland, vol. 2, p415
153. André, Bernard, p33
154. Cokayne vol. 1, p331-2
155. Smyth, p154,p172
156. Smyth, p128
157. Smyth, p173
158. Cokayne vol. 1, p324

159. Hookham, p348
160. Smyth, piii
161. Smyth, p173-5

Chapter Four: Raising the Children
162. Stow, p687
163. Holinshed, p277
164. Stow, p736
165. 'Spain: 1493', in *Calendar of State Papers, Spain*, Volume 1, 1485-1509, ed. G A Bergenroth (London, 1862), pp. 43-51 www.british-history.ac.uk [accessed 11 August 2022].
166. Robinson, Rev. Charles. *A History of the Castles of Herefordshire and Their Lords*, Longmsn and Co., London, 1869) Appendix, pv.
167. Davis, Rev. F.N. *The Canterbury and York Society, Canterbury and York Series* vol. 25, 1909. p89
168. Stow, p789
169. Stow, p789
170. Visit to Hereford Cathedral, January 2023
171. Leland, *Itinerary*, vol.1, p45
172. Strickland, vol. 2, p410
173. Commines, p396-397
174. Vergil, p134-135
175. *Testamenta Vetusta*, p304
176. Fenn, vol. 1, p179-180
177. Fenn, vol. 1, p83
178. Fenn, vol. 2, p34
179. Nineteenth-century casts of the Norbury effigies of Elizabeth and Ralph Fitzherbert can also be seen at the Victoria and Albert Museum in London.
180. Cox, Charles J., p237-238
181. CPR 1461-67, p102
182. CPR 1467-77, pp349
183. CPR 1467-77, p405, CPR 1476-1485 p395, p400
184. Dom Bede Camm, *Forgotten Shrines: an account of some old Catholic halls and families in England, and of relics and memorials of the English martyrs*, (MacDonald and Evans, London,1910), p6
185. Skeat, Walter, p95-98
186. Derbyshire Archaeological and Natural History Society, 'The Will of Elizabeth Fitzherbert', pp32-39
187. Cox, p236-7
188. The Will of Elizabeth Fitzherbert, pp32-39
189. *Journal of the Derbyshire Archaeological and Natural History Society*, vol 17, 1897. 'The Abstract of The Will of Ralph Fitzherbert', p94-100
190. Cothi, Lewis Glyn, *The Poetical Works of Lewis Glyn Cothi*, (London, 1837), p1
191. Prichard, p435-7
192. White, John, *Guide to the town and neighbourhood of Abergavenny*, (J.H.Morgan, 1845), p84-86

193. *Guide to Raglan castle, including many interesting particulars connected with its history,* (Waugh and Son, Monmouth,1880), p32

Chapter Five: Women of the Wars in Work
194. Vyner, p17
195. Jesse, p238
196. Ashton, John. *The Fleet: its river, prison and marriages,* Scribner, New York, 1888), p235-236
197. Howard, Henry. *The poems of Henry Howard, Earl of Surrey,* (Bell and Daldy, London, 1871), pxxix
198. Jonathan Mackman and Matthew Stevens, 'CP40/825: Michaelmas term 1467', in Court of Common Pleas: the National Archives, Cp40 1399-1500 (London, 2010), www.british-history.ac.uk [accessed 17 May 2022].
199. *Calendar of Inquisitions Post Mortem And Other Analogous Documents Preserved In the Public Record Office.* (Makie, London, 1904), p30
200. Stow, p645
201. Devon, Frederick. *Issues of the Exchequer, Henry III to Henry VI Inclusive, with Appendix.* (John Murray, London, 1837), p488. Modern currency equivalent calculated at www.nationalarchives.gov.uk/currency-converter
202. CPR 1467-1477, p50
203. Fenn, vol. 1, p191
204. Fenn, vol. 2, p42
205. Commines, p192
206. Cely Papers, p46, p48, p54-55
207. Commines, p198
208. Vergil, p143
209. CPR 1452-1461, p438, p436 and CPR 1461-1467, p36
210. Holinshed, p333
211. Stow, p798
212. Stow, p665
213. Rozmital, p63 and Cely papers, p57
214. Cely Papers, p82-83
215. Burgess, Clive, Part 3, p21
216. Scofield, vol. 2, p420
217. Sellers, Maud. *The York Mercers and Merchant Adventurers, 1356-1917,* (The Surtees Society, 1918), p64
218. Fabyan, p633
219. CPR 1467-1477, p354
220. Evans, p19
221. Scofield, vol. 2, p416
222. Burgess, Clive, Part 3, p22
223. Burgess, Clive, Part 3, p396
224. Burgess, Clive, Part 3, p374-5
225. Burgess, Clive, Part 1, p17
226. Burgess, Clive, Part 3, p22
227. Botfield, p165

228. 'Lichfield: History to c.1500', in *A History of the County of Stafford*: Volume 14, Lichfield, ed. M W Greenslade (London, 1990), pp. 4-14. www.british-history. ac.uk/vch/staffs/vol14/pp4-14 [accessed 25 August 2022]. Modern equivalent of currency obtained at www.nationalarchives.gov.uk/currency-converter
229. Telford, p147 also in Goldberg, P.J.P., (1995) p213
230. Fabyan, p670
231. Karras, p35
232. Fenn, vol.1, p22
233. Flenley, p133
234. Rendle, William and Norman, Phillip. *The Inns of Southwark and Their Associations*, (Longmans, Green and Co, London, 1888), p130
235. Stow, p645
236. Nichols, *Chronicle of the Greyfriars*, p19
237. Shakespeare, *Henry VI Part Two,* Act 4, Scene 8
238. Gregory, p194
239. CCR, 1450, p174 and 1452, p348
240. Rozmital, p54
241. Percy Society, *Early English Poetry*, p50, p53
242. Collier, p245
243. Botfield, p160-161 and p151
244. Hall, p236
245. Fenn, vol. 2, p65
246. Stonor Letters, vol. 1, p110
247. CCR, 1454-1461, p401
248. Stow, p686
249. 'Milan: 1461', in *Calendar of State Papers and Manuscripts in the Archives and Collections of Milan 1385-1618*, ed. Allen B Hinds (London, 1912), pp. 37-106. www.british-history.ac.uk [accessed 25 January 2023].
250. Davies, J.S., *An English Chronicle*, p79
251. Croyland, p444
252. Botfield, p230
253. Leland, *Itinerary* vol. 1, p41
254. Holinshed, p418

Chapter Six: The Wheel of Fortune
255. Hall, p241
256. Shakespeare, William, *Henry VI Part 2,* Act 3, Scene 1
257. Cokayne, vol. 6, p371
258. Mancini, p77
259. Gristwood, p163
260. Mancini, p89
261. Cokayne, vol. 2, p64
262. CPR 1476-1485, p436
263. Cokayne, vol. 1, pp293-295
264. Cokayne, vol. 4, pp369-70
265. McCaffrey, Carmel, *In Search of Ireland's Heroes: the story of the Irish from the*

English invasion to the present day. (Ivan R. Dee, Chicago, 2006), p41

266. Cokayne, vol. 6, p276

267. Healy, John, *Maynooth College, its centenary history,* (Browne and Nolan, Dublin, 1895), p129-130

268. Leinster, Charles William Fitzgerald, *The Earls of Kildare and their Ancestors from 1057-1773,* (Hodges, Smith and Co, Dublin, 1858), p58 and p79

269. MacCarthy, *Annals of Ulster,* p315

270. Leinster, Charles William Fitzgerald, *The Earls of Kildare and their Ancestors from 1057-1773,* (Hodges, Smith and Co, Dublin, 1858), p56-57

271. Cokayne, vol. 4, p370

272. Cokayne, vol. 6, p167

273. 'Henry VII: November 1485, Part 1', in *Parliament Rolls of Medieval England,* www.british-history.ac.uk [accessed 25 January 2023], article 8

274. 'Henry VII: November 1485, Part 1', in *Parliament Rolls of Medieval England,* www.british-history.ac.uk [accessed 25 January 2023], article 8

275. Cokayne, vol. 7, p39

276. 'Henry VIII: June 1541, 1-10', in *Letters and Papers, Foreign and Domestic, Henry VIII,* Volume 16, 1540-1541, ed. James Gairdner and R H Brodie (London, 1898), pp. 429-437, www.british-history.ac.uk/letters-papers-hen8/vol16/pp429-437 [accessed 9 August 2022]

Part Two, Chapter Seven: Overlooked Royal Women

277. Gairdner, James (ed). *Letters and Papers Illustrative of the Reigns of Richard III and Henry VII,* (Longman, Green, Longman and Roberts, London, 1861), vol. 1, p32

278. Strickland vol. 2, p328 and *A Collection of Ordinances* 'Cecily Neville', p37 and Wood, *Letters of Illustrious Ladies,* p107

279. Cokayne, vol. 8, p214-215

280. Wood, *Illustrious Ladies,* p117

281. Cokayne, vol. 8, p214-215

282. Gregory, p208

283. Licence, Amy, *Cecily, Mother of Kings,* Kindle ebook, Location 1101. For mention of the St Christopher see Nichols, *Wills of Eminent Persons*, p2

284. Fabyan, p635

285. Wood, *Illustrious Ladies,* p106

286. Nichols, *Wills of Eminent Persons* p7

287. Nichols, *Wills of Eminent Persons,* p2-3

288. *A Collection of Ordinances,* 'Cecily Neville', p37

289. Nichols, *Wills of Eminent Persons,* p2

290. Strickland, vol. 2, p336

291. Cokayne, vol. 3, p298

292. CPR 1461-1467, p104

293. See, for example CPR 1461-1467, p7 and Stow, p707

294. Fabyan, p663

295. Croyland, p464

296. Fenn, vol. 2, p9

297. Croyland, p464 and Commines p201, p368
298. Baker, p239 and André, Bernard, p45
299. Hall, p433
300. Hall, p462-463
301. Hall, p472
302. Strickland, vol. 2, p236
303. Stow, p684
304. 'Milan: 1461', in *Calendar of State Papers and Manuscripts in the Archives and Collections of Milan 1385-1618*, ed. Allen B Hinds (London, 1912), pp. 37-106. www.british-history.ac.uk [accessed 21 October 2022].
305. Stow, p693
306. More, p110
307. Hall p407, Vergil p211
308. Strickland, vol. 2, p382
309. Rous, John. Part 62
310. Commines, p188
311. 'Milan: 1467', in Calendar of State Papers and Manuscripts in the Archives and Collections of Milan 1385-1618, ed. Allen B Hinds (London, 1912), pp. 117-122. www.british-history.ac.uk [accessed 27 September 2022]
312. Cokayne, vol. 4, p45
313. Strickland, vol. 2, p382
314. Croyland, p498
315. CPR 1476-1485 p477 and Mancini, p89
316. Gristwood, p144
317. Rous, John. Part 62
318. Croyland, p497
319. Weir, Alison. *Elizabeth of York The First Tudor Queen*. Audible audiobook, 2013
320. Watts, Alaric Alexander (ed) *The Literary Souvenir*. 'The Young Novice', Mary Russell Mitford. (Longman, Rees, Brown and Green, London, 1829), p290
321. Privy Purse Accounts of Elizabeth of York, p29
322. Strickland, vol. 2, p371

Chapter Eight: Religious Sanctuary
323. Croyland, p419
324. Cokayne, vol. 7, p138
325. Cokayne, vol. 8, 143
326. 'The ancient parish of Barking: Abbeys and churches founded before 1830', in *A History of the County of Essex*: Volume 5, ed. W R Powell (London, 1966), pp. 222-231, www.british-history.ac.uk/vch/essex/vol5/pp222-231 [accessed 6 August 2022].
327. CPR 1446-1452 p320
328. Blacman, p30
329. 'Rymer's Foedera with Syllabus: November 1440', in Rymer's *Foedera* Volume 10, ed. Thomas Rymer (London, 1739-1745), pp. 817-834. www.british-history.ac.uk/rymer-foedera/vol10/pp817-834 [accessed 6 August 2022]. Currency calculated at www.nationalarchives.gov.uk/currency-converter/

330. CPR 1446-1452, p355
331. Alice Raw. Gender and Protest in Late Medieval England, c.1400–c.1532. *The English Historical Review*, Volume 136, Issue 582, October 2021, Pages 1148–1163, https://doi.org/10.1093/ehr/ceab280
332. CPR 1467-1477, p388
333. CPR 1461-1467, p428
334. 'Houses of Cistercian nuns: Priory of Whistones', in *A History of the County of Worcester*, Volume 2, ed. J W Willis-Bund and William Page (London, 1906) p155
335. Warkworth, p15. The brass monument to Chief Justice Sir Thomas Urswyk and Lady, Saint Peter and Paul Dagenham, Essex (1479) can be seen in *Illustrations of Monumental Brasses*, (Camden Society, Cambridge, 1846)
336. Croyland, p422-423
337. Rozmital, p60
338. CPR 1467-1477, p392
339. CPR 1446-1452, p86
340. CPR 1467-1477, p138
341. *Testamenta Vetusta*, p404. Currency calculation made at www.nationalarchives.gov.uk/currency-converter
342. *Testamenta Vetusta* p357
343. Clay, William Keatinge. *A History of the Parish of Waterbeach in the County of Cambridge*. (C.J. Clay, University Press, 1859), p112-113
344. Bourdillon, A. F. C. *The Order of Minoresses in England*. (Manchester University Press, 1926) p119-120
345. Buck, N. *The North-East View of Denny Priory*, Near Cambridge. S & N Buck, London. 1730
346. Clay, William Keatinge, *A History of the Parish of Waterbeach in the County of Cambridge*. (C.J. Clay, University Press, 1859), p112-113
347. 'House of Benedictine nuns: The priory of King's Mead', in *A History of the County of Derby*: Volume 2, ed. William Page (London, 1907), pp. 43-45, www.british-history.ac.uk/vch/derbs/vol2/pp43-45 [accessed 18 August 2022].
348. Clay, William Keatinge, *A History of the Parish of Waterbeach in the County of Cambridge*. (C.J. Clay, University Press, 1859), p111
349. CPR 1467-1477, p190
350. Power, Eileen, p459
351. Thompson, *Visitations*, p112
352. CPR 1467-1477, p190
353. CPR 1467-1477, p190
354. CPR 1452-1461, p481
355. Power, Eileen, p61
356. Davies, J. S., *An English Chronicle*, p96
357. Davies, J. S., *An English Chronicle*, p97
358. Leland, *Itinerary*, vol. 1, p8-9
359. Davies, J. S., *An English Chronicle*, p98
360. CPR 1476-1485, p280

Chapter Nine: Overcoming Adversity

361. André, Bernard, p12
362. Vergil, p177
363. Baker, Richard, p226
364. Rickert, Edith, p45
365. Moore, J.S., p182
366. Wood, Mary Everett, *Letters of Royal and Illustrious Ladies,* p101-103
367. Wood, Mary Everett, *Letters of Royal and Illustrious Ladies,* p104
368. Fenn, vol. 2, p81
369. CPR 1467-1477, p455
370. Wood, Mary Everett, *Letters of Royal and Illustrious Ladies,* p101
371. Rous, John. Part 56
372. Rous, John. Introduction p2
373. Rous, John. Part 56
374. Croyland, p470
375. Moore, J.S., p42
376. Leland, *Itinerary,* p263-4
377. Cokayne, vol. 4, p276 and Hoare, p96
378. Hoare, p105
379. Cokayne, vol. 4, p276-277
380. Hoare, p99
381. Hoare, p101
382. Hoare, p101
383. Hoare, p93
384. Hoare p97-98
385. Napier, p25 and p29
386. Napier, p30-31
387. Flenley, p118
388. CPR 1446-1452, p174
389. Strickland, vol. 2, p178, p192
390. 'Henry VI: November 1449', in *Parliament Rolls of Medieval England,* www.
     british-history.ac.uk/no-series/parliament-rolls-medieval/november-1449
     [accessed 4 August 2022].
391. Hall, p217
392. Fenn, vol. 1, p18
393. Leland, *Itinerary,* vol. 1, p112
394. 'Henry VI: November 1450', in *Parliament Rolls of Medieval England,* www.
     british-history.ac.uk/no-series/parliament-rolls-medieval/november-1450
     [accessed 9 August 2022].
395. CPR 1446-1452, p431
396. Napier, p96, p108, p100
397. Gairdner, James. *The Paston Letters 1422-1509, Volume 4,* (Chatto and Windus,
     London, 1904), p221
398. Public Record Office. *A Descriptive Catalogue of Ancient Deeds in the Public Record
     Office. vol. 5,* (Mackie and Co, London, 1906), p95-96
399. Ashmole, Elias. *The History of the Most Noble Order of the Garter,* Printed 1715

400. Ashmole, Elias. *The History of the Most Noble Order of the Garter*, Printed 1715, p276
401. Amin, Nathen, p218
402. 'Spain: December 1495', in Calendar of State Papers, Spain, Volume 1, 1485-1509, ed. G A Bergenroth (London, 1862), pp. 72-79. www.british-history. ac.uk/cal-state-papers/spain/vol1/pp72-79 [accessed 29 January 2023].
403. André, Bernard, p65
404. Hall, p483
405. Hall, p485
406. Holinshed p519 and Grafton Continuation in Hardyng, p581
407. André, Bernard, p68
408. André, Bernard, p69
409. Traherne, p12
410. Traherne, p10
411. Traherne, p16
412. Traherne, p24-25
413. CPR 1461-1467, p231
414. CPR 1467-1477, p584-585
415. CPR, 1467-1477, p329 also 'Edward IV: November 1461', in *Parliament Rolls of Medieval England*, www.british-history.ac.uk/no-series/parliament-rolls-medieval/november-1461 [accessed 29 January 2023].
416. CPR 1452-1461, p237 and CPR 1476-1485, p72. Also 'Edward IV: November 1461', in *Parliament Rolls of Medieval England*, www.british-history.ac.uk/no-series/parliament-rolls-medieval/november-1461 [accessed 29 January 2023].

Part Three, Chapter Ten: The Organiser, Margaret Paston

417. Landry, p28
418. Landry, p120
419. Stow, p780
420. Fenn, vol. 1, p88-89
421. Fenn, vol. 1, p191-192
422. Fenn, vol. 2, p34-35
423. Fenn, vol. 1, p118
424. Fenn, vol. 2, p11
425. Cokayne, vol. 6, p167-168
426. Fenn, vol. 2, p45
427. Fenn, vol. 2, p61
428. Fenn, vol. 2, p61
429. Fabyan, Robert, p663
430. Fenn, vol. 2, p114
431. CPR 1476-1485, p254
432. 'Henry VII: November 1485, Part 1', in *Parliament Rolls of Medieval England*, www.british-history.ac.uk/no-series/parliament-rolls-medieval/november-1485-pt-1 [accessed 29 January 2023].
433. Wood, *Letters of Illustrious Ladies,* p113
434. Cokayne, vol. 7, p36

435. Vergil, p19 and Baker, p200
436. Cokayne, vol. 7, p36-37
437. 'Henry VI: November 1459', in *Parliament Rolls of Medieval England*, www. british-history.ac.uk/no-series/parliament-rolls-medieval/november-1459 [accessed 19 October 2022].
438. 'Henry VI: November 1459', in *Parliament Rolls of Medieval England*, www. british-history.ac.uk/no-series/parliament-rolls-medieval/november-1459 [accessed 19 October 2022].
439. Fenn, vol. 1, p103-104
440. CPR 1452-1461, p 572, 551
441. Cokayne, vol. 7, p37
442. CPR 1461-1467, p15
443. Cokayne, vol. 1, p330
444. Fosbroke, p152
445. Baker, p200
446. Smyth, p65
447. Fosbroke, p153
448. Cokayne, vol. 1, p330
449. *Collections for a History of Staffordshire* 1914. p197-198
450. *Collections for A History of Staffordshire* 1914. p201-202
451. *Collections for a History of Staffordshire* 1914. p201-202

Chapter Eleven: The Defender, Alice Knyvet

452. Christine de Pisan, p110
453. Moore, J.S., p183
454. CPR 1461-1467, p67
455. Barrett, p185
456. CPR 1461-1467, p67
457. CPR 1461-1467, p83
458. alton, Robert Bell. *Annals and Legends of Calais,* (John Russell Smith, London, 1852), p154-155
459. CPR 1467-1477 p455
460. CPR 1476-1485, p276
461. More, p107
462. More, p112
463. More, p112
464. CPR 1476-1485, p526 and CPR 1485-1494, p99
465. Fenn, vol. 2, p11
466. Leland, *Itinerary*, vol. 1, p323
467. Carew, Richard. *The Survey of Cornwall and An Epistle Concerning the Excellencies of the English Tongue.* (B. Law, London, 1769), p133
468. Carew, p122
469. Carew, p136
470. Leland, *Itinerary*, vol. 1 p204
471. Leland, *Itinerary*, vol. 1 p204
472. Carew, p133-134

473. Ewing, Juliana Horatio. *Verses for Children and Songs for Music.* (London, 1895), p37
474. Rous, John. Part 51
475. Smyth, p65
476. Smyth, p65
477. Smyth, p66-69
478. Leland Itinerary, vol. 7-8, p105
479. Lloyd, William Valentine. *Description of the armorial insignia of the Vaughans of Llwydiarth; which once surrounded their family pew in Llanfihangel Church, but are now in Wynnstay Chapel; with memorials of the Lloyds of Dolobran and other cognate families.* (1881), p32
480. CPR 1452-1461 p367
481. Lewis, Samuel. *A topographical dictionary of Wales*, 'Glasbury', 1834.
482. Cothi, Lewis Glyn. *Poetical Works,* (The Royal Cambrian Institution, 1837), 'Marwnad Thomas ab Rhosser, Arglwydd Hera St', p18-19
483. Mancini, p99
484. Berners, Dame Juliana, *The Treatyse of Fysshynge With An Angle.* (Geo W Van Siclen ed, New York, 1880), p36-37
485. Starling, Elizabeth, *Noble Deeds of Woman, or Examples of Female Courage and Virtue,* (Phillips, Sampson and Co., Boston, 1859), p44
486. Moore, J. S., p183
487. CPR 1446-1452, p338
488. CPR 1446-1452, p338-374
489. Fenn, vol. 1, p22
490. CPR 1452-1461, p55
491. CPR 1452-1461, p491
492. CPR 1452-1461, p493
493. CPR 1467-1477, p215-216
494. CPR 1467-1477, p288
495. CPR 1476-1485, p50
496. CPR 1452-1461, p518
497. CPR 1452-1461, p527
498. Flenley, p140
499. Flenley, p126 note 3
500. Flenley, p126 note 3
501. CPR 1446-1452, p135

Part Four, Chapter Twelve: Trade and Industry
502. Flenley, p119-120
503. Croyland, p481-482
504. Leland, John, Thomas Hearne, *Joannis Lelandi Antiquarii De Rebvs Britannicis Collectanea.* Editio altera. Londini (J. Richardson, 1770), p219
505. Croyland, p482
506. Fortescue., Sir John. *The Governance of England: otherwise called the difference between an absolute and a limited monarchy.* Plummer, Charles ed. (Clarendon Press, Oxford, 1885) p.129

507. Nicolas, *Privy Purse Expenses*, p117-118
508. Lowry, p67
509. Warner, Frank, *The Silk Industry of the United Kingdom : its origin and development.* (Drane's, London, 1921), p535-536
510. MacGibbon, p45-46
511. Nicolas, *Privy Purse Expenses*, p92, p27, p51
512. *A Collection of Ordinances*, 'Henry VII' p126
513. Nicolas, *Privy Purse Expenses*, p82
514. Tighe, Robert Richard, Davis, James Edward. *Annals of Windsor : being a history of the castle and town : with some account of Eton and places adjacent.* (Longman, Brown, Green, Longmans and Roberts, London, 1858), p370
515. *A Collection of Ordinances*, 'Henry VI' p23
516. *A Collection of Ordinances*, 'Edward IV' p85
517. Nicolas, *Privy Purse Expenses*, p122
518. Nicolas, *Privy Purse Expenses*, p46
519. Leyser, p152
520. *A Collection of Ordinances*, 'Edward IV' p85 and 'Henry VIII', p215
521. Fabyan, p653
522. CPR 1461-1467, p203, p277
523. Botfield, p193, p207, p212 p350
524. Collier, p221
525. Bentley, *Excerpta* p89, p119, p122
526. Nicolas, Privy Purse Expenses, p16, p38
527. Blacman p30
528. Withington, Robert, *English pageantry; an historical outline* (Cambridge Harvard University Press, London, 1918), p144
529. Rickart, pxviii
530. Bentley, *Excerpta* p94, p104, p105
531. Stow, p709
532. Baker, p216
533. Fabyan, p664

Chapter Thirteen: Companionship

534. CPR 1452-1461, p608
535. CPR 1461-1467, p22, p91
536. CPR 1461-1467, p373 and 1467-1477, p567
537. *A Collection of Ordinances,* 'Edward IV', p36
538. *A Collection of Ordinances*, 'Henry VII', p118
539. 'Richard III: January 1484', in *Parliament Rolls of Medieval England*, www.british-history.ac.uk/no-series/parliament-rolls-medieval/january-1484 [accessed 11 August 2022]. also
540. 'Henry VII: November 1485, Part 1', in *Parliament Rolls of Medieval England*, www.british-history.ac.uk/no-series/parliament-rolls-medieval/november-1485-pt-1 [accessed 11 August 2022].
541. Leland, John, and Thomas Hearne. *Joannis Lelandi Antiquarii De Rebvs Britannicis Collectanea. Editio altera. Londini:* (J. Richardson, 1770), p220, p222

542. Strickland, vol. 2, p210
543. Rozmital, p47
544. Rozmital, p47
545. Bentley, *Excerpta*. p382
546. Fenn, vol. 2, p60
547. More, p59
548. Bentley, *Excerpta*. p381
549. *A Collection of Ordinances*, 'Cecily Neville', p37
550. Warkworth, John, p19
551. Fenn, vol. 2, p71 also Davis, Norman. *The Paston Letters, A Selection in Modern Spelling*. (Oxford University Press, London, 1963), p250
552. Commines, p189
553. Commines, p189
554. Baker, p208
555. Commines, p200
556. Stow, p687
557. Baker, p198
558. CPR 1461-1467, p177, p285
559. 'Lateran Regesta 502: 1455-1456', in *Calendar of Papal Registers Relating To Great Britain and Ireland*: Volume 11, 1455-1464, ed. J A Twemlow (London, 1921), pp. 224-229. British History Online: www.british-history.ac.uk/cal-papal-registers/brit-ie/vol11/pp224-229 [accessed 1 April 2022].
560. 'Close Rolls, Edward IV: July 1470', in *Calendar of Close Rolls, Edward IV*: Volume 2, 1468-1476, ed. W H B Bird and K H Ledward (London, 1953), pp. 121-125. British History Online: www.british-history.ac.uk/cal-close-rolls/edw4/vol2/pp121-125 [accessed 1 April 2022].
561. *A Collection of Ordinances*, 'George, Duke of Clarence', p89-94
562. *A Collection of Ordinances*, 'George Duke of Clarence', p100
563. CPR, 1476-1485, p72
564. CPR, 1476-1485, p73
565. Stow, p716-717
566. Vergil, p140
567. Strickland, vol. 2, p351
568. CPR 1476-1485, p72
569. Blacman, p30
570. Stow, p705 and Blacman, p29
571. *Third Report of the Royal Commission of Historical Manuscripts*. 'Copy of a Paper Roll, Temp H.6., Containing Charges Against the Duke of Suffolk', (London, 1872. Kraus Reprint, 1979), p279
572. Croyland, p484 and Vergil, p117
573. Commines, p200
574. 'Richard III: January 1484', in *Parliament Rolls of Medieval England*, www.british-history.ac.uk/no-series/parliament-rolls-medieval/january-1484 [accessed 29 October 2022].
575. Cokayne, vol.7, p296-297
576. Cokayne, vol.7, p297

577. Commines, p396
578. More, p61
579. Buck, p121
580. Stow, p756
581. Baker, p217
582. 'Lateran Regesta 761: 1475-1476', in *Calendar of Papal Registers Relating To Great Britain and Ireland*: Volume 13, 1471-1484, ed. J A Twemlow (London, 1955), pp. 487-495. British History Online: www.british-history.ac.uk/cal-papal-registers/brit-ie/vol13/pp487-495 [accessed 31 January 2023].
583. More, p54
584. Drayton, quoted in Thornbury, Walter. *Old and New London : a narrative of its history, its people, and its places.* (Cassell, Petter and Galpin, London, 1873)
585. More, p54-55
586. Stow, p750 and CPR 1465-1485, p371
587. More, p54
588. Baker, p234
589. More, p54-p55
590. More, p55

Chapter Fourteen: Birthing A New Dynasty

590. Percy Society, *Early English Poetry*, p78
591. 'Milan: 1469', in *Calendar of State Papers and Manuscripts in the Archives and Collections of Milan 1385-1618*, ed. Allen B Hinds (London, 1912), pp. 128-134. British History Online: www.british-history.ac.uk/cal-state-papers/milan/1385-1618/pp128-134 [accessed 31 January 2023].
592. Fortescue., Sir John. *The Governance of England: otherwise called the difference between an absolute and a limited monarchy.* Plummer, Charles ed. (Clarendon Press, Oxford, 1885) p356, p353
593. Mancini, p77
594. Leland, vol. 1, p72
595. 'Henry VII: November 1485, Part 1', in *Parliament Rolls of Medieval England*, www.british-history.ac.uk/no-series/parliament-rolls-medieval/november-1485-pt-1 [accessed 1 February 2023].
596. CPR 1467-1477, p154
597. CPR 1467-1477, p547
598. Strickland, vol. 2, p341-2
599. Leyser, p127
600. Raynauld, Thomas, *The Birth of Mankynde, Otherwise Called The Woman's Booke,* 1565, 'The Second Book'
601. Nicolas, Privy Purse Accounts, p78
602. Fiddyment, Sarah et al. "Girding the loins? Direct evidence of the use of a medieval English parchment birthing girdle from biomolecular analysis." *Royal Society Open Science* vol. 8,3 202055. 10 Mar. 2021, doi:10.1098/rsos.20205513.
603. CPR 1446-1452, p244
604. Fabyan, p655
605. CPR 1452-1461, p535

606. CPR 1476-1485, p191
607. CPR 1452-1461, p462
608. CPR 1461-1467, p520 and 1476-1485, p374
609. CPR 1422-1429, p322
610. CPR 1452-1461, p567
611. *A Collection of Ordinances,* 'Edward V', p28
612. *A Collection of Ordinances,* 'Edward V', p29
613. Page, William. *The Victoria History of the County of Buckingham.* (Archibald Constable and Co, London, 1908) vol. 2, p150
614. Bentley, *Excerpta*, p150
615. *A Collection of Ordinances,* 'Henry VII', p127
616. Ellis, Henry. *Original Letters, Illustrative of English History : including numerous royal letters; from autographs in the British Museum, and one or two other collections. With notes and illus. by Henry Ellis.* 2d series, vol. 1, (Harding and Lepard, London, 1827), p170
617. Ellis, p170
618. Ellis, p171
619. CPR 1485-1494 p152
620. CPR 1485-1494 p312
621. A Collection of Ordinances, 'Henry VII', p127

ACKNoWLEDGEMENTS

Writing this book has been an absolute joy; I have loved getting to know these fascinating women who lived through one of the most turbulent periods in our medieval history. I am grateful to the Pen and Sword team for all their help and for bringing this book into being. Thanks also to Danielle Burton from the *Voyager of History* blog for her assistance with my research into fifteenth-century effigies, particularly that of Elizabeth Fitzherbert, and for sharing her knowledge about Elizabeth Scales. Thanks to author Sharon Bennett-Connolly who blogs at *History... The Interesting Bits* for her assistance, support, and enthusiasm, which meant so much to me while I was writing. I am grateful too, to Claire Miles from the *Hisdoryan* blog for looking at some medieval Welsh poetry for me and to Dr Joanna Laynesmith for sharing some advice about Anne, Duchess of Exeter. A huge thanks to all the staff at museums, record offices, cathedrals and churches who helped with my many enquiries and visits, and for their warmth and excitement about the project. Additionally, I must thank my followers on social media for their help and encouragement. A special mention goes to Javier, Georgina, Sofia, Viv, Rob, Dave and Malcolm for their never-ending support. Finally, thanks must go to Professor Barbara English, who sparked my life-long passion for medieval women's history many years ago at Hull.

SELECT BIBLIOGRAPHY

More specialist sources referred to only once or twice in the text can be found in the corresponding endnotes.

All modern currency equivalents were calculated using The National Archives Currency Converter at www.nationalarchives.gov.uk/currency-converter/ which gives a general guide to historic values.

Primary Sources

André, Bernard. *The Life of Henry VII*, ed. Hobbins, Daniel, (Italica Press, New York, 2011)

Bentley, Samuel. *Excerpta Historica; or Illustrations of English History*, (Samuel Bentley, London, 1831)

Blacman, John. *Henry The Sixth. A reprint of John Blacman's memoir with translation and notes*, ed. James, M.R., (Cambridge University Press, 1919)

Botfield, Beriah. The Expenses of Sir John Howard, Knight in Stoke by Nayland, 1461-1469 In: *Manners and Household Expenses of England in the Thirteenth and Fifteenth Centuries, illustrated by original records* pp149-621, (Shakspeare Press, London, 1841)

Bruce, John. *Historie of the Arrivall of Edward IV in England and the Finall Recouerye of his Kingdomes from Henry VI A.D. M.CCCC.-LXXI* (Nichols, London, 1838)

Burgess, Clive (ed.). *The Pre-Reformation Records of All Saints Church Volume 47, Part 1.* (Bristol Record Society, 1995)

Burgess, Clive (ed.). *The Pre-Reformation Records of All Saints Church Volume 56, Part 3.* Wills, the Halleway Chantry Records and Deeds, (Bristol Record Society, 2004)

Burgess, L.A. (ed.), Harvey, P.D.A. and Saunders, A.D. *The Southampton Terrier of 1454*, Southampton Records Series Vol XV. (HMSO, London,1976)

Calendar of the Close Rolls: Henry VI 1447-1454, Volume 5, (Public Record Office, London, 1971)

Calendar of the Close Rolls: Henry VI 1454-1461, Volume 6, (Public Record Office, London, 1947)

Calendar of the Patent Rolls, Preserved in the Public Record Office: Henry VI, 1422-1429, (H. M. Stationery Office, London, 1901)

Calendar of the Patent Rolls, Preserved in the Public Record Office: Henry VI, 1446-1452, (H. M. Stationery Office, London, 1901)

Calendar of the Patent Rolls, Preserved in the Public Record Office: Henry VI, 1452-1461, (H. M. Stationery Office, London, 1910)

Calendar of the Patent Rolls, Preserved in the Public Record Office: Edward IV, 1461-1467, (H. M. Stationery Office, London, 1897)

Calendar of the Patent Rolls, Preserved in the Public Record Office: Edward IV, Henry VI, 1467-1477, (H. M. Stationery Office, London, 1900)

Calendar of the Patent Rolls, Preserved in the Public Record Office: Edward IV, Edward V, Richard III, 1476-1485, (H. M. Stationery Office, London, 1901)

Calendar of the Patent Rolls, Preserved in the Public Record Office: Henry VII, 1485-1494, (H. M. Stationery Office, London, 1914)

Calendar of the Patent Rolls, Preserved in the Public Record Office: Henry VII, 1494-1509, (H. M. Stationery Office, London, 1916)

Collier, J. Payne (ed.). *Household Books of John, Duke of Norfolk and Thomas Earl of Surrey*, (William Nicol, Shakspeare Press, London 1844)

Commines, Philip de, Lord of Argenton. *Containing the histories of Louis XI and Charles VIII Kings of France and of Charles the Bold, Duke of Burgundy*, ed. Scoble, Andrew R. Volume 1, (Bell and Sons, London, 1911)

Davies, John Silvester (ed.). *An English Chronicle of the Reigns of Richard II, Henry IV, Henry V and Henry VI Written Before the Year 1471*, (The Camden Society, London, 1968)

Davis, Norman. *The Paston Letters*, (Oxford University Press, London, 1963)

Fabyan, Robert. *The New Chronicles of England and France, in two parts*, edited by Ellis, Sir Henry, (F. C. and J. Rivington, London,1811)

Fenn, John. *The Paston Letters: original letters written during the reigns of Henry VI, Edward IV and Richard III by various persons of rank or consequence, Volumes 1 and 2*, ed. Ramsay, A. (Charles Knight and Co, London, 1840)

Fitzherbert, Master. *The Book of Husbandry,* ed. Skeat, Walter W. (Trubner and Co, London, 1882)

Flenley, Ralph. *Six Town Chronicles of England*, (Clarendon Press, Oxford, 1911)

Gairdner, James. *Three Fifteenth-Century Chronicles, with historical memoranda by John Stowe, the antiquary, and contemporary notes of occurrences written by him in the reign of Queen Elizabeth*, (Camden Society, London, 1880)

Gairdner, James and Brodie, R.H. (eds.). Letters and Papers: Books of the Court of Augmentations, in *Letters and Papers, Foreign and Domestic, Henry VIII, Volume 14 Part 1, January-July 1539* (London, 1894) British History Online

Gerard, John. *The Herball, or Generall Historie of Plantes*, (John Norton, London, 1597)

'Gregory's Chronicle' in *The Historical Collections of a Citizen of London in the Fifteenth Century*, ed. James Gairdner (Camden Society, London, 1876)

Hall, Edward. *Hall's Chronicle: containing the history of England, during the reign of Henry the Fourth, and the succeeding monarchs, to the end of the reign of Henry the Eighth, in which are particularly described the manners and customs of those periods. Collated with the editions of 1548 and 1550.* (J. Johnson, London, 1809)

Hardyng, John. *The Chronicle of John Hardyng with the Continuation of Richard Grafton*, ed. Henry Ellis, (F.C. and J. Rivington, London, 1812)

Hinds, Allen B., (ed.). 'Milan: 1469', in *Calendar of State Papers and Manuscripts in the Archives and Collections of Milan 1385-1618*, (London, 1912) British History Online

Holinshed, Raphael. *Holinshed's Chronicles of England, Scotland and Ireland. Volume 3*, (J. Johnson, London, 1808)

Kerry, Rev Charles. The Will of Elizabeth Fitzherbert, In: *Journal of the Derbyshire Archaeological and Natural History Society, Volume 10*, contributed by Rev Reginald H.C. FitzHerbert, (Bemrose and Sons, London, 1898)

Kingsford, Charles Lethbridge (ed.). *Two London Chronicles from the Collections of John Stow* (London, 1910)

Kingsford, Charles Lethbridge (ed.). *The Stonor Letters and Papers 1290-1483, Volumes 1 and 2*, (Royal Historical Society, London, 1919)

Landry, G de la Tour. *The Book of the Knight of the Tower: compiled for the instruction of his daughters.* ed. Wright, Thomas, (Trübner and Co, London, 1868)

Leland, *John. Joannis Lelandi Antiquarii De Rebvs Britannicis Collectanea*, ed. Hearne, Thomas, (J. Richardson, London, 1770)

Leland, John. *The Itinerary of John Leland in or about the Years 1535-1543*, ed. Smith, Lucy Toulmin, Parts 1-11, (G. Bell and Sons, London, 1906-1910)

Letts, Malcolm. *The Travels of Leo of Rozmital, Through Germany, Flanders, England, France, Spain, Portugal and Italy 1465-1467*, (The Hakluyt Society, Cambridge, 1957)

MacCarthy, B. (ed.). *The Annals of Ulster: A Chronicle of Irish Affairs Volume 3, AD 1379-1541*, (Alex Thom and Co., Dublin, 1895.)

Malden, Henry Elliot (ed.). *The Cely Papers: selections from the correspondence and memoranda of the Cely family, merchants of the staple, A.D. 1475-1488*, (Longmans, Green and Co., London, 1900)

Mancini, Dominic. *The Usurpation of Richard III*, ed. C. A. J. Armstrong, (Clarendon Press, London, 1969)

Moore, Joseph S. (ed.). *The Pictorial Book of Ancient Ballad Poetry of Great Britain: Historical, Traditional, and Romantic,* (Henry Washbourne and Co., London, 1853)

More, Sir Thomas. *History of King Richard III*, Lumby, J. Rawson (ed.), (Cambridge University Press, 1924)

Nicolas, Nicholas Harris. *Testamenta Vetusta: being illustrations from wills, of manners, customers, etc as well as of the descents and possessions of many distinguished families. From the reign of Henry the Second to the accession of Queen Elizabeth, Volume 1,* (Nichols and Son, London, 1826)

Nicolas, Sir Nicholas Harris (ed.), *Privy purse Expenses of Elizabeth of York, Wardrobe Accounts of Edward the Fourth. With a memoir of Elizabeth of York, and notes.* (Pickering, London, 1830)

Nichols, John Gough (ed.), *Chronicle of the Rebellion in Lincolnshire 1470,* (Camden Society, London, 1847)

Nichols, John Gough (ed.). *Chronicle of the Greyfriars of London*, (Camden Society, London, 1851)

Nichols, John Gough and Bruce, John (eds.). *A Selection from the Wills of Eminent Persons Proved in the Prerogative Court of Canterbury 1495-1695,* (Camden Society, London, 1863)

Parliament Rolls of Medieval England, ed. Chris Given-Wilson, Paul Brand, Seymour Phillips, Mark Ormrod, Geoffrey Martin, Anne Curry and Rosemary Horrox (Woodbridge, 2005), British History Online: www.british-history.ac.uk/no-series/parliament-rolls-medieval/

Percy Society. *Early English Poetry, Ballads and Popular Literature of the Middle Ages, Edited from Original Manuscripts and Scarce Publications, Volume XX,* (T. Richards, London, 1840)

Pisan, Christine de, *The Treasure of the City of Ladies*, Translated by Sarah Lawson, (Penguin, London, 2003)

Public Record Office. *List of Early Chancery Proceedings, Volume 1,* (Kraus Reprint Corporation, New York, 1963)

Rickart, Robert. *The Maire of Bristowe is Kalendar*, ed. Smith, Lucy Toulmin, (Camden Society, 1872)

Rickert, Edith. *The Babees' Book: Medieval Manners for the Young*, (Furnivall, Frederick James, London, 1923)

Riley, Henry T. (ed.). *Ingulph's Chronicle of the Abbey of Croyland, with the continuations by Peter of Blois and anonymous writers, translated by Henry T. Riley,* (George Bell and Sons, London 1908)

Rous, John, *The Rous Roll, This rol was laburd & finished by Master John Rows of Warrewyk*, (W. Pickering, London, 1845)

Society of Antiquaries in London. *A Collection of Ordinances and Regulations for the Government of the Royal Household, Made in Divers Reigns from King Edward III to King William and Queen Mary, also Receipts in Ancient Cookery,* (John Nichols, London, 1790)

Stow, John. *Annals of England to 1603,* (London, 1603)

The Chronicles of the White Rose of York: a series of historical fragments, proclamations, letters and other contemporary documents relating to the reign of Edward the Fourth, (James Bohn, London, 1845)

The Home Treasury. *The Ancient and Modern Ballads of Chevy Chase,* (J. Cundall, London, 1844)

Thompson, Alexander Hamilton (ed.). *Visitations of Religious Houses in the Diocese of Lincoln, 1420-1436, Volume 1,* (The Canterbury and York Society, London, 1915)

Vergil, Polydore. *Three Books of Polydore Vergil's English History, comprising the reigns of Henry VI, Edward IV and Richard III from an early translation preserved among the MSS of the old royal library in the British Museum,* ed. Sir Henry Ellis. (Camden Society, London, 1844)

Warkworth, John. *A Chronicle of the First Thirteen Years of the Reign of King Edward the Fourth,* (Camden Society, John Bowyer Nichols and Son, London, 1839)

Wood Green, Mary Anne Everett (ed.). *Letters of Royal And Illustrious Ladies of Great Britain: From the Commencement of the Twelfth Century to the Close of the Reign of Queen Mary, Volume 1,* (H. Colburn, London, 1846)

Secondary Sources

Amin, Nathen. *Henry VII and the Tudor Pretenders, Simnel, Warbeck and Warwick,* (Amberley, Stroud, 2020)

Baker, Sir Richard. *A Chronicle of the Kings of England, from the time of the Romans government to the death of King James the First, with a Continuation to the Year 1660 by E. Phillips,* (Samuel Ballard, London, 1733)

Baldwin, David. *The Kingmaker's Sisters, Six Powerful Women in the Wars of the Roses,* (The History Press, Stroud, 2011) Kindle ebook.

Barrett, Jonathan. *Memorials of the Parochial Church and Collegiate Chantry and The Chapel of St Mary,* (John W. Parker, London, 1848)

Bennett-Connolly, Sharon. *Heroines of the Medieval World,* (Amberley, Stroud, 2019)

Bicheno, Hugh. *Battle Royal, The Wars of Lancaster and York, 1464-1487* (Head of Zeus, London, 2015)

Buck, George. *The History of the Life and Reign of Richard the Third*, (W. Wilson, London, 1647)

Castor, Helen, *Blood and Roses: The Paston family and the Wars of the Roses*, (Faber and Faber, London, 2005)

Clark, K.L. *The Nevilles of Middleham, England's Most Powerful Family in the Wars of the Roses*, (The History Press, Stroud, 2016)

Cokayne, George Edward. *The Complete Peerage, Edition 1, Volumes 1-7*, (George Bell and Sons, London, 1887-1896)

Cox, Charles J. *Notes on the Churches of Derbyshire, Volume 3, The Hundreds of Appletree and Repton and Gresley*, (W. Edmunds, Chesterfield, 1877)

Dallaway, James. *Antiquities of Bristow in the Middle Centuries Including the Topography of William Wyrcester and the Life of William Canynges*, (Mirror Office, Bristol, 1834)

Davies, J.S., *A History of Southampton*, (Gilbert and Co, Southampton, 1883)

Dresser, Madge, (ed.). *Women and the City, Bristol 1373-2000*, (Redcliffe Press, Bristol, 2016)

Evans, H.T. *Wales in the Wars of the Roses*, (Sutton Publishing, Stroud 1998)

Fleming, Peter. *Bristol and the Wars of the Roses*, Pamphlet no. 113, (Bristol Branch of the Historical Association, 2005)

Fosbroke, Thomas Dudley. *Berkeley Manuscripts, Abstracts and Extracts of Smyths Lives of the Berkeleys, Illustrative of the Ancient Manners and the Constitution including All Their Pedigrees in that Ancient Manuscript, which are annexed A Copious History of the Castle and Parish of Berkeley*, (John Nichols and Son, London, 1821)

Goldberg, P.J.P. (ed.). *Women in England c1275-1525*, (Manchester University Press, 1995)

Goldberg, P.J.P. (ed.). *Women in Medieval English Society*, (Alan Sutton, Stroud, 1997)

Gristwood, Sarah. *Blood Sisters: The Women Behind the Wars of the Roses*, (Harper Press, London, 2013)

Harcourt, Edward William. *The Harcourt Papers, Volume 1*, (James Parker, Oxford, 1880)

Higginbotham, Susan. *The Indomitable Duchess Alice Chaucer, Duchess of Suffolk* (article), www.susanhigginbotham.com/posts/the-indomitable-duchess-alice-chaucer-duchess-of-suffolk/

Higginbotham, Susan, *The Mysterious Margaret Beaufort, Countess of Stafford* [article], www.susanhigginbotham.com/posts/the-mysterious-margaret-beaufort-countess-of-stafford/[accessed 20 January 2023]

Higginbotham, Susan. *The Woodvilles, The Wars of the Roses and England's Most Infamous Family*, (The History Press, Stroud, 2015)

Hoare, Sir Richard Colt. *The History of Modern Wiltshire 'Hundred of Heytesbury'* (John Nicholas and Sons, London, 1824) p96

Holland, Bernard Henry. *The Lancashire Hollands*, (J. Murray, London, 1917)

Hookham, Mary Ann. *The Life and Times of Margaret of Anjou, Queen of England and France Volume 1*, (Tinsley Brothers, London, 1872)

Jesse, J. Heneage. *London and its Celebrities, Volume 2*, (Richard Bentley, London, 1850)

Johnson, Lauren. *Noblewomen in the Wars of the Roses: Turning Fortune's Wheel* (article), The Historical Society Blog, www.histsociety.blogspot.com, (6 December 2013)

Johnson, Lauren. *Shadow King: The Life and Death of Henry VI*, (Audible audiobook, 2020)

Jones, Dan. *The Hollow Crown: The Wars of the Roses and the Rise of the Tudors*, (Audible audiobook, 2018)

Karras, Ruth Mazo, *Common Women: Prostitution and Sexuality in Medieval England*, (Oxford University Press, Oxford, 1996)

Kingsford, C.L. *Prejudice and Promise in Fifteenth Century England, The Ford Lectures 1923-24*, (Clarendon Press, Oxford, 1925)

Knowles, Dom David. *The Religious Orders in England, Volume 2, The End of the Middle Ages*, (Cambridge University Press, Cambridge, 1955)

The University of Leicester. 'Richard III: Discovery and Identification', le.ac.uk

Leyser, Henrietta. *Medieval Women, A Social History of Women in England 450-1500*, (Phoenix Giant, London, 1997)

Licence, Amy. *Cecily Neville Mother of Kings*, (Amberley, Stroud, 2014)

Licence, Amy. *Red Roses, Blanche of Gaunt to Margaret Beaufort*, (The History Press, Stroud, 2017)

Lowry, Priscilla. *The Secrets of Silk, From the Myths and Legends to the Middle Ages*, (St John's Press, London, 2003)

McSheffrey, Dr Shannon. Sanctuary Seekers in England (website) sanctuaryseekers.ca

MacGibbon, David. *Elizabeth Woodville: A Life*, (Amberley, Stroud, 2014)

McCaffrey, Carmen. *In Search of Ireland's Heroes, the story of the Irish from the English invasion to the present day*, (Ivan R. Dee, Chicago, 2006)

Mayhew, Mickey. *House of Tudor, A Grisly History*, (Pen and Sword, Yorkshire, 2022)

Napier, Henry Alfred. *Historical Notices of the Parishes of Swyncombe and*

Ewelme in the County of Oxford, (James Wright, Oxford, 1858)

Norton, Elizabeth. *The Boleyn Women: The Tudor Femmes Fatales Who Changed English History.* (Amberley, Stroud, 2013)

Noorthouck, John. 'Book 1, Ch. 6: Cade's Rebellion to Henry VII', in *A New History of London Including Westminster and Southwark* (London, 1773) British History Online

Penn, Thomas. *The Brothers York: An English Tragedy,* (Audible audiobook, 2019)

Power, Eileen. *Medieval English Nunneries c1275-1535,* (Cambridge University Press, Cambridge, 1922)

Prichard, T.J. Llewellyn. *Heroines of Welsh History: Memoirs and Biographical Notices of the Celebrated Women of Wales,* (W. and F. G. Cash, London, 1854)

Pryce, George. *Memorials of the Canynges' Family and their Times,* (George Wright, Bristol, 1854)

Raw, Alice. Gender and Protest in Late Medieval England, c.1400–c.1532, *The English Historical Review, Volume 136, Issue 582,* (October 2021)

Roger, Euan. *The Birth (and Death?) of Edward V* [article], https://blog.nationalarchives.gov.uk/the-birth-and-death-of-edward-fifth/ [accessed 1 February 2023]

Scofield, Cora L. *The Life and Reign of Edward the Fourth, King of England and of France and Lord of Ireland, Volumes 1 and 2,* (Longmans, London, 1923)

Seward, Desmond. *A Brief History of the Wars of the Roses. The Bloody Rivalry for the Throne of England,* (Robinson, London, 2007)

Skidmore, Chris. *Richard III, Brother, Protector, King,* (Audible audiobook, 2017)

Smith, Albert. 'The Legend of Chertsey Church' in *Pictures of Life at Home and Abroad,* (Richard Bentley, London, 1852)

Smyth, John. *The Berkeley Manuscripts, The Lives of the Berkeleys Lords of the Honour, Castle and Manor of Berkeley in the County of Gloucester From 1066-1618, with a Description of the Hundred of Berkeley and its Inhabitants, Volume 2,* ed., Sir John Maclean, (John Bellows, Gloucester, 1883)

Stanley, Peter Edmund, *The House of Stanley: the history of an English family from the twelfth century,* (Pentland Press, Edinburgh, 1998)

Starr, Eliza Allen. *Isabella of Castile 1492-1892,* (C.V. Waite and Co, Chicago, 1889)

Strickland, Agnes. *Lives of the Queens of England Volume 2,* (Hurst and Blackett, London, 1854)

Telford, Lynda. *Medieval Women in England,* (Amberley, Stroud, 2021)
thehistoryjar.com

The William Salt Archaeological Society. *Collections for a History of Staffordshire*, (Harrison and Sons, London, 1914)

Torlesse, Charles Martin. *Some account of Stoke by Nayland, Suffolk*, (Harrison & Sons, London,1877)

Traherne, John Montgomery. *Historical Notices of Sir Matthew Cradock, Knt of Swansea*, (William Rees, London, 1840)

Vyner, Charles James. *Vyner Family History*, (1885)

Watson, Gemma Louise. (2013) 'Roger Machado: A Life in Objects', PhD Thesis, The University of Southampton, Faculty of Humanities, Archaeology, English and History, Southampton

Weir, Alison. *Elizabeth of York, The First Tudor Queen*, (Audible audiobook, 2013)

Weir, Alison. *Lancaster and York, The Wars of the Roses*, (Vintage Books, London, 2009)

Notes

The Calendar of Patent Rolls is abbreviated to CPR
The Calendar of Court Rolls is abbreviated to CCR

INDEX